SELECT LAB SERIES PLUS

PROJECTS FOR MICROSOFT® ACCESS

Philip A. Koneman
Colorado Christian University

Pamela R. Toliver

Yvonne Johnson

▲ **ADDISON-WESLEY**

An imprint of Addison Wesley Longman, Inc.

Reading, Massachusetts • Menlo Park, California • New York • Harlow, England
Don Mills, Ontario • Sydney • Mexico City • Madrid • Amsterdam

Senior Editor: Carol Crowell
Associate Editor: Amy Golash
Production Supervision: Juliet Silveri/Diane Freed
Copyeditor: Susan Middleton
Proofreader: Holly McLean-Aldis
Technical Editor: Samantha Penrod
Indexer: Bernice Eisen
Composition: Michael Strong, Sally Simpson
Cover Design Supervisor: Gina Hagen
Marketing Manager: Michelle Hudson
Manufacturing Manager: Hugh Crawford

Copyright © 1998 by Addison Wesley Longman, Inc.

All rights reserved. No part of this publication may be reproduced, stored in a retrieval system, or transmitted, in any form or by any means, electronic, mechanical, photocopying, recording, or otherwise, without the prior written permission of the publisher. Printed in the United States of America.

ISBN 0-201-37205-3

Ordering from the SELECT System
For more information on ordering and pricing policies for the SELECT Lab Series and supplements, please contact your Addison Wesley Longman sales representative or call 1-800-552-2499.

Addison-Wesley Publishing Company
One Jacob Way
Reading, MA 01867
http://hepg.awl.com/select
is@awl.com

1 2 3 4 5 6 7 8 9 10-DOW-00999897

Preface to the Instructor

Welcome to the *SELECT Lab Series*. This applications series is designed specifically to make learning easy and enjoyable, a natural outcome of thoughtful, meaningful activity. The goal for the series is to create a learning environment in which students can explore the essentials of software applications, use critical thinking, and gain confidence and proficiency.

Greater access to ideas and information is changing the way people work. With today's business and communication application software, you have greater integration capabilities and easier access to Internet resources than ever before. The *SELECT Lab Series* helps you take advantage of these valuable resources, with special assignments devoted to the Internet and with additional connectivity resources that can be accessed through our Web site, **http://hepg.awl.com/select/**.

The *SELECT Lab Series* offers dozens of proven and class-tested materials, from the latest operating systems and browsers, to the most popular applications software for word processing, spreadsheets, databases, presentation graphics, desktop publishing, and integrated packages, to HTML, to programming. For your lab course, you can choose what you want to combine; your choice of lab manuals will be sent to the bookstore, combined in a TechSuite, allowing students to purchase all books in one convenient package at a discount.

The most popular *SELECT Lab Series* titles are available in three levels of coverage. The *SELECT Brief features* 4 projects that quickly lay the foundation of an application in 3 to 5 contact hours. The *standard edition SELECT* expands on material covered in the brief edition with 5 to 8 projects that teach intermediate skills in just 6 to 9 contact hours. *SELECT Plus* provides 10 to 12 projects that cover intermediate to advanced material in 12 to 14 contact hours.

Your Addison Wesley Longman representative will be happy to work with you and your bookstore manager to provide the most current menu of *SELECT Lab Series* offerings, outline the ordering process, and provide pricing, ISBNs, and delivery information. Or call 1-800-447-2226 or visit our Web site at http://www.awl.com/.

Organization

The "Overview of Windows 95," which appears in some *SELECT Lab Series* modules, familiarizes students with Windows 95 before launching into the application. Students learn the basics of starting Windows 95, using a mouse, using the essential features of Windows 95, getting help, and exiting Windows 95.

Each application is then covered in depth in a number of projects that teach beginning to intermediate skills. An overview introduces the basic concepts of the application and provides hands-on instructions to put students to work using the application immediately. Students learn problem-solving techniques while working through projects that provide practical, real-life scenarios that they can relate to.

Web assignments appear throughout the text at the end of each project, giving students practice using the Internet.

Approach

The *SELECT Lab Series* uses a document-centered approach to learning. Each project begins with a list of measurable objectives, a realistic scenario called the Challenge, a well-defined plan called the Solution, and an illustration of the final product. The Setup enables students to verify that the settings on the computer match those needed for the project. Each project is arranged in carefully divided, highly visual objective-based tasks that foster confidence and self-reliance. Each project closes with a wrap-up of the project called the Conclusion, followed by summary questions, exercises, and assignments geared to reinforcing the information taught through the project.

Other Features

In addition to the document-centered, visual approach of each project, this book contains the following features:

- An overview of the application so that students feel comfortable and confident as they function in the working environment.
- Keycaps and toolbar button icons within each step so that the student can quickly perform the required action.
- A comprehensive and well-organized end-of-the-project Summary and Exercises section for reviewing, integrating, and applying new skills.
- An illustration or description of the results of each step so that students know they're on the right track all the time.

Preface to the Instructor ACC-V

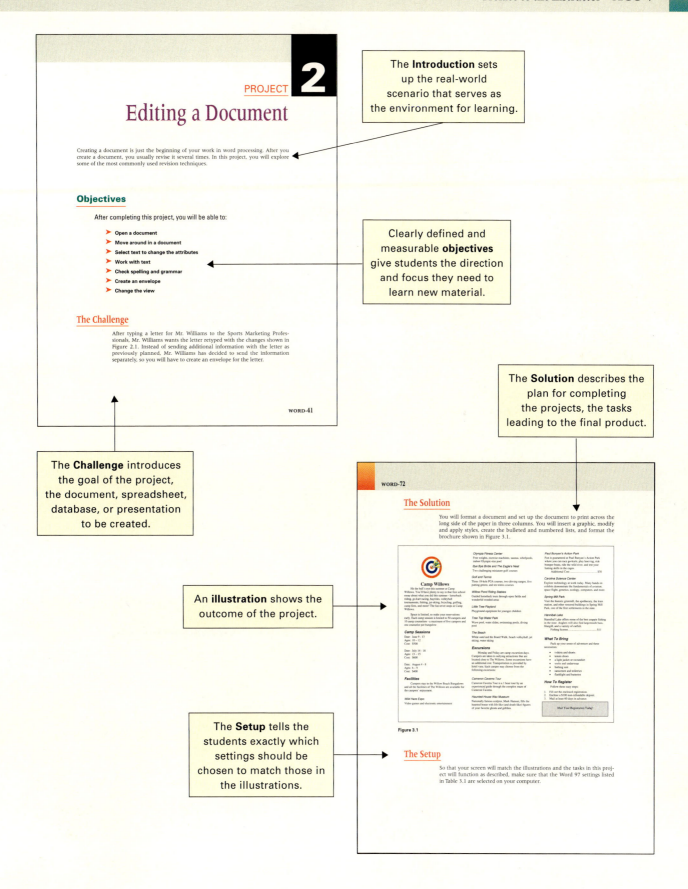

ACC-vi

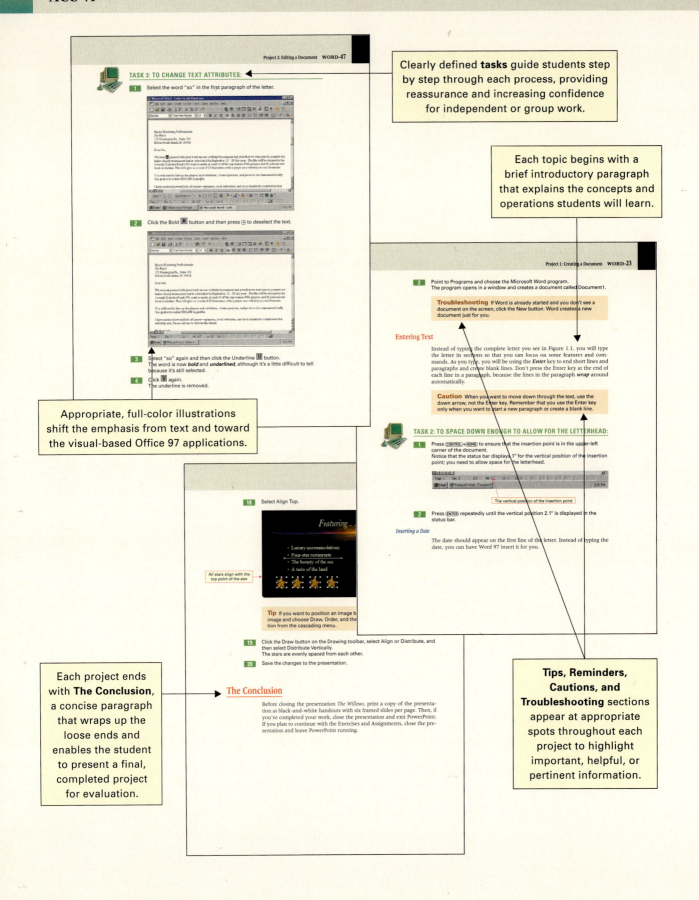

Preface to the Instructor ACC-vii

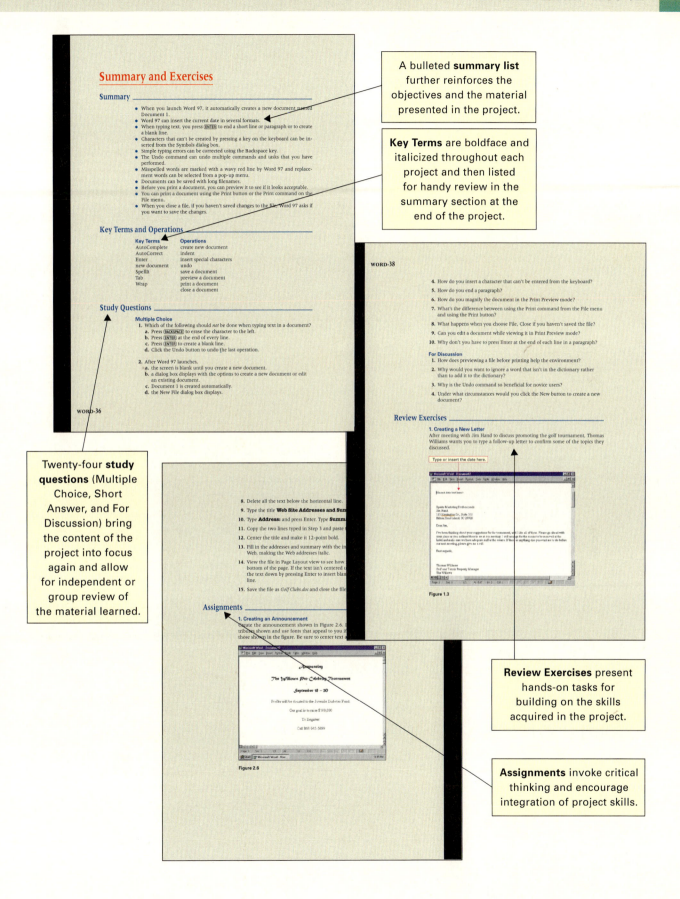

Supplements

You get extra support for this text from supplemental materials, including the *Instructor's Manual* and the Instructor's Data Disk.

The *Instructor's Manual* includes a Test Bank for each project in the student text, Expanded Student Objectives, Answers to Study Questions, and Additional Assessment Techniques. The Test Bank contains two separate tests with answers and consists of multiple-choice, true/false, and fill-in questions referenced to pages in the student text. Transparency Masters illustrate key concepts and screen captures from the text.

The Instructor's Data Disk contains student data files, completed data files for Review Exercises and assignments, and the test files from the *Instructor's Manual* in ASCII format.

For Internet and browser-related lab manuals, see the SELECT Web site for supplementary materials.

Thanks to . . .

When team members combine their knowledge and skills to produce a work designed to meet the needs of students and professors across the country, they take on an unenviable challenge.

To **Carol Crowell** and **Barb Terry,** thanks for the steady focus and refocus needed to get this project off the ground.

Thanks to **Martha Johnson, Robin Edwards,** and **Deborah Minyard,** who were more than just technical editors, but who also made sure things worked the way we said they would. Thanks to **Robin Drake**—without your great help and comments during development, nothing in this book would match; and to **Chuck Hutchinson,** for excellent editing. To those in production, especially to **Pat Mahtani,** your design efforts have paid off in a highly user friendly book!

To **Michelle Hudson,** thanks for your strong marketing insights for this book.

And, finally, thanks to everyone at Addison Wesley Longman who has followed this project from start to finish.

P. T.
Y. J.

Special thanks to my wife Tanya, and our children, Megan, Jonathan, and Andrew. They have been very patient and supportive during this project.

P. K.

Acknowledgments

Addison-Wesley Publishing Company would like to thank the following reviewers for their valuable contributions to the *SELECT Lab Series*.

James Agnew
Northern Virginia Community College

Joseph Aieta
Babson College

Dr. Muzaffar Ali
Bellarmine College

Tom Ashby
Oklahoma CC

Bob Barber
Lane CC

Robert Caruso
Santa Rosa Junior College

Robert Chi
California State Long Beach

Jill Davis
State University of New York at Stony Brook

Fredia Dillard
Samford University

Peter Drexel
Plymouth State College

David Egle
University of Texas, Pan American

Linda Ericksen
Lane Community College

Jonathan Frank
Suffolk University

Patrick Gilbert
University of Hawaii

Maureen Greenbaum
Union County College

Sally Ann Hanson
Mercer County CC

Sunil Hazari
East Carolina University

Gloria Henderson
Victor Valley College

Bruce Herniter
University of Hartford

Rick Homkes
Purdue University

Lisa Jackson
Henderson CC

Martha Johnson
(technical reviewer)
Delta State University

Cynthia Kachik
Santa Fe CC

Bennett Kramer
Massasoit CC

Charles Lake
Faulkner State Junior College

Ron Leake
Johnson County CC

Randy Marak
Hill College

Charles Mattox, Jr.
St. Mary's University

Jim McCullough
Porter and Chester Institute

Gail Miles
Lenoir-Rhyne College

Steve Moore
University of South Florida

Anthony Nowakowski
Buffalo State College

Gloria Oman
Portland State University

John Passafiume
Clemson University

Leonard Presby
William Paterson College

Louis Pryor
Garland County CC

Michael Reilly
University of Denver

Dick Ricketts
Lane CC

Dennis Santomauro
Kean College of New Jersey

Pamela Schmidt
Oakton CC

Gary Schubert
Alderson-Broaddus College

T. Michael Smith
Austin CC

Cynthia Thompson
Carl Sandburg College

Marion Tucker
Northern Oklahoma College

JoAnn Weatherwax
Saddleback College

David Whitney
San Francisco State University

James Wood
Tri-County Technical College

Minnie Yen
University of Alaska Anchorage

Allen Zilbert
Long Island University

About the Authors

Pam Toliver has over fifteen years of experience teaching students and adults of all ages about the sometimes mysterious world of software. She bought her first computer for a high school classroom in 1979, and through necessity, began to develop teaching materials and exercises designed to strengthen student productivity and make learning fun. Since those early days, she has moved from teaching business education classes at the high school level to teaching software applications at the community college and university levels.

Pam has a bachelor's degree in business teacher education from Southern Illinois University, Carbondale and a master's degree in vocational education from Louisiana State University, Baton Rouge. She divides her personal time among her favorite activities: writing, learning new software, and teaching — but more often lately she finds herself "caught in the Web".

Yvonne Johnson has been involved in teaching and writing about PCs since they first came into use. For 12 years she owned and operated a successful computer training school, the first school of its kind in Kentucky. She authored all the training material for the school and has written 17 books published by Que, Osborne/McGraw-Hill and other publishers. Her training and writing background has made her exceptionally well-versed in database, word processing, graphic, spreadsheet, presentation, integrated, and publishing software.

She holds a BA degree from Centre College of Kentucky with a major in Education and English. She did her post graduate work at the University of South Florida.

Philip Koneman has over 10 years of experience in computers and education. In addition to being an associate professor of Computer Information Systems at Colorado Christian University, Dr. Koneman is the president of Instructional Design Consultants, Inc., a company that develops educational multimedia. His company was awarded the 1995 *Denver Business Journal*'s "Most Innovative New Products Award in Biotechnology" for *GermWare Bacteriology*, a CD-ROM computer learning system for medical technology training.

Dr. Koneman received his Ph.D. in Instructional Technology from the University of Colorado at Denver. His research interests include computer-based learning and assessment, and the ethical implications of computers and technology.

Contents

Overview of Windows 95   WIN-1

Objectives   WIN-1
Launching Windows 95   WIN-2
Identifying the Desktop Elements   WIN-2
Using a Mouse   WIN-3
Using the Basic Features of Windows 95   WIN-4
   Using the Start Menu   WIN-4
   Using Windows   WIN-5
   Using Menu Bars and Toolbars   WIN-7
   Using Dialog Boxes   WIN-8
Getting Help   WIN-10
Exiting Windows 95   WIN-16

Overview   2

Objectives   2
   Defining Database Terminology   2
      Defining Database Terms   3
   Designing a Database   6
   Launching Microsoft Access   7
   Creating and Saving a Database   8
   Identifying Microsoft Access
      Screen Elements   10
   Working with Menus, Dialog Boxes,
      and Toolbars   11
      Identifying Menu Features   11
      Working with Toolbars   12
      Working with Dialog Boxes   12
   Getting Help   14
      Using the Office Assistant   14
      Using What's This? Help   16
      Using Help Contents   17
      Using the Help Index   18
      Getting Help from the Microsoft
         Web Site   19
   Closing a Database and Exiting
      Microsoft Access   20
Summary and Exercises   21
Summary   21
Key Terms and Operations   21
   Key Terms   21
   Operations   21
Study Questions   21
   Multiple Choice   21
   Short Answer   22
   For Discussion   23
Review Exercises   23
   1. Designing a New Database   23
   2. Getting Help About Wizards   23

Assignments   23
   *1. Identifying Fields to Include in Database for
      The Willows*   23
   *2. Exploring the Microsoft Access Forum to Look for
      Jobs on the Web*   24

Project 1 Building a Database   25

Objectives   25
The Challenge   25
The Solution   26
The Setup   26
   Opening an Access Database   27
   Creating an Access Database Table   28
      Defining Table Fields   29
      Saving and Closing a Database Table   32
   Opening an Access Database Table   33
   Adding Records to an Access
      Database Table   34
   Checking the Spelling of Data in a
      Database Table   36
   Creating and Saving an AutoForm   37
   Navigating Datasheets and Forms   38
   Previewing and Printing Database Data   40
The Conclusion   42
Summary and Exercises   43
Summary   43
Key Terms and Operations   43
   Key Terms   43
   Operations   43
Study Questions   43
   Multiple Choice   43
   Short Answer   44
   For Discussion   45
Review Exercises   45
   1. Creating a Database and a Database Table   45
   2. Adding Records to a Database Table   47
Assignments   47
   *1. Creating a New Table and Adding Records to
      the Table*   47
   2. Finding Competitors on the Internet   49

Project 2 Maintaining a Database   50

Objectives   50
The Challenge   50
The Solution   51
The Setup   51
   Finding Records   52
   Updating Records   53

ACC-xi

Inserting Records 55
Using the Replace Feature 57
Deleting Records 59
Sorting Records 60
Filtering Records by Selection 62
Filtering Records by Form 63
The Conclusion 66
Summary and Exercises 67
Summary 67
Key Terms and Operations 67
   Key Terms 67
   Operations 67
Study Questions 67
   Multiple Choice 67
   Short Answer 69
   For Discussion 69
Review Exercises 69
   1. Sorting Data, Finding and Replacing Data, and Updating a Database Table 69
   2. Filtering Data in a Database Table 72
Assignments 73
   1. Sorting, Filtering, Finding, and Updating Database Records 73
   2. Updating and Sorting a Database 73

Project 3 Altering the Table Design 74

Objectives 74
The Challenge 74
The Solution 75
The Setup 76
   Inserting Table Fields 76
   Rearranging Fields in a Table 78
   Deleting Table Fields 81
   Creating a Key Field 82
   Creating and Saving an AutoReport 83
   Copying a Table Structure 84
The Conclusion 85
Summary and Exercises 86
Summary 86
Key Terms and Operations 86
   Key Terms 86
   Operations 86
Study Questions 86
   Multiple Choice 86
   Short Answer 87
   For Discussion 88
Review Exercises 88
   1. Insert and Delete Fields, Assign a Key Field, and Update a Table 88
   2. Rearranging Fields in a Table and Creating an AutoReport 89

Assignments 90
   1. Insert Fields, Delete Fields, Set Key Field, and Set Field Properties 90
   2. Editing and Copying the Structure of a Database Table 90

Project 4 Creating Queries 92

Objectives 92
The Challenge 92
The Solution 93
The Setup 93
   Creating a New Query 94
   Adding Fields to the Query Grid 96
   Running a Query 97
   Saving and Closing a Query 98
   Opening and Running a Query 99
   Setting Query Sort Order and Criteria 100
   Editing a Query 104
The Conclusion 108
Summary and Exercises 109
Summary 109
Key Terms and Operations 109
   Key Terms 109
   Operations 109
Study Questions 109
   Multiple Choice 109
   Short Answer 110
   For Discussion 110
Review Exercises 111
   1. Creating and Saving a Simple Query 111
   2. Creating, Running, Saving, Editing, and Using Criteria in a Multi-Table Query 112
Assignments 113
   1. Creating a Query; Saving, Editing, Opening, and Running a Query 113
   2. Creating Queries from Data on the World Wide Web 114

Project 5 Creating and Modifying Forms 115

Objectives 115
The Challenge 116
The Solution 116
The Setup 116
   Creating a New Form and Displaying Form Design View 117
   Identifying Form Design View Features 118
   Selecting and Removing Fields from a Form 119
   Rearranging Fields on a Form 120
   Saving a Form 122
   Aligning Fields on a Form 122
   Changing Form Field Labels 123

Adjusting Field Length on a Form   124
Adding Titles to Forms   125
The Conclusion   128
Summary and Exercises   129
Key Terms and Operations   129
   Key Terms   129
   Operations   129
Study Questions   129
   Multiple Choice   129
   Short Answer   130
   For Discussion   131
Review Exercises   131
   1. Creating a New Form, Rearranging Fields, and Saving a Form   131
   2. Editing Field Labels, Adjusting Field Length, and Adding a Form Title   132
Assignments   132
   1. Creating a Form: Rearranging Fields, Removing Fields, Changing Field Labels, Adjusting Field Length, Adding a Title, and Saving   132
   2. Locating Forms on the Internet   133

Project 6 Customizing AutoReports   134

Objectives   134
The Challenge   134
The Solution   135
The Setup   135
   Opening a Report and Identifying Report Design Screen Features   135
   Selecting and Removing Fields from a Report   137
   Saving and Viewing Reports   139
   Modify a Report Design   140
   Printing Reports   148
The Conclusion   149
Summary and Exercises   150
Summary   150
Key Terms and Operations   150
   Key Terms   150
   Operations   150
Study Questions   150
   Multiple Choice   150
   Short Answer   152
   For Discussion   152
Review Exercises   152
   1. Creating a new AutoReport, rearranging fields, and saving a report   152
   2. Editing fields labels, adjusting field length, and adding a report title   153
Assignments   154
   1. Creating a new query to use for creating, designing, modifying, and saving a report   154
   2. Locating report layouts on the Internet   155

Beyond the basics   159

Project 7 Designing a Relational Database   161

Objectives   161
The Challenge   161
The Solution   162
The Setup   162
File Processing Systems   163
The Database Approach   163
   The Database Design Process   164
   Using the Entity-Relationship Model in Database Design   166
   Designing a Simple Data Dictionary   168
   Creating a Microsoft Access Database   169
   Creating a Table Object by Importing Data   170
   Modifying the Design of the Customers Table   176
The Conclusion   179
Summary and Exercises   180
Summary   180
Key Terms and Operations   180
   Key Terms   180
   Operations   180
Study Questions   181
   Multiple Choice   181
   Short Answer   182
   For Discussion   182
Review Exercises   182
   1. Creating an Employee Database   182
   2. Adding a Primary Key and Input Mask to a Table Design   183
Assignments   185
   1. Creating a Student File   185
   2. Finding Information on the Internet (Optional Assignment)   185

Project 8 Creating Additional Tables and Establishing Relationships   186

Objectives   186
The Challenge   187
The Solution   187
The Setup   187
Understanding Relationships   188
   Kinds of Cardinalities   189
   Reading Cardinalities in E-R Diagrams   190
   The Updated Data Dictionary   192
   Database Normalization   192
Designing the Database   195
   Creating the Products Table   195
   Creating the *Orders* Table   197
   Establishing Relationships   198
The Conclusion   201
Summary and Exercises   202

Summary 202
Key Terms and Operations 202
   Key Terms 202
   Operations 202
Study Questions 202
   Multiple Choice 202
   Short Answer 204
   For Discussion 204
Review Exercises 204
   1. Modifying the Employee Database 204
   2. Adding Records to the Employees Time Card Table 205
Assignments 206
   1. Updating the Student Database 206
   2. Updating the Vail Eating Establishments Database 206

Project 9 Creating a Sales Transaction Query and a Customer Form 207

Objectives 207
The Challenge 208
The Solution 208
The Setup 209
   Working with Queries 209
   Working with Forms 222
The Conclusion 229
Summary and Exercises 230
Summary 230
Key Terms and Operations 230
   Key Terms 230
   Operations 230
Study Questions 230
   Multiple Choice 230
   Short Answer 231
   For Discussion 232
Review Exercises 232
   1. Adding a Query to the Employees Database 232
   2. Creating a Calculated Field in the Gross Pay Query 232
Assignments 232
   1. Updating the Student Database 232
   2. Adding a Query to the Vail Eating Establishments Database 232

Project 10 Creating Forms Based on Multiple Tables 233

Objectives 233
The Challenge 233
The Solution 234
The Setup 235
   Learning More about Controls on Forms 236
   Modifying the *Customers* Form 237
   Creating a Form Based on a Multitable Query 239
   Creating a Form That Includes a Subform 242
The Conclusion 250
Summary and Exercises 251
Summary 251
Key Terms and Operations 251
   Key Terms 251
   Operations 251
Study Questions 251
   Multiple Choice 251
   Short Answer 253
   For Discussion 253
Review Exercises 253
   1. Creating an Employee Main Form and Subform 253
   2. Adding the Employees Subform to the Main Form 254
Assignments 254
   1. Creating a Form Displaying Student Course Data 254
   2. Creating a Form Displaying Restaurant Information 254

Project 11 Creating a Database Application 255

Objectives 255
The Challenge 255
The Solution 256
The Setup 256
   Creating a Report Based on a Query 257
   Customizing the *Add Customer Orders* Form by Altering Its Properties 267
   Creating a Startup Form 273
   Adding an Image Control to the Startup Form 274
The Conclusion 276
Summary and Exercises 277
Summary 277
Key Terms and Operations 277
   Key Terms 277
   Operations 277
Study Questions 277
   Multiple Choice 277
   Short Answer 279
   For Discussion 279
Review Exercises 280
   1. Adding a Time Card Report to the Employees Database 280
   2. Adding a Startup Form to the Employees Database 280
Assignments 281

1. Creating a Grade Report for the Student Database 281
2. Adding a Startup Form Displaying Restaurants in Vail, Colorado 281

Project 12 Using Microsoft Access Data in Other Applications 282

Objectives 282
The Challenge 283
The Solution 283
The Setup 284
    Publishing Access Data on the World Wide Web or a Corporate Intranet 285
    Creating a Database Front-End Application with Microsoft Visual Basic 295
The Conclusion 316
Summary and Exercises 317
Summary 317
Key Terms and Operations 317
Key Terms 317
Operations 317
Study Questions 317
    Multiple Choice 317
    Short Answer 319
    For Discussion 319
Review Exercises 319
    1. Creating a Visual Basic Front-End Application for the Employees *Database 319*
    2. Creating a Distribution Set to Install the Gross Pay *Database Front-End Application 320*
Assignments 320
    1. Creating a Visual Basic Front-End Application for the Student Database 320
    2. Create an HTML Page of Restaurants 320

Operations Reference EM-1

Glossary EM-4

Index EM-8

Overview of Windows 95

Microsoft Windows 95 is an *operating system,* a special kind of computer program that performs three major functions. First, an operating system controls the actual *hardware* of the computer (the screen, the keyboard, the disk drives, and so on). Second, an operating system enables other software programs such as word processing or spreadsheet *applications* to run. Finally, an operating system determines how the user operates the computer and its programs or applications.

As an operating system, Windows 95 and all other programs written to run under it provide *graphics* (or pictures) called *icons* to carry out commands and run programs. For this reason, Windows 95 is referred to as a *Graphical User Interface* or GUI (pronounced *gooey*). You can use the keyboard or a device called a *mouse* to activate the icons.

This overview explains the basics of Windows 95 so that you can begin using your computer quickly and easily.

Objectives

After completing this project, you will be able to:

- Launch Windows 95
- Identify the desktop elements
- Use a mouse
- Use the basic features of Windows 95
- Organize your computer
- Work with multiple programs
- Get help
- Exit Windows 95

Launching Windows 95

Because Windows 95 is an operating system, it launches immediately when you turn on the computer. Depending on the way your computer is set up, you may have to type your user name and password to log on — to get permission to begin using the program.) After Windows 95 launches, the working environment, called the *desktop*, displays on the screen.

Identifying the Desktop Elements

Figure W.1 shows the Windows 95 desktop with several icons that represent the hardware and the software installed on the computer. ***My Computer*** enables you to organize your work. The ***Recycle Bin*** is a temporary storage area for files deleted from the hard disk. At the bottom of the desktop is the ***Taskbar*** for starting programs, accessing various areas of Windows 95, and switching among programs.

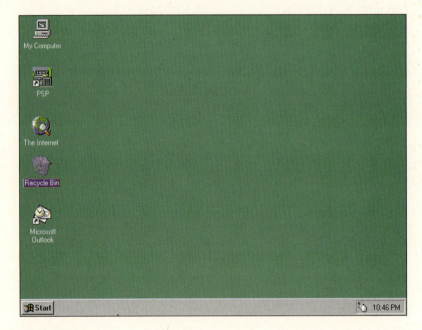

Figure W.1

> **Note** The desktop can be customized, so the desktop on the computer you're using will not look exactly like the one shown in the illustrations in this overview.

Overview   WIN-3

Using a Mouse

A pointing device is almost an indispensable tool for using Windows 95. Although you can use the keyboard to navigate and make selections, using a mouse is often more convenient and efficient.

When you move the mouse on your desk, a pointer moves on the screen. When the pointer is on the object you want to use, you can take one of the actions described in Table W.1 to give Windows 95 an instruction.

Table W.1   Mouse Actions

Action	Description
Point	Slide the mouse across a smooth surface (preferably a mouse pad) until the pointer on the screen is on the object.
Click	Press and release the left mouse button once.
Drag	Press and hold down the left mouse button while you move the mouse, and then release the mouse button to complete the action.
Right-click	Press and release the right mouse button once. Right-clicking usually displays a shortcut menu.
Double-click	Press and release the left mouse button twice in rapid succession.

TASK 1: TO PRACTICE USING THE MOUSE:

1. Point to the My Computer icon, press and hold down the left mouse button, and then drag the mouse across the desk.
   The icon moves.
2. Drag the My Computer icon back to its original location.
3. Right-click the icon.

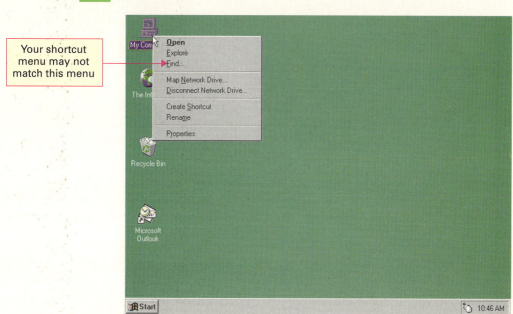

Your shortcut menu may not match this menu

WIN-4

4 Click a blank space on the screen. The shortcut menu closes.

5 Double-click the My Computer icon.

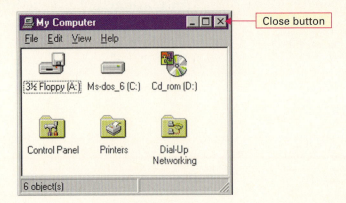

6 Click the Close ⊠ button to close the My Computer window.

Using the Basic Features of Windows 95

The basic features of Windows 95 are menus, windows, menu bars, dialog boxes, and toolbars. These features are used in all programs that are written to run under Windows 95.

Using the Start Menu

Menus contain the commands you use to perform tasks. In Windows 95, you can use the Start menu shown in Figure W.2 to start programs and to access other Windows options.

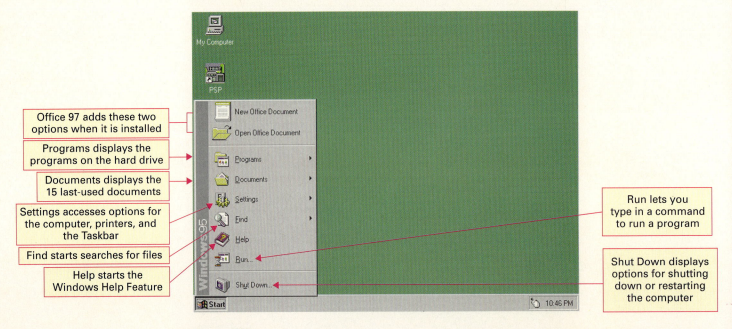

Figure W.2

Overview WIN-5

TASK 2: TO USE THE START MENU TO LAUNCH A PROGRAM:

1. Click the Start button.
   The triangles beside several of the menu options indicate that the options will display another menu.

2. Point to Programs and click the Windows Explorer icon.
   The Exploring window opens (see Figure W.3). You can use this feature of Windows 95 to manage files.

Using Windows

Clicking on the Windows Explorer icon opened a ***window,*** a Windows 95 feature that you saw earlier when you opened the My Computer window. Figure W.3 shows the common elements that most windows contain.

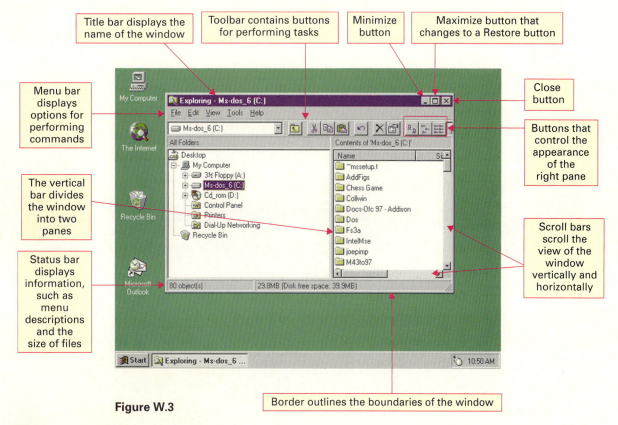

Figure W.3

TASK 3: TO WORK WITH A WINDOW:

1. Click the Maximize ☐ button if it is displayed. If it is not displayed, click the Restore ☐ button, and then click the Maximize button.
   The Maximize button changes to a Restore ☐ button.

2. Click the Minimize ☐ button.

WIN-6

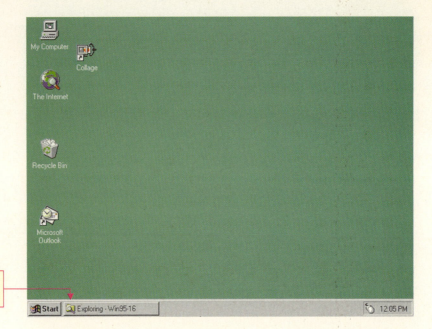

Warning When you minimize a window, the program in the window is still running and therefore using computer memory. To exit a program that is running in a window, you must click the Close button, not the Minimize button.

3 Click the Exploring button on the Taskbar and then click 🗗.

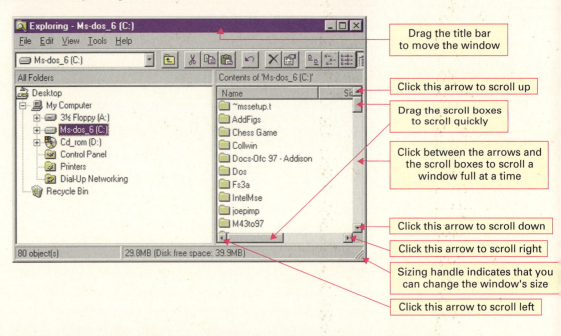

4 Point to the border of the Exploring window until the pointer changes to a double-headed black arrow, and then drag the border to make the window wider. (Be sure that all the buttons in the toolbar are visible.)

5 Practice scrolling.

6 When you are comfortable with your scrolling expertise, click 🗖.

Overview WIN-7

Using Menu Bars and Toolbars

Menu bars and toolbars are generally located at the top of a window. You can select a menu option in a menu bar by clicking the option or by pressing ALT and then typing the underlined letter for the option. When you select an option, a drop-down menu appears. Figure W.4 shows a menu with many of the elements common to menus.

> **Note** Because you can select menu commands in two ways, the steps with instructions to select a menu command will use the word choose instead of dictating the method of selection.

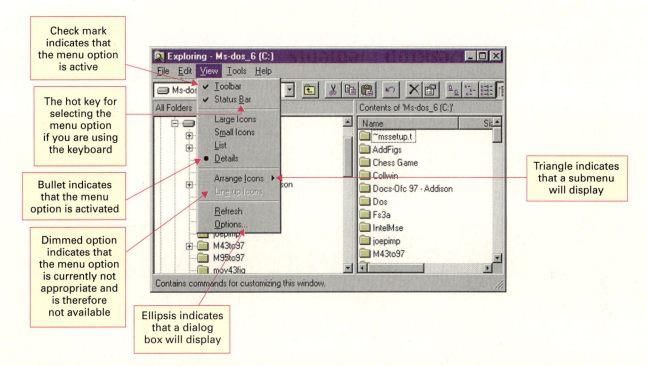

Figure W.4

Toolbars contain buttons that perform many of the same commands found on menus. To use a toolbar button, click the button; Windows 95 takes an immediate action, depending on the button's function.

> **Tip** If you don't know what a button on the toolbar does, point to the button; a ToolTip, a brief description of the button, appears near the button.

TASK 4: TO USE MENUS AND TOOLBARS:

1. Choose View in the Exploring window.
   The View menu shown in Figure W.4 displays.

2. Choose Large Icons.

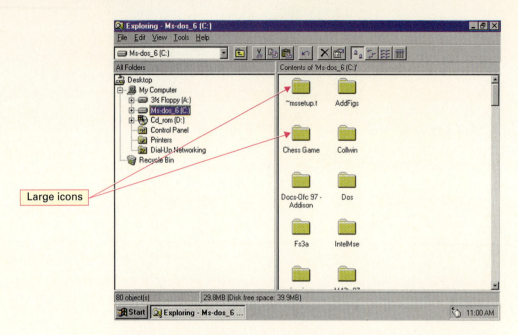

3 Click the Details button on the toolbar.

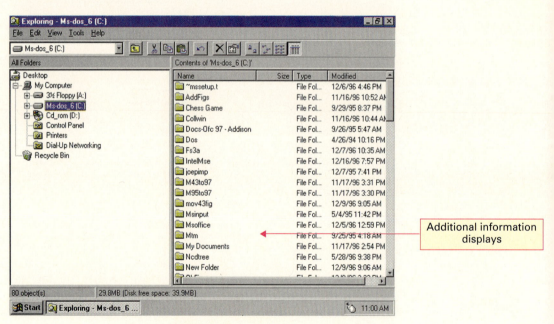

Using Dialog Boxes

When many options are available for a single task, Windows 95 conveniently groups the options in one place, called a *dialog box*. Some functions have so many options that Windows 95 divides them further into groups and places them on separate pages in the dialog box. Figures W.5 and W.6 show dialog boxes with different types of options. Throughout the remainder of this project, you practice using dialog boxes.

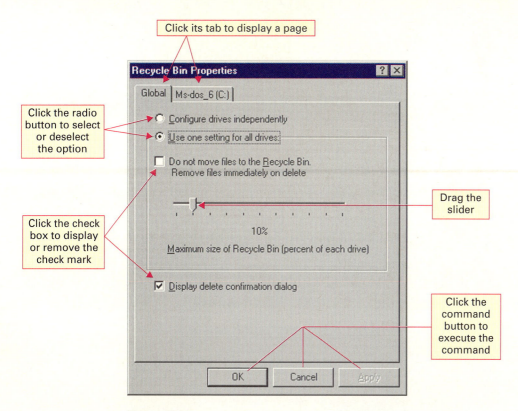

Figure W.5

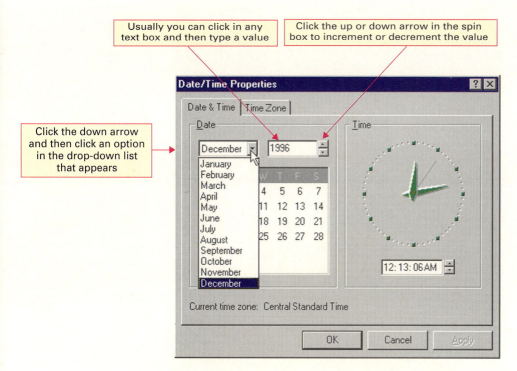

Figure W.6

Getting Help

Windows 95 provides you with three methods of accessing help information: You can look up information in a table of contents; you can search for information in an index; or you can find a specific word or phrase in a database maintained by the Find feature.

Additionally, Windows 95 provides *context-sensitive help,* called *What's This?* for the topic you are working on. This type of help is generally found in dialog boxes.

After you learn to use Help in Windows 95, you can use help in any Windows program because all programs use the same help format.

TASK 12: TO USE HELP CONTENTS, INDEX, AND FIND:

1 Click the Start button on the Taskbar and click Help.

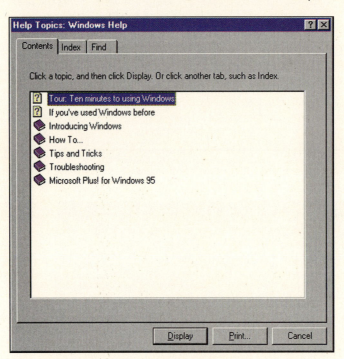

2 Click the Contents tab if a different page is displayed. The Contents page displays.

Overview **WIN-11**

3 Double-click Tips and Tricks.

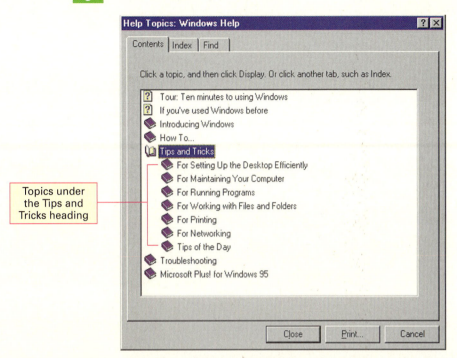

Topics under the Tips and Tricks heading

4 Double-click Tips of the Day.

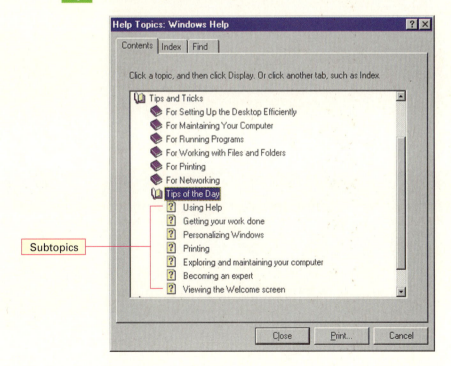

Subtopics

WIN-12

5 Double-click Using Help.

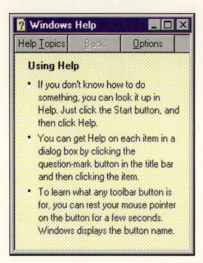

6 Read the information, click the Help Topics button, and then click the Index tab.

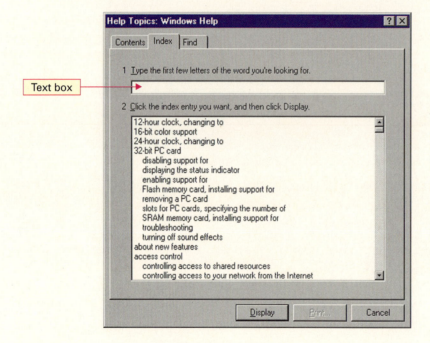

Overview **WIN-13**

7 Type **shortcut** in the textbox.

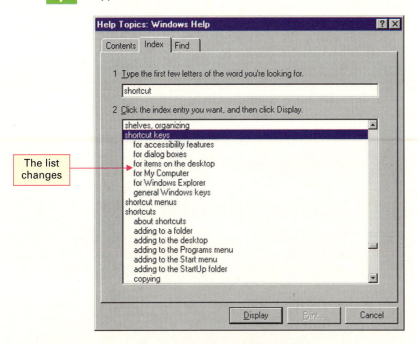

8 Double-click "shortcut menus" in the list.

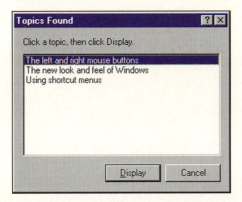

9 Double-click "Using shortcut menus."

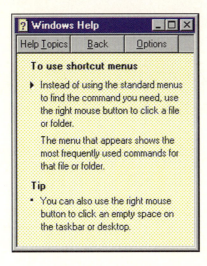

10 Read the information, click the Help Topics button, and then click the Find tab.

11 Click the What's This 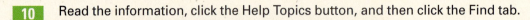 button in the Help Topics title bar. A question mark is attached to the mouse pointer.

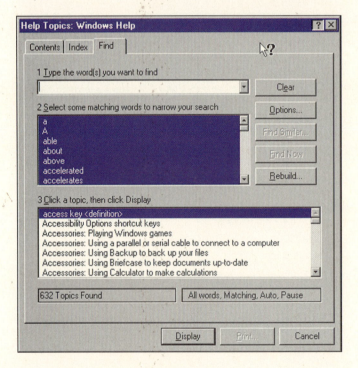

12 Click the Options button.

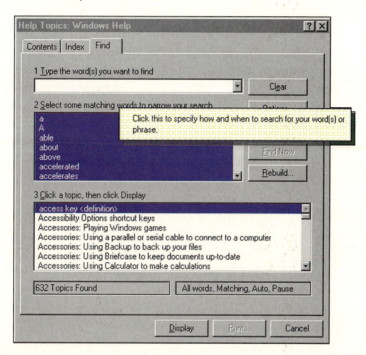

13 Read the pop-up message and then click it. The message closes.

14 Type **printing help.** (If the list at the bottom of the screen doesn't change, click the Find Now button.

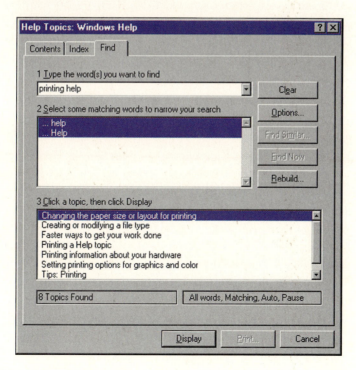

15 If necessary, scroll to "Printing a Help topic" in the list that displays and then double-click it.

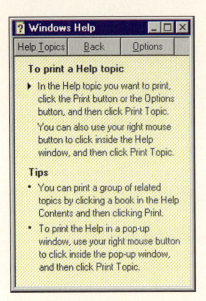

16 Click ⊠. The Help dialog box closes.

> **Tip** You can print any help article by right-clicking anywhere in the article and choosing Print Topic.

Exiting Windows 95

When you are ready to turn off the computer, you must exit Windows 95 first. You should never turn off the computer without following the proper exit procedure because Windows 95 has to do some utility tasks before it shuts down. Unlike most of us, Windows 95 likes to put everything away when it's finished. When you shut down improperly, you can cause serious problems in Windows 95.

TASK 13: TO EXIT WINDOWS 95:

1 Click the Start button and then click Shut Down.

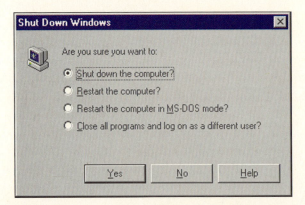

2 Click Shut down the computer? and then click Yes.

3 When the message "It's now safe to turn off your computer" appears, turn off the computer.

Databases
Using Microsoft Access 97

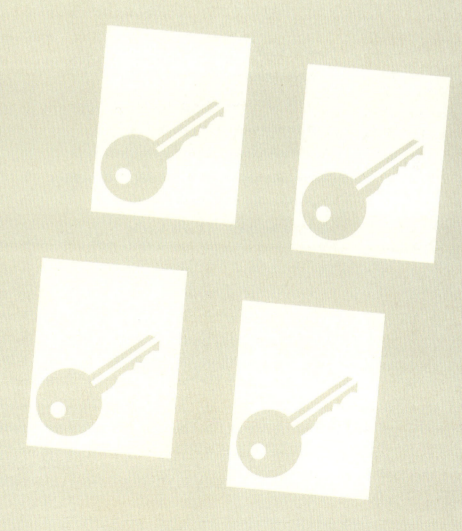

Overview

Microsoft Access is the database application that comes with Microsoft Office 97. This module identifies many of the basic concepts associated with databases and acquaints you with features of Microsoft Access in particular.

Objectives

After completing this project, you will be able to:

- ▶ **Define database terminology**
- ▶ **Design a database**
- ▶ **Launch Microsoft Access**
- ▶ **Create and save a database**
- ▶ **Identify Microsoft Access screen elements**
- ▶ **Work with menus, dialog boxes, and toolbars**
- ▶ **Get Microsoft Access Help**
- ▶ **Close a database and exit Access**

Defining Database Terminology

Databases are large collections of related data stored together to provide useful information about related topics. You work with a database each time you look up a telephone number or thumb through a catalog.

Microsoft Access is a *relational database management system* (RDBMS) for organizing and storing large volumes of data in a relatively small space so that you can find data more efficiently. Imagine what it would be like if we could use a computer database program to organize our closets!

ACC-2

Defining Database Terms

Database management systems use the basic terms listed in Table O.1.

Table O.1   Database Terms

Term	Description	Examples
Field	One unit or piece of data; the more precise each field is, the more efficient the database management system is when you start searching and manipulating data	First name, middle initial, phone number, catalog number
Record	A collection of all related fields about one person, place, or thing	A driver's license, all the information about each catalog item
File	A collection of records related to the same topic	All drivers licenses for a state, all items in a catalog
Key field	A field containing different (unique) information for each record in a database; if you don't identify a key field, Access can assign one	Social Security number, catalog item number, filename, customer number, numeric count
Objects	Items attached to a database to hold data stored in the database	Tables, forms, reports, queries, macros, modules
Relationship	An association established between tables using fields that the tables have in common	Using Social Security number, item number, or Vendor No. to tie data from one table to data from another table.

Notice how each of these terms applies to information contained in the objects pictured in Figure O.1.

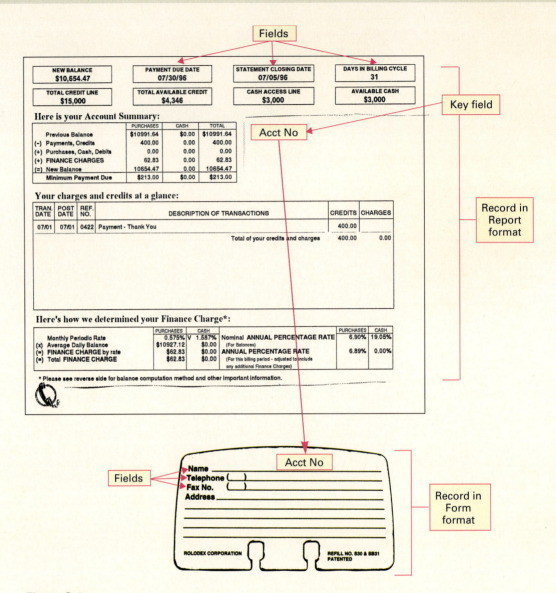

Figure O.1

Access is called an *object-oriented* relational database program because each database you create can contain more than one of each **object** listed in Table O.2.

Table O.2   Database Objects

Object	Description
Table	The primary unit of a database that stores field names, field descriptions, field controls, and field data. Tables display multiple records in a row/column format similar to a spreadsheet layout.
Query	A structured guideline used to search database tables and retrieve records that meet specific conditions.
Form	An aesthetically pleasing layout of table data designed to display one record on-screen at a time.
Report	An organized format of database data designed to generate printouts that provide meaningful information.
Macros *	A mini program that stores a set of instructions designed to perform a particular task.
Module *	A collection of Visual Basic programming procedures stored together to customize the Access environment.

* Macros and modules are advanced topics that extend beyond the scope of this text.

Figures O.2a-O.2c show how different objects display the same data.

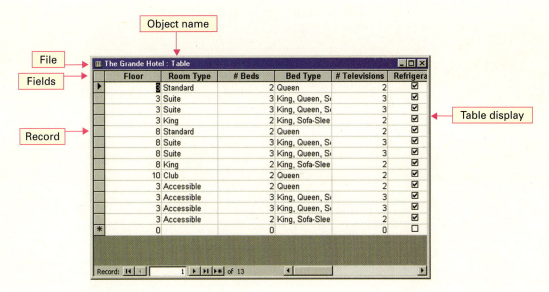

Figure O.2a

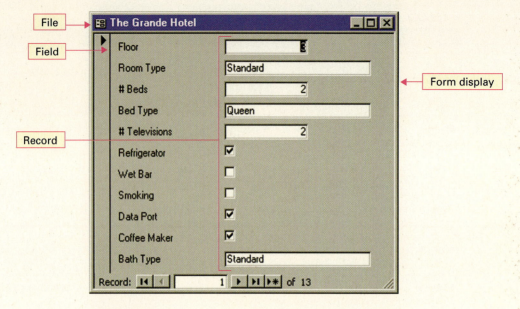

Figure O.2b

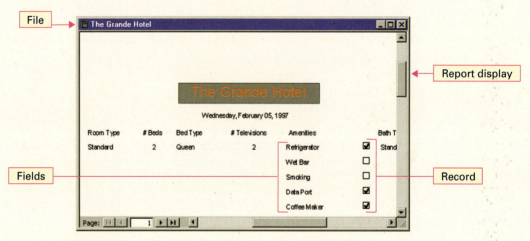

Figure O.2c

Because a database can contain numerous objects, only one database can be open at a time.

Designing a Database

Making the database easier to manage requires careful planning—and the time you spend planning the database reduces the amount of time you spend creating and maintaining the database. Determine the purpose of the database, the data you want to store, and the type of information you want to pull from the database. To print information from a database onto the Rolodex card pictured in Figure O.1, for example, the data must be contained in fields in one of the database tables. You can then create a report format that places the data on the Rolodex-size card.

After you determine the purpose of the database, you're ready to design it. Consider these points as you design the database:

- Determine how many objects (tables, forms, and reports) you need to include in the database file.
- Identify the pieces of information you want to include in each object.
- List the fields you want to include in each object in the database, breaking the information into its smallest pieces; for example, break *Name* into three fields (*First Name, Middle Name, Last Name*).
- Assign names to fields that clearly identify the data the field contains.
- In a table, place key fields first and organize remaining fields in order of importance for each database object.
- Group together similar or related fields, such as those that make up an address, for each database object.
- List all fields for each database object on paper, and next to each field, jot down the maximum number of spaces each field requires and the type of data (text characters, numbers, or dates) each field contains.

Figure O.3 displays field information to be included in an address book.

Field Name	Field Type	Field Length
Last Name	Text	20
First Name	Text	15
Middle Initial	Text	2
Street	Text	25
City	Text	20
State	Text	2
ZIP	Number	5 (or 9)
Home Telephone	Number	12
Business Telephone	Number	12
E-Mail Address	Text	25

Figure O.3

Launching Microsoft Access

After you power up the computer, log onto required networks, and respond to message windows built into the system, Windows 95 starts automatically. Think of the Start button as the launch pad and you'll be able to quickly get Access up and running.

TASK 1: TO LAUNCH ACCESS:

1. Click the Start **Start** button.
2. Point to Programs.

ACC-8

3 Point to Microsoft Access and click.

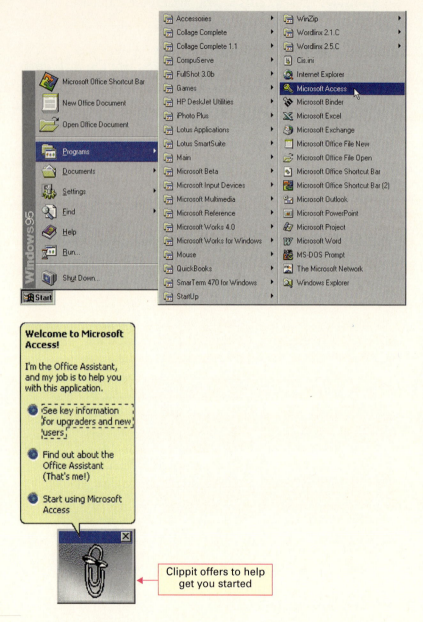

Clippit offers to help get you started

4 Click Start Using Microsoft Access if the Office Assistant displays.

Creating and Saving a Database

The first time you launch Access, the **Office Assistant** pops up, introduces itself, and offers assistance. After the first launch, the Office Assistant takes a seat up on the toolbar and waits for you to call for help. If you don't see the Office Assistant, that's okay. You learn more about it later in this overview; for now you just want to get started. The dialog box shown in Figure O.4 presents options that enable you to create a new database or open an existing one.

Overview ACC-9

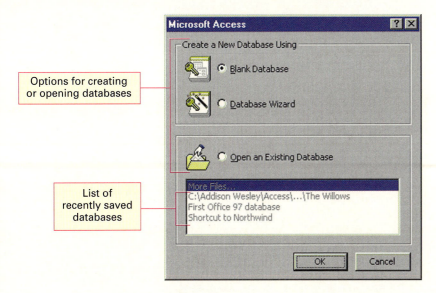

Figure O.4

When you create a new database, you have to do your part: you have to name the database and identify the folder you want to use to store the database. Eventually, you will create objects within the database, and Access will store the objects together in the same database file.

> **Note** If you're not ready to create or open a database but just want to learn more about using Access, you can click Cancel in the Access dialog box and then open the Help menu.

TASK 2: TO CREATE AND SAVE A NEW DATABASE FILE:

1 Click Blank Database and then click OK.

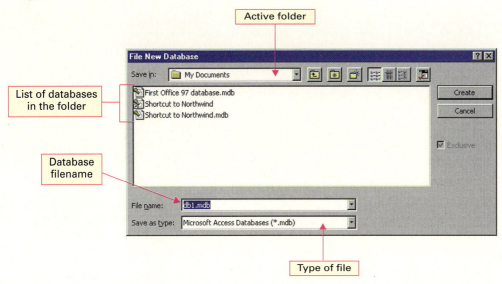

2 Select the folder you want to use to store the database from the Save in drop-down list as directed by your instructor.

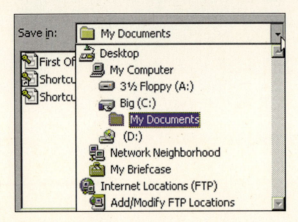

3 Type **The Willows** in the File name text box and press (ENTER). Access automatically saves the file. Unless someone has customized your Microsoft Access environment, the screen should resemble the screen shown in Figure O.5.

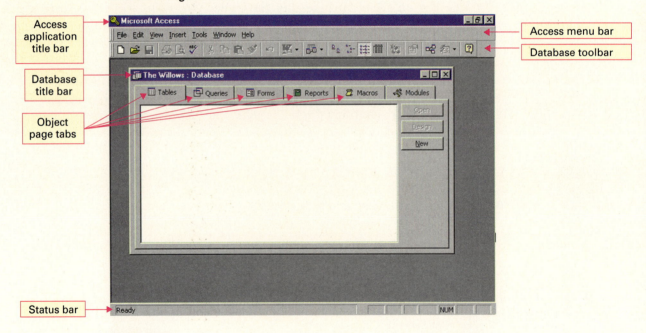

Figure O.5

Identifying Microsoft Access Screen Elements

The Microsoft Access screen features a number of elements found in other application windows as well as several elements unique to Microsoft Access, as you can see in Table O.3.

Table O.3 Access Screen Features

Screen Feature	Description
Menu bar	Provides access to commands used to perform tasks. The menu bar changes, depending on the task you're performing and the object that is active.
Application title bar	Identifies the application name and contains the application icon, Maximize/Restore, Minimize, and Close buttons. If the database window is maximized, the application title bar also contains the name of the active database.
Database toolbar	Contains buttons that serve as shortcuts for performing the most common tasks.
Database window	Organizes objects by type to make accessing objects more efficient.
Object Page tabs	Provide access to objects contained in the database.
Status bar	Displays information about the program status, instructions for performing selected tasks, active key information, and trouble messages.

Working with Menus, Dialog Boxes, and Toolbars

Menus and toolbars provide access to features and commands you use as you perform tasks in Access. Dialog boxes present options for you to choose as you create database files and objects, format forms and reports, and build databases.

Identifying Menu Features

The Access *menu bar* appears just below the *title bar* in the Access window. Menu items contained on the menu bar group commands for performing tasks according to type. Don't be surprised when your Access screen seems to change for no reason: in Access, the menu bar changes as you work with different database objects. To display a list of menu commands, point to the menu item and click. Figure O.6 identifies the standard features of Access menus you see.

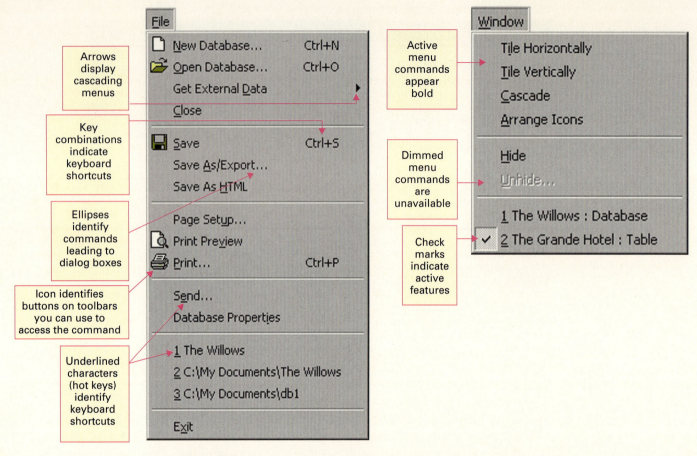

Figure O.6

Working with Toolbars

You can perform many of the most frequently used menu commands or display dialog boxes by clicking buttons on the Access **toolbars**. A **Screen-Tip** pops up when you point to any toolbar button, identifying the task that that button performs. The toolbar displayed in the Access window changes automatically as you work with objects and perform different tasks, just as the menu changes.

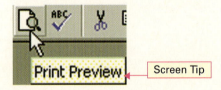

Working with Dialog Boxes

A dialog box appears when you choose a menu command followed by an ellipsis or when you click certain toolbar buttons. Figure O.7 identifies features that you'll see as you work with dialog boxes. Not all features appear in every dialog box.

Overview ACC-13

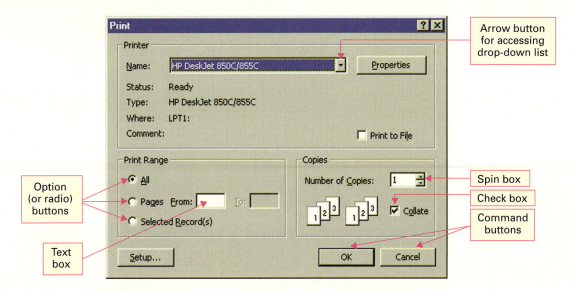

Figure O.7

TASK 3: TO DISPLAY MENUS AND DIALOG BOXES AND USE THE TOOLBAR:

1 Point to the File menu and click.
The File menu shown in Figure O.6 displays.

2 Click Open Database.

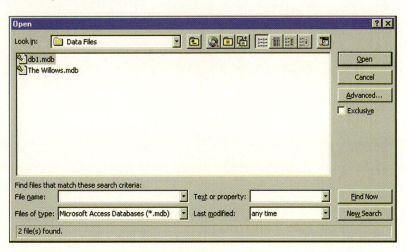

3 Press ESC to close the dialog box.

4 Point to the Spelling button on the toolbar and pause to see the ScreenTip.

5 Click the Open button on the toolbar. The Open dialog box opens again.

6 Close the dialog box again.

Getting Help

Microsoft Access provides numerous ways for you to get *online help* as you work. Simply display the Microsoft Access Help menu and choose the help feature you want to use:

- The Office Assistant, which enables you to ask questions about the task you want to perform.
- The standard three-page Windows 95 Help dialog box, which displays Contents, Index, and Find to search for information on the topic or procedure you need.
- The What's This? feature to obtain a brief description of a button, feature, or command.
- Microsoft on the Web to explore information about new products, obtain answers to frequently asked questions, recommend improvements to the program, and so forth.

In addition, Microsoft Access provides context-sensitive help and tips as you work. Because the Office Assistant automatically pops up as you work with Access, it's the Help feature used to obtain Help in this book.

> **Note** Online help has proven to be a more efficient method for obtaining help than searching through voluminous manuals for tips and information about specific programs and tasks. However, "online help" doesn't refer to connecting to the Internet or communications provider; it simply refers to the help provided by the software that is accessible from the computer.

Using the Office Assistant

The Office Assistant is a feature new to Microsoft Office 97 applications. Because you can type questions or topics for which you want help in the Office Assistant's text box, this feature is already growing in popularity. Office Assistant is easy to use, personably animated, and provides a more focused list of help topics than the list displayed when you use the Find or Contents features.

TASK 4: TO DISPLAY, USE, AND CLOSE THE OFFICE ASSISTANT:

1 Click the Office Assistant button.

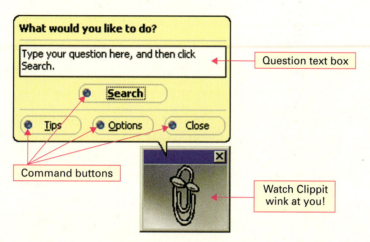

2 Type **Create a Table** in the Question text box; then press (ENTER).

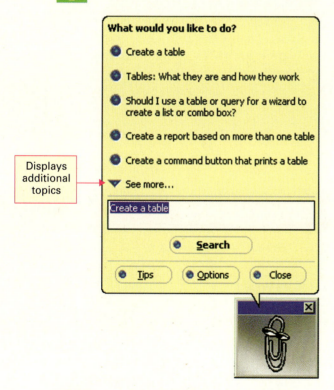

3 Click the button beside Create a table, at the top of the related topics list.

ACC-16

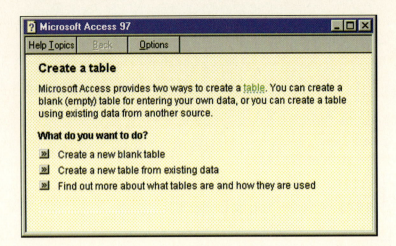

4 Review the information in the help dialog box and then click the Close ⊠ button.
The list of related topics disappears; the Office Assistant remains on-screen until you close it.

5 Click ⊠ on the Office Assistant window.

Using What's This? Help

The What's This? Help feature provides a simple, straightforward way for you to point to something on-screen and get a quick definition in a pop-up box. In Access 97, you can select What's This? Help from the Help menu or press Shift+F1.

TASK 5: TO USE WHAT'S THIS? HELP:

1 Press (SHIFT)+(F1).
The pointer changes to an arrow with a question mark attached.

2 Click the Forms tab on the database window.

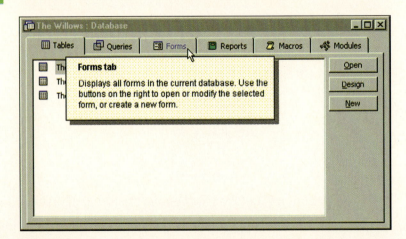

3 Click again.
The pop-up box closes.

Overview   ACC-17

Using Help Contents

The "Getting Help" section of the Overview of Windows 95 provides a comprehensive overview of how Help features work in most Windows 95 products. This quick review will give you a peek at some of the topics you'll find when you use the Help feature in Access.

TASK 6: TO LOOK UP THE NEW FEATURES OF ACCESS 97:

1 Choose Help.
The Help menu drops down.

2 Choose Contents and Index and click the Contents tab if necessary.

3 Double-click Welcome to Microsoft Access 97 - What's New?

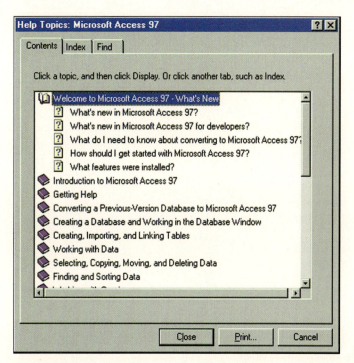

4 Double-click How should I get started with Microsoft Access 97?

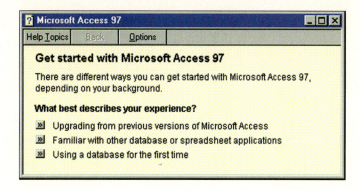

ACC-18

5 Click the button beside Using a database for the first time.
Another list of possible topics opens.

6 Review the list of topics and then click ☒ in the Help window.

Using the Help Index

The Help Index feature resembles the Office Assistant in the way it lets you type a topic and see a list of related topics. The basic difference is that you see a comprehensive listing of all Help topics in the Index window—not just the few that Office Assistant identifies when you ask it for help.

TASK 7: TO SEARCH FOR TOPICS IN THE INDEX ABOUT RELATIONSHIPS:

1 Choose Help, Contents and Index, and click on the Index tab if necessary. The Index list opens.

2 Type **relationships** and review the list of topics related to relationships.

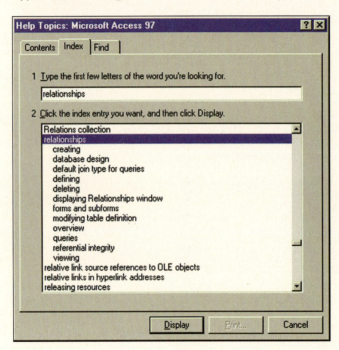

Overview ACC-19

3 Double-click the word *overview* in the list.

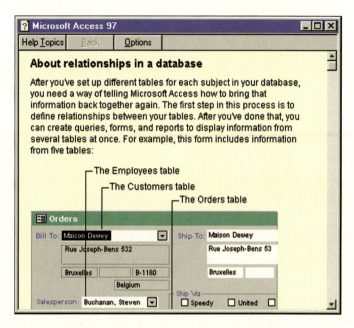

4 Read the Help dialog box and then click ⊠.
The dialog box closes.

Getting Help from the Microsoft Web Site

If you're connected to the Internet, you can access the Microsoft World Wide Web site to obtain additional help information. The site provides information directly from Microsoft support team members as well as information from other users.

TASK 8: TO ACCESS ONLINE SUPPORT FROM THE MICROSOFT WEB SITE:

1 Choose Help, Microsoft on the Web.

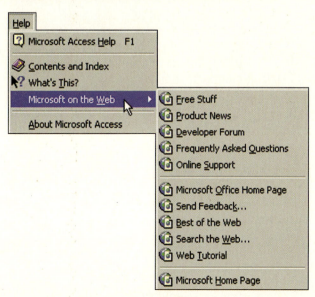

2 Choose Online Support.

3 Complete the standard procedure for logging onto the Internet using your service provider, if necessary.

4 Review the available help topics and then log off the Internet.

Closing a Database and Exiting Microsoft Access

After you've completed your work on a database, you need to close it. When you finish using Access, you need to close the database and exit Access.

TASK 9: TO CLOSE A DATABASE AND EXIT ACCESS:

1 Click ⊠ on the database window.

> **Tip** As you close a database, Access examines each object in the database and reminds you to save changed objects by displaying a message window. Click Yes to save changes to the object, No to discard changes, or Cancel to return to the database.

2 Click ⊠ on the application window.

Summary and Exercises

Summary

- Microsoft Access is an object-oriented relational database program.
- Databases are collections of related data stored together to provide useful information about related topics.
- You must name new databases as you create them.
- Each database can contain numerous tables, forms, reports, queries, macros, and modules, each designed to focus on a particular aspect of the broad-based database theme.
- Only one database can be open at a time.
- The toolbar that contains tools needed for specific tasks appears automatically.
- Access offers a variety of resources from which you can get online help.
- Microsoft Access reminds you to save changes to objects you create before you exit the program.

Key Terms and Operations

Key Terms
form
macro
menu bar
module
object
Office Assistant
online help
query
relational database
report
status bar
table
title bar
toolbar
ScreenTips

Operations
exit Microsoft Access
launch Microsoft Access
name and save a Microsoft Access database
retrieve help from the Web
use Office Assistant

Study Questions

Multiple Choice

1. To display the Help dialog box,
   a. choose Help, Contents and Index.
   b. click the Office Assistant button.
   c. press Shift+F1.
   d. choose Help, About Microsoft Access.

2. To start Microsoft Access,
   a. double-click the Outlook icon on the desktop.
   b. click Start and choose Programs, Microsoft Access.
   c. start Windows 95 and then press Alt+A.
   d. open My Computer.

3. What feature identifies toolbar buttons?
   a. the Tipster
   b. Office Assistant
   c. the Objects button
   d. ScreenTips

4. All the following are features of dialog boxes *except*
   a. option buttons.
   b. text boxes.
   c. drop-down lists.
   d. ScreenTips.

5. When you launch Microsoft Access,
   a. a new database appears.
   b. the Open dialog box appears.
   c. the Microsoft Access dialog box appears so that you can tell Access whether you want to create a new database or open an existing database.
   d. a blank table appears so that you can enter field names.

6. How many databases can be open at the same time?
   a. one
   b. ten
   c. as many as the memory installed on the computer can handle
   d. an infinite number

7. All the following procedures can be used to exit Microsoft Access *except*
   a. choosing File, Exit.
   b. clicking the Close button in the menu bar.
   c. pressing Alt+F4.
   d. double-clicking the application control icon.

8. What database term represents a unit of data, such as *First Name?*
   a. field
   b. record
   c. file
   d. key field

9. A unique unit of data can be used as a
   a. field.
   b. record.
   c. file.
   d. key field.

10. To set aside room on a disk to contain the database,
    a. you must save the database as you create it.
    b. type **reserved** in the title field.
    c. open an existing database.
    d. check with your instructor.

Short Answer
1. Why is it necessary to save and name a database as you create it?
2. What's the basic object of a database?
3. How are fields related to files?
4. How many toolbars are available in Microsoft Access?

5. Where does the filename you assign to a database appear?
6. What's the default toolbar displayed in Microsoft Access?
7. How do you find out what task a toolbar button performs?
8. Which Help feature enables you to type a question and displays a narrow range of topics in response to your question?
9. What does an ellipsis following a menu command mean?
10. What's a database management system?

For Discussion
1. How does the procedure for launching Microsoft Access differ from the procedure for launching other Windows 95 applications?
2. Why is planning your database important?
3. What factors should you keep in mind when planning a database?
4. Describe each of the different objects that can be created in a database?

Review Exercises

1. Designing a New Database
One of the databases that The Willows wants you to create is an employee database. It will be used to keep track of names, addresses, salary information, employment history, and other pertinent information about the people who work for each facility at The Willows. Create a list of data fields you would recommend be included in The Willows' employee table. Include an estimated number of characters required by the data to be entered into each field, and record an example of data that might be typed into the field.

2. Getting Help About Wizards
Because Microsoft Office 97 incorporates the use of wizards to help you create databases and objects within databases, you need to learn more about how wizards can help you with your work. Ask the Office Assistant to locate information about creating a database by using a wizard. Follow these steps:

1. Click the Office Assistant button on the toolbar.

2. Type **Tell me about the Database Wizard** in the question text box of the Office Assistant window and then press (ENTER).

3. Click Create a database in the list of items displayed by the Office Assistant.

4. Click Create a database using a Database Wizard at the bottom of the Create a Database Help window, and then review the information and steps displayed in the Help window.

Assignments

1. Identifying Fields to Include in Database for The Willows
The reception desk of The Grande Hotel at The Willows Resort wants to use the database for The Willows to identify characteristics of the different rooms available at the hotel. Develop a list of field names, field types, and field sizes you think should be included in a table to provide useful information to reception clerks. These data fields will be used in Project 1 to create one of the table objects in the database.

2. Exploring the Microsoft Access Forum on the Web to Look for Jobs
The Microsoft Access Web page contains links to many interesting and helpful sites. (The Microsoft home page is www.Microsoft.com.) One site to which the Microsoft Access page is linked is the Microsoft Access Job Forum. (Click on Product.) Using Microsoft Access on the Web help, locate the Job Forum and copy job information for five jobs listed on the Forum. If the system permits, you may want to download detailed job descriptions from this forum.

PROJECT 1

Building a Database

Now that you've created a Microsoft Access 97 database, you're ready to build the database by adding objects to the database. In this project, you will create a table to store data and a form to view the data on-screen.

Objectives

After completing this project, you will be able to:

- ➤ Open an Access database
- ➤ Create an Access database table
- ➤ Open an Access database table
- ➤ Add records to an Access database table
- ➤ Check the spelling of data in a database table
- ➤ Create and save a form
- ➤ Navigate datasheets and forms
- ➤ Preview and print database data

The Challenge

As the data-entry specialist for The Willows, you build and maintain databases for The Willows. The first *table* you need to add to the database called *The Willows* will be used by reception clerks at The Grande Hotel to check room descriptions when guests check in. Mr. Gilmore, manager of The Grande Hotel, has developed a list of information he wants you to place in the database table.

ACC-25

ACC-26

The Solution

Your job is to create a new table in the database *The Willows* and define the table fields to hold the information provided by Mr. Gilmore. The table fields are shown in Figure 1.1. After saving the table, you need to enter records in the table, create a form to display table data, and print database data.

The Setup

Just to make sure that you're on the same screen as those pictured in this module, you may want to check some of the settings before you get started. This module assumes that the default settings were in place when the lab guru installed the program on the machine. Because many students work with the lab computers, though, some of the settings may have changed.

If you don't see a toolbar on the screen when you open the Access database, choose View, Toolbars. Then click the toolbar listed at the top of the cascading menu. If you see extra toolbars, close them. After you activate one toolbar, Access should automatically display appropriate toolbars as you work with various features.

If you don't see a status bar, choose Tools, Options. When the Options dialog box displays, click the View page tab and then click the check box beside Status Bar at the top of the page. While you're in the Options dialog box, check the Keyboard page to see which options are selected. Ensure that Next Field is selected in the Move After Enter section in the upper-left corner, so you can press Enter as well as Tab to move from one field to the next.

Most of the pictures you see in this project display the screen with objects in their own windows. If you have objects maximized, click the Restore button on each object window.

> **Tip** If your screen still doesn't match the ones shown here, ask your instructor to help you locate those features that appear to be missing.

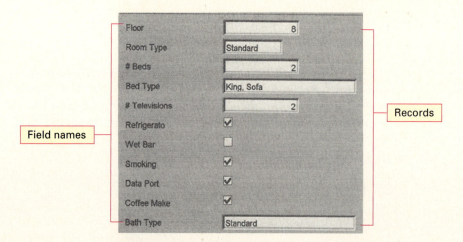

Figure 1.1

Opening an Access Database

When you launch Access, the Microsoft Access dialog box contains an option for opening an existing database. In addition, the last five databases saved on the computer appear in the list box at the bottom of the Microsoft Access dialog box.

TASK 1: TO OPEN A DATABASE:

1. Launch Access.

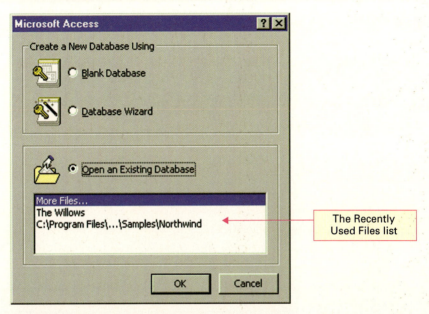

2. Double-click *The Willows* in the list at the bottom of the Microsoft Access dialog box.

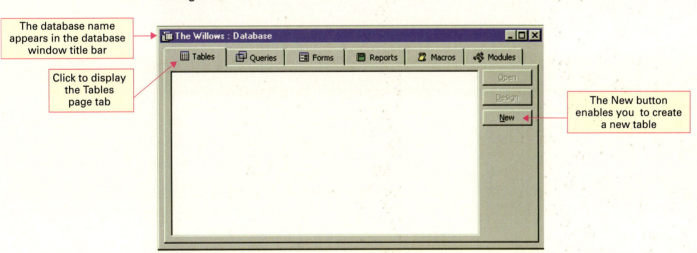

Note If the file you want doesn't appear on the dialog box list, select More Files. From the Open dialog box that appears, select the folder that has the database you want to open and then double-click the database filename.

Creating an Access Database Table

The primary object used to store data in a database is the *database table*. Tables hold the field names, field descriptions, and data for each field of each record. Tables make up the underlying structure for data stored in a database.

The first object you create in the database *The Willows* is a table to hold room descriptions for The Grande Hotel.

TASK 2: TO CREATE A NEW DATABASE TABLE:

1. Click the New button on the tables page in the database window.

2. Select Design View in the New Table dialog box; then click OK.

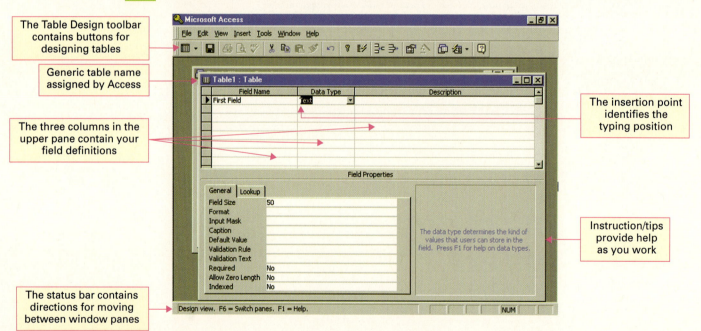

- The Table Design toolbar contains buttons for designing tables
- Generic table name assigned by Access
- The three columns in the upper pane contain your field definitions
- The status bar contains directions for moving between window panes
- The insertion point identifies the typing position
- Instruction/tips provide help as you work

Defining Table Fields

Table 1.1 describes the data types available in Access.

Table 1.1 Access Data Types

Data Type	Description
Text	Any combination of alphabetic and numeric characters, such as names, addresses, and telephone numbers, that aren't used in calculations. Text is the default data type.
Memo	Long entries that require multiple lines of text, such as detailed descriptions and performance notes.
Number	Numeric values, such as the number of items or number of days worked, that might be used in calculations.
Date/Time	Dates, such as date hired, and times, such as 1:00.
Currency	Monetary values, such as a salary, consisting of numbers that might be used in calculations.
AutoNumber	Numbers assigned by Access to uniquely identify each record; these values can't be changed, deleted, or edited.
Yes/No	Single-character entry fields that are marked when the status of the field is true (yes) or left blank when the status is false (no).
OLE Object	Fields that may contain embedded or linked objects, such as a picture or a document.
Hyperlink	Fields linked to other objects, Web pages, or documents that appear when the field is clicked.
Lookup Wizard	Fields that enable you to access a value from a table or list of values.

TASK 3: TO DEFINE FIELDS IN THE TABLE DESIGN WINDOW:

 Type **Floor** in the Field Name column of the first row of the top pane; then press `TAB`.

> **Tip** Being human, you're bound to make mistakes as you're typing. To correct your errors, press Backspace to remove the incorrect characters and then type the correct characters. If you discover a mistake after you've moved the insertion point to the next column, point to the column containing the error and double-click to select the field contents. Typing the correct data while the field contents are selected automatically replaces the selected data.

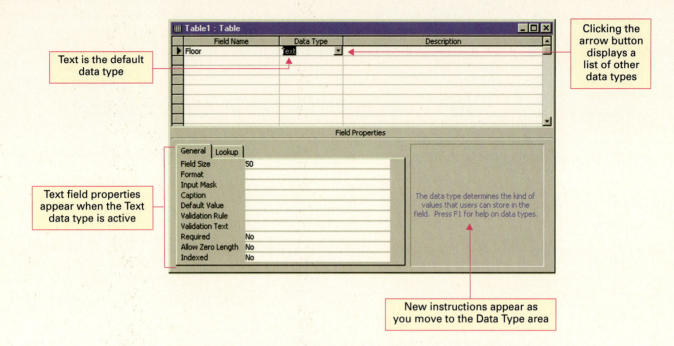

2 Click the arrow button at the right side of the Data Type column.

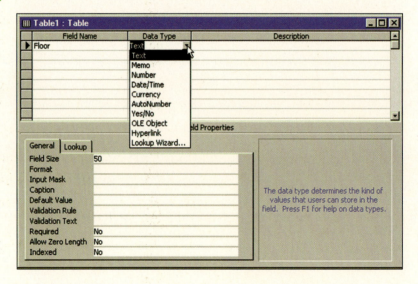

3 Click Number to tell Access that the Floor field will contain numeric data.

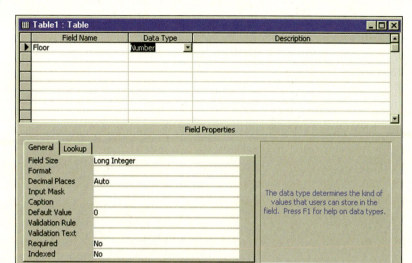

4 Press TAB to move to the Description field. Then type **Valid entries range from 3 through 12** in the text box.

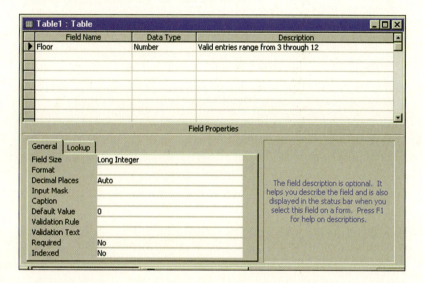

5 Press TAB to move to the Field Name column of the second row.

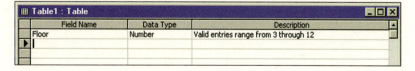

6 Type **Room Type,** press TAB twice, and type **Standard Room or Suite** in the Description text box.

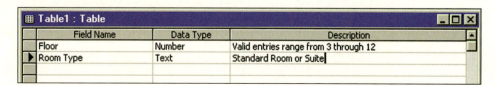

7 Press F6 to move to the Field Properties pane.

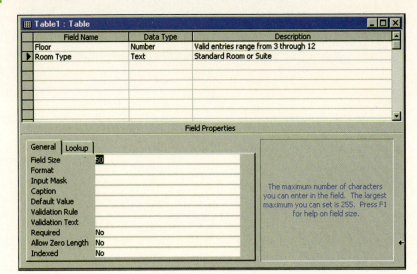

8 Type **10** in the Field Size text box; then press F6 to return to the top pane.

9 Press TAB to move to the next row of the Field Name column.

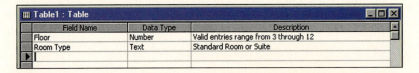

10 Follow the same procedures to add the remaining fields shown in Figure 1.2 to the table design. Accept the default values for field sizes.

Field Name	Data Type	Description
Floor	Number	Valid entries range from 3 through 12
Room Type	Text	Standard Room or Suite
# Beds	Number	
Bed Type	Text	King, Queen, Sofa, Double, Rollaway
# Televisions	Number	
Refrigerator	Yes/No	
Wet Bar	Yes/No	
Smoking	Yes/No	
Data Port	Yes/No	
Coffee Maker	Yes/No	
Bath Type	Text	Standard, Shower, Jacuzzi

Figure 1.2

Saving and Closing a Database Table

After you enter all fields and field descriptions, you need to save the table and close it until you're ready to start entering data into the table.

Project 1: Building a Database   ACC-33

TASK 4: TO SAVE AND CLOSE A DATABASE TABLE:

1 Click the Save button.

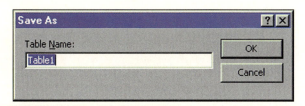

2 Type **The Grande Hotel** in the Table Name text box and press (ENTER).

3 Click No to tell Access that you don't want to name a key field.

4 Click the Close button on the table window.

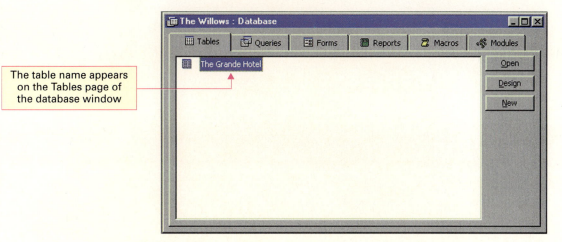

The table name appears on the Tables page of the database window

Opening an Access Database Table

Before you can add data to a database table, you need to open the table. Access places an Open button on each page of objects in the database window to make opening objects more efficient.

TASK 5: TO OPEN A DATABASE TABLE:

1 Select The Grande Hotel on the Tables page of the database window, if necessary.

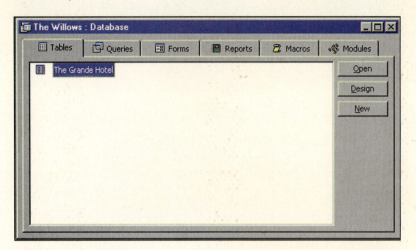

2 Click the Open button.

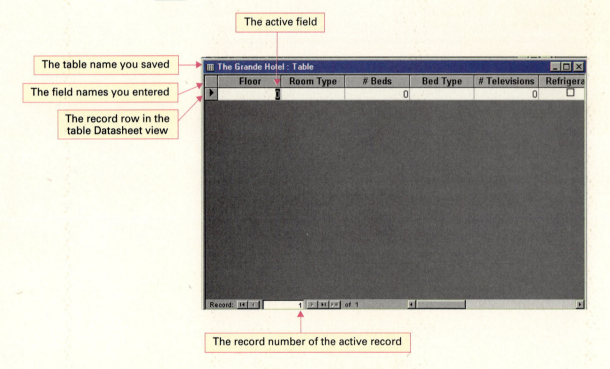

Adding Records to an Access Database Table

Mr. Gilmore provided a list of features that describe the rooms in The Grande Hotel. You can use the list to add records to the table. As you enter the data, be consistent in the way you position commas and capitalize words. Any inconsistencies will crop up later when you use the data to create reports and search for data.

Project 1: Building a Database   ACC-35

> **Tip** As you're typing, use the same techniques to correct mistakes that you used to correct errors earlier.

TASK 6: TO ADD RECORDS TO THE DATABASE TABLE:

1 For the first record, type the following entries in the designated fields, pressing TAB to move from one field to the next:

Floor	Room Type	# Beds	Bed Type	# Televisions
3	**Standard**	**2**	**Queen**	**2**

> **Tip** If you set your options to move to the next field when you press Enter, you can press either Enter or Tab to move to the next field.

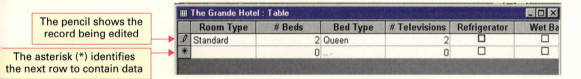

The pencil shows the record being edited

The asterisk (*) identifies the next row to contain data

2 Click the check box (or press SPACE) in the Refrigerator column to select the check box; then press TAB three times.
The Data Port field is active.

3 Select the check box in the Data Port column and press TAB.
The Coffee Maker field is active now.

4 Select the check box in the Coffee Maker column.

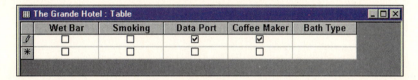

5 Type **Standard** in the Bath Type column, and press TAB to move to the next record.

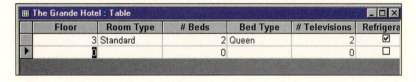

The first record is complete, and you're ready to enter data into the next record. Use the same method to add data to the records as shown in Figure 1.3.

ACC-36

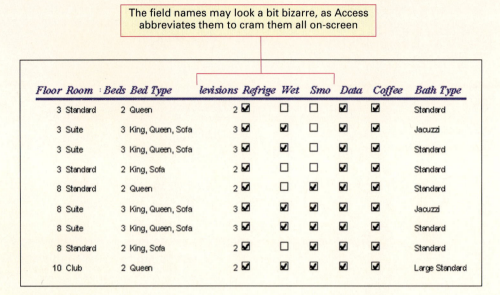

Figure 1.3

> **Note** As you add data to each record, Access saves the data as part of the table. Therefore, after you have completed all records for the table, you don't need to save the table again before closing it.

Checking the Spelling of Data in a Database Table

Access is equipped with a spelling checker that contains a few unique features designed to check the spelling of data in tables.

TASK 7: TO SPELL-CHECK TABLE DATA:

1 Click the Spelling button on the toolbar.

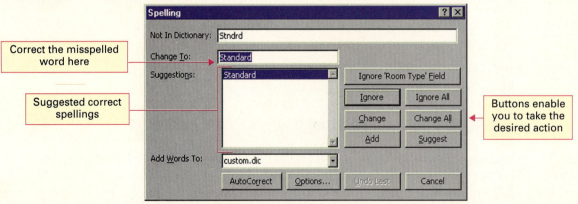

2 Click the button for the action you want to take, or select the correct spelling for the word and then click Change.

Project 1: Building a Database   ACC-37

> **Tip** When Access pauses on a word in a field that contains coded data or proper nouns, click the Ignore 'field name' Field button to tell Access not to spell-check the field. You'll get through the table quicker by limiting the fields checked to those that contain meaningful text.

3 Repeat Step 2 each time Access selects a word until all words have been checked.

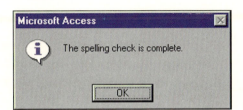

4 Click the OK button to close the message box.

Creating and Saving an AutoForm

Access automatically displays new tables using the **Datasheet view** so that you see field names as column headings and records as rows. The Datasheet view enables you to see multiple records on-screen at the same time and makes data entry more efficient. When you want to view records on-screen one at a time, you need to create a *form*. Forms use the fields and data that are stored in database tables. Therefore, you must have a table open to create a form using the AutoForm procedures outlined here. You can save forms as separate objects in the database.

TASK 8: TO CREATE AND SAVE A FORM:

1 Click the New Object: AutoForm button on the Table Datasheet toolbar.

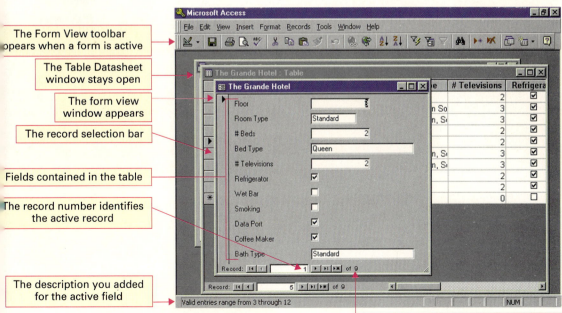

- The Form View toolbar appears when a form is active
- The Table Datasheet window stays open
- The form view window appears
- The record selection bar
- Fields contained in the table
- The record number identifies the active record
- The description you added for the active field
- The total number of records in the table

ACC-38

2 Click 💾.

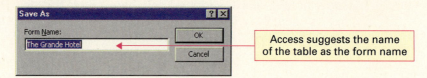

Access suggests the name of the table as the form name

3 Press (ENTER) to assign the table name to the form; then press (CTRL)+(F6) to display the database window.
Access saves the form and places the form name on the Forms page of the database window.

Navigating Datasheets and Forms

Access displays navigation buttons at the bottom of each form or datasheet; these buttons make moving among the records of a database easy. Figure 1.4 explains the purpose of each navigation button and how to use each one.

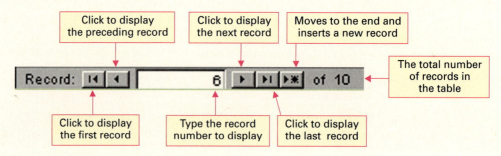

Figure 1.4

TASK 9: TO USE NAVIGATION BUTTONS TO NAVIGATE RECORDS:

1 Press (CTRL)+(F6) until the form *The Grande Hotel* appears.

2 Click ▶|.

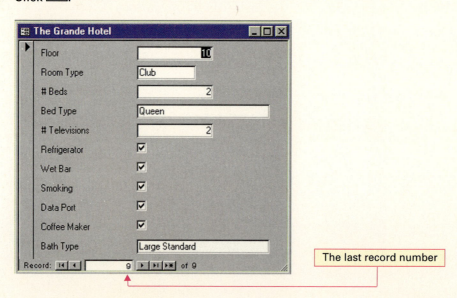

The last record number

3 Click the Previous Record button.

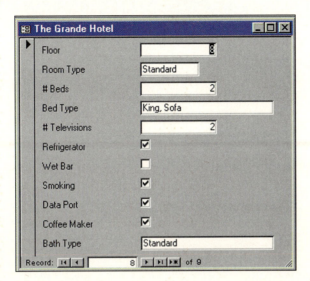

4 Select the Record Number text box, type **5,** and press (ENTER). Record 5 appears.

5 Choose View, Datasheet View to display the form *The Grande Hotel* as a datasheet.
Notice that record 5 is the active record.

6 Click the Next Record button.

7 Click .
The first table record becomes active.

You can also use keyboard techniques to navigate records in Datasheet view or *Form view.* The records displayed using keyboard techniques depend, to some extent, on whether you're working with the table datasheet or the form and whether you have field data selected, as shown in Table 1.2.

Table 1.2   Keyboard Techniques for Form and Datasheet Views

Keystroke	Form	Datasheet
← →	Left/right one character or to next or previous field if field is highlighted	Left/right one field
↑ ↓	To next or previous field if field is highlighted	Up/down one record (row)
HOME	Beginning of active field or first field in record if data is selected	First field in record (row)
END	End of active field or last field if data is selected	Last field in record (row)
CTRL+HOME	Beginning of active field or first field in active record if data is selected	First field in first record
CTRL+END	End of field or last field in active record if field is selected	Last field in last record
PGUP PGDN	Previous/next record	Previous/next screen of records
CTRL+← CTRL+→	Previous/next field	Previous/next field
CTRL+↑ CTRL+↓	First/last record	First record in same column Last record in same column

Practice each of these keystrokes in both the form and datasheet for The Grande Hotel to see how they work.

Previewing and Printing Database Data

Using the Print Preview feature in Access, you can display data on-screen as it will appear when you print the data on paper. What you see when you preview the printouts in Access depends on which object is active: the table in Datasheet view or the form. After you preview the data, you can print it by clicking the Print button on the Print Preview toolbar, or you can close the Print Preview window and print from the datasheet or form.

TASK 10: TO PREVIEW AND PRINT FORMS AND DATASHEETS:

1 Press CTRL+F6 to display the form *The Grande Hotel.*

Project 1: Building a Database   ACC-41

2 Click the Print Preview button on the toolbar.

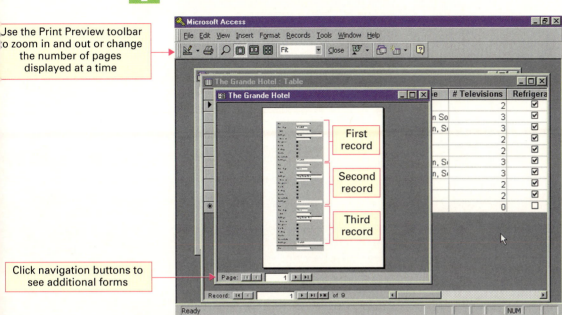

3 Click the Close button on the preview window title bar. The form *The Grande Hotel* displays.

4 Press CTRL+F6 until the datasheet for The Grande Hotel displays.

5 Click.

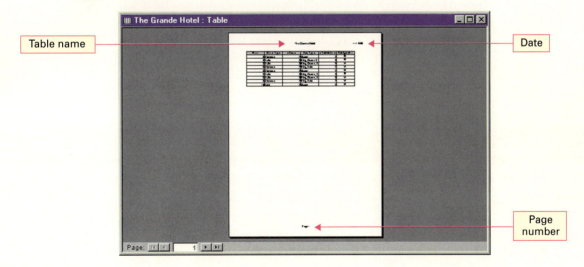

6 Click ▶ to display the next page of the printout.

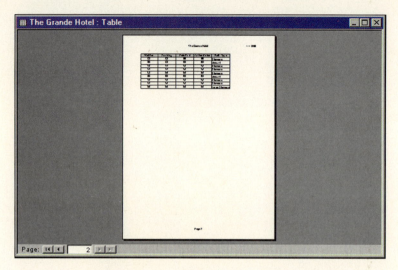

7 Click the Print 🖨 button on the Print Preview toolbar.

The Conclusion

After completing work in the database, you need to close each object that's open, save changes to objects when reminded to do so, and then close the database. You can click the Close button to close each object as well as to close the database. If you're finished working in Access, exit properly by clicking the Close button for the application. If you plan to continue working on the exercises and assignments, leave Access open.

Summary and Exercises

Summary

- Tables are used to store data in a database.
- You enter field names, field types, field lengths, and field descriptions in the Table Design view.
- To create a new table, you must first open the database that will contain the table.
- After you create a table structure, you must save the table so that you can begin adding data to the table.
- Database tables display information in the Datasheet view by default. The Datasheet view displays multiple records on-screen at a time.
- You create forms by using field definitions and descriptions contained within a table. Forms display information from only one record on-screen at a time.
- Forms are saved as separate objects in a database and appear in the Forms page of the database window.
- Navigation buttons located at the bottom of the form and datasheet windows make navigating records easy. You also can use the keyboard to move among records in a database table.
- You can print table data from both the Datasheet view and Form view.
- The spelling checker in Access enables you to skip fields that contain proper nouns or coded information.

Key Terms and Operations

Key Terms
AutoForm
Datasheet view
Form view
table

Operations
add records to a database table
create and save a database form
create and save a database table
open a database
open a database table
preview and print database data
spell-check database data

Study Questions

Multiple Choice

1. What's the basic object of a database used to store data?
   a. table
   b. form
   c. datasheet
   d. preview

2. To create a table,
   a. you must also create a new database.
   b. you may either create a new database or open an existing one.
   c. you first create a form.
   d. you press Enter.

ACC-43

3. To design your own database table and enter your field names and descriptions, click the New button on the table page in the database window and then
   a. press Enter.
   b. click New Form Wizard.
   c. select Design View and press Enter.
   d. select Datasheet View and press Enter.

4. To create a straightforward form that contains all the fields in a table,
   a. display the Forms page of the dialog box and click New.
   b. click the Design View button on the Datasheet toolbar.
   c. choose File, New, and select Form.
   d. click the New Object: AutoForm button on the toolbar.

5. The Table Design window is divided into which of the following panes?
   a. field entry, properties, instructions
   b. field entry, properties
   c. field entry, properties, instructions, help
   d. field description pane only

6. To move from one field to another in a table or form, press
   a. Tab.
   b. Esc.
   c. F6.
   d. Shift+right arrow.

7. To move to specific records in a database table,
   a. press Ctrl+Page Down.
   b. press F6.
   c. press Ctrl+Home.
   d. click the navigation buttons at the bottom of the window.

8. What special button in the Spelling dialog box lets you skip fields in a database while spell-checking?
   a. Skip button
   b. Ignore button
   c. Ignore *'field name'* Field button
   d. Change button

9. Forms can be saved
   a. as part of a table datasheet.
   b. as separate objects, using the name of the table.
   c. only if they contain different data from data in tables.
   d. outside the database only.

10. What field type uses a check box to contain field data?
    a. Text
    b. Number
    c. Date
    d. Yes/No

Short Answer

1. What's the difference between a database and a table?

2. If a table isn't open when you try to create a form, what happens?

3. What page of the database window contains AutoForms?
4. What's the most common data type?
5. What does the Yes/No data type do?
6. What's the quickest way to open a database you've saved recently?
7. To open a database table, what must be open first?
8. What navigation procedure would you use to go directly to a specific record in a database?
9. How do you add a field size to a field in Design view?
10. What's the easiest way to start the Spelling Checker in Access?

For Discussion
1. What are the different field types, and how would you use each?
2. Describe the types of information you might want to include in the Description column of the Table Design view. Where does information entered into the Description column appear when you're entering data?
3. How do the procedures required to create and save a form differ from the procedures for creating and saving a database? A table?
4. What additional information would you include in the table *The Grande Hotel?*
5. What additional tables, if any, could be added to the database *The Willows?*

Review Exercises

1. Creating a Database and a Database Table

Use the Employee database design you created in Exercise 1 in the Overview to create a new database named *The Willows Personnel*. Then create a table named *The Willows Managers* to store employee information contained in Figure 1.5 on the next page. Include fields from the information presented below in the table design.

Field Name	Data Type
First Name	Text
Middle Name	Text
Last Name	Text
Street	Text
City	Text
State	Text
ZIP	Text
Date Employed	Date/Time
Position	Text
Department	Text
Salary	Text
Business Phone	Text
Home Phone	Text

Figure 1.5

First Name	Middle Name	Last Name	Street	City	State	ZIP	Date	Position	Department	Salary	Business Phone	Home Phone
John	Richard	Gilmore	13951 Field Court	Willow Grove	SC	223	2/4/90	Manager	The Grande Hotel	120000	803-555-1200	803-555-1597
Rebecca	Rae	Jackson	10054 Ruler Court	Smithfield	SC	224	1/19/85	Manager	Willows Beach Cottages	85000	803-555-0850	803-555-3547
Ruth	Smith	Lindsey	15065 Knicker Drive	Willow Grove	SC	223	3/1/81	Manager	All Shops	101000	803-555-1010	803-555-2546
Mark	Edward	Taylor	14419 Brook Street	James Way	SC	243	5/31/88	Manager	The Atrium Grill	65000	803-555-0650	803-555-7854
Brian	Anthony	Atkinson	110 Crozet Street	Smithfield	SC	224	7/5/87	Manager	Willow Top	80000	803-555-0800	803-555-6874
Philip	James	Holmes	15018 Cordell Avenue	James Way	SC	243	8/7/93	Manager	The 18th Hole	70000	803-555-0700	803-555-9658
Marcela	Ann	Bradbury	5622 Forest Glen Road	Willow Grove	SC	223	8/13/96	Manager	Wind in the Willows	50000	803-555-0500	803-555-3574
Henry	Chung	Cho	13411 Reardon Lane	Altamont	SC	222	11/22/86	Manager	All Sandwich Shops	80000	803-555-0801	803-555-1597
Thomas	Nicholas	Williams	9007 Leesburg Pike	Willow Grove	SC	223	9/12/89	Manager	Golf/Tennis Property & Pro Shop	75000	803-555-0750	803-555-8624
Laura	Rene	Carr	9575 Kingsley Road	Smithfield	SC	224	5/16/92	Manager	Exercise/Aerobic Facility	50000	803-555-0501	803-555-9713
Frank	Robert	Davis	14563 Greenridge	James Way	SC	243	6/27/96	Manager	Miniature Golf & Little Tree Playground	30000	803-555-0300	803-555-3179
Chuck	Mercer	Bailey	1275 Garrison Road	Willow Grove	SC	223	4/28/86	Manager	Willow Pond Riding Stables	48000	803-555-0480	803-555-6482
Maria	Suarez	Sanchez	250 Windjammer Drive	Altamont	SC	222	10/15/90	Manager	Willows Water Park	36000	803-555-0360	803-555-3516

Project 1: Building a Database ACC-47

Follow these steps to create the database and table:

1. Launch Access and select Blank Database from the Microsoft Access dialog box. Then press (ENTER).
2. Type the name of the database in the File name text box, select the folder you want to use to store the database, and then press (ENTER).
3. Display the Tables page of the database dialog box, and click New.
4. Select Design View from the New Table list, and press (ENTER).
5. Type the field names and select field types in the Table Design window.
6. Click the Save button to save the table, type the table name in the Save As dialog box, press (ENTER), and respond No to the message about the key field.

2. Adding Records to a Database Table

Record the data from Figure 1.5 in the table *The Willows Managers* in the database *The Willows Personnel*. Follow these steps to add records to the table:

1. Open the database *The Willows Personnel*, and then open the table *The Willows Managers*. Hint: For fields that contain the same data in each record, press (CTRL) + " to copy data from the same field in the previous record.
2. Type the information for each field of the first record, pressing (TAB) to move to the next field.
3. Repeat Step 2 until all records are complete.
4. Spell-check the table, making any necessary changes.
5. Close the table and the database.

Assignments

1. Creating a New Table and Adding Records to the Table

The database called *The Willows* currently contains only one table—called *The Grande Hotel*. Create a new table named *The Grande Hotel Rooms* in the database *The Willows*. Add the following three fields to the table: Floor, Room Number, and Room Type. Use the data in Table 1.3 to add records to the new table. Notice that the Room Number field contains multiple room munbers for some records. Each row in Table 1.3 is a table record.

Table 1.3 Rooms in The Grande Hotel by Type

Floor	Room Number	Room Type
3	3010, 3110, 3210, 3310	Suite
3	3020–3100	Standard
3	3120–3200	King
3	3220–3300	King
3	3320–3400	Standard
4	4010, 4110, 4210, 4310	Suite
4	4020–4100	Standard
4	4120–4200	King
4	4220–4300	King
4	4320–4400	Standard
5	5010, 5110, 5210, 5310	Suite
5	5020–5100	Standard
5	5120–5200	King
5	5220–5300	King
5	5320–5400	Standard
6	6010, 6110, 6210, 6310	Suite
6	6020–6100	Standard
6	6120–6200	King
6	6220–6300	King
6	6320–6400	Standard
7	7010, 7110, 7210, 7310	Suite
7	7020–7100	Standard
7	7120–7200	King
7	7220–7300	King
7	7320–7400	Standard
8	8010, 8110, 8210, 8310	Suite
8	8020–8100	Standard
8	8120–8200	King
8	8220–8300	King
8	8320–8400	Standard

Table 1.3 *(Continued)*

Floor	Room Number	Room Type
9	9010, 9110, 9210, 9310	Suite
9	9020–9100	Standard
9	9120–9200	King
9	9220–9300	King
9	9320–9400	Standard
10	1001–1014	Club King
10	1015–1028	Club Standard
11	1101, 1111, 1121, 1131	Suite
11	1102–1110	Standard
11	1112–1120	King
11	1122–1130	King
11	1132–1140	Standard
12	1201, 1211, 1221, 1231	Suite
12	1202–1210	Standard
12	1212–1220	King
12	1222–1230	King
12	1232–1240	Standard

2. Finding Competitors on the Internet (Optional assignment)

In an effort to ensure that The Willows remains competitive with other resorts along the Atlantic coast, Mr. Gilmore would like for you to search the Internet for information about resorts in the three-state area (North Carolina, South Carolina, and Virginia) that offer golf, water recreation, and beaches. You should download pricing information. Then create a database named Competitors, and add a table that contains fields you can use to record names, locations, facilities, and prices for three of the competitors. Enter data for each of the resorts you locate, and then print a copy of the datasheet data for Mr. Gilmore's approval before adding data for additional records.

PROJECT 2

Maintaining a Database

As addresses and other data stored in the database change and employees come and go, you need to update table data to ensure that the information is accurate and to maintain the usefulness of the database. In this project, you learn how to locate records in large databases, update field data, insert and delete records in database tables, and sort and select records.

Objectives

After completing this project, you will be able to:

➤ Find records
➤ Update records
➤ Insert records
➤ Use the Replace feature
➤ Delete records
➤ Sort records
➤ Filter records by selection
➤ Filter records by form

The Challenge

As the data-entry specialist for The Willows, you are the jack-of-all-trades: you must edit, update, and maintain the database *The Willows*. Some of the equipment in rooms of The Grande Hotel has changed, and some rooms are now accessible to the handicapped. Mr. Gilmore also wants you to replace the term *Sofa* with *Sofa Sleeper* throughout the table for The Grande Hotel. After you finish making the changes to the table, he wants you to prepare a list of rooms organized by room type, a list of nonsmoking rooms, and a separate list of rooms with king-size beds. He would also like to see a list of nonsmoking rooms with king-size beds. Seems an almost overwhelming task, doesn't it?

The Solution

Access contains features that make updating the table *The Grande Hotel* in the database *The Willows* almost painless. In only a short time you can make the changes in the equipment contained in the guest rooms, change the room type for some of the rooms, and identify those rooms in The Grande Hotel that are accessible to the handicapped. After you make the changes, you can sort and select records to provide the lists that Mr. Gilmore wants. The revised table is shown in Figure 2.1.

Floor	Room Type	# Beds	Bed Type	# Televisions
3	Standard	2	Queen	2
3	Suite	3	King, Queen, Sofa Sleeper	3
3	Suite	3	King, Queen, Sofa Sleeper	3
3	King	2	King, Sofa Sleeper	2
8	Standard	2	Queen	2
8	Suite	3	King, Queen, Sofa Sleeper	3
8	Suite	3	King, Queen, Sofa Sleeper	3
8	King	2	King, Sofa Sleeper	2
10	Club	2	Queen	2
3	Accessible	2	Queen	2
3	Accessible	3	King, Queen, Sofa Sleeper	3
3	Accessible	3	King, Queen, Sofa Sleeper	3
3	Accessible	2	King, Sofa Sleeper	2

Refrigerator	Wet Bar	Smoking	Data Port	Coffee Maker	Bath Type
✓	☐	☐	✓	✓	Standard
✓	✓	☐	✓	✓	Jacuzzi
✓	✓	☐	✓	✓	Standard
✓	☐	☐	✓	✓	Standard
✓	☐	✓	✓	✓	Standard
✓	✓	✓	✓	✓	Jacuzzi
✓	✓	✓	✓	✓	Standard
✓	☐	✓	✓	✓	Standard
✓	✓	✓	✓	✓	Large Standard
✓	☐	☐	✓	✓	Standard
✓	✓	☐	✓	✓	Jacuzzi
✓	✓	☐	✓	✓	Standard
✓	☐	☐	✓	✓	Standard

Figure 2.1

The Setup

So that the screen will match the illustrations and the tasks in this project will function as described, make sure that your Access 97 settings are the same as those listed here:

ACC-52

- If you don't see a toolbar on the screen, choose View, Toolbars, and then select the toolbar listed at the top of the cascading menu.
- If you have objects maximized, click the Restore button on the window for each object.
- If you don't see the status bar, choose Tools, Options and click the View page tab. Click the check box beside Status Bar at the top of the page tab.

Check the data in your database table before you start these activities to ensure that you were consistent in your placement of commas and capitalization. Field data must be consistent to achieve the desired results.

Finding Records

To change the information contained in a database record, you must first display the record in Form view or make it the active row in the Table Datasheet view. The Access Find feature helps you locate specific records.

TASK 1: TO FIND RECORDS IN A DATABASE TABLE:

1. Open the database *The Willows* and then open the table *The Grande Hotel* in Datasheet view.
   A list of records you entered earlier appears in Datasheet view.

2. Click the Find button on the toolbar.

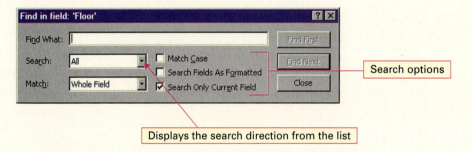

3. Type **King** in the Find What text box, select Any Part of Field from the Match drop-down list, and remove the check mark from the Search Only Current Field check box.

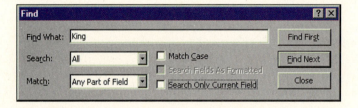

Project 2: Maintaining a Database   ACC-53

4   Click the Find First button.

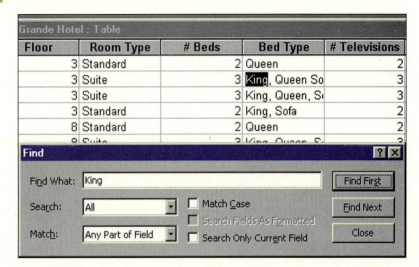

> **Note** If your records are arranged differently, Access may find a different first record.

5   Click the Find Next button until you locate a record for a Standard room containing a king-size bed.

> **Tip** Drag the title bar of the Find dialog box to move the dialog box out of the way so that you can see the complete form.

6   Press `ESC` or click the Close ⊠ button to close the Find dialog box.

Updating Records

The primary objective of finding data is generally to *update* or change the field data contained in the record. In the table *The Grande Hotel*, you need to change the room type for all Standard rooms with king-size beds to King. You can use either Datasheet view or Form view to edit the data.

TASK 2: TO UPDATE RECORDS:

1   Double-click the word *Standard* in the Room Type field.

Floor	Room Type	# Beds	Bed Type	# Televisions
3	Standard	2	Queen	2
3	Suite	3	King, Queen So	3
3	Suite	3	King, Queen, S	3
3	Standard	2	King, Sofa	2
8	Standard	2	Queen	2

ACC-54

2 Type **King.**

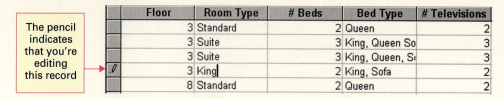

The pencil indicates that you're editing this record

3 Press ⬇ on the keyboard to save changes to the record.

4 Click 🔍 and click Find Next until you find the next occurrence of a record for a Standard room with a king-size bed.

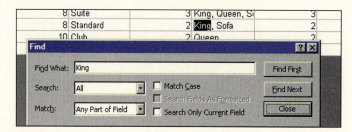

5 Press ESC to close the Find dialog box, double-click the word *Standard* in the Room Type field, and type **King.**
The Room Type data changes.

6 Click the Database Window 🗔 button to display the database window, click the Forms tab, and double-click *The Grande Hotel* to open the form.

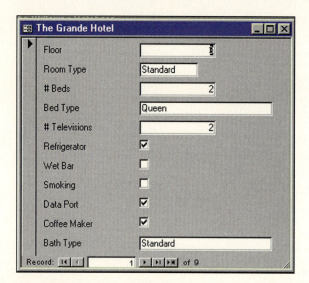

7 Click 🔍.
The Find window opens again.

8 Click the Find Next button until you identify the next Standard room with a king-size bed and press ESC.
Access identifies the next record containing the word *King* in any field.

9 Change the room type to King.

10 Continue finding Standard rooms containing king-size beds and change the room type to *King*.

11 Press ESC to close the Find dialog box when all records are complete.

12 Close the form.

Inserting Records

In Access, you can add records to a database by using the Datasheet view or by entering records on a form. Records you add in either view appear at the bottom of the database table. You can also create new records by copying existing records and updating field data.

TASK 3: TO INSERT RECORDS INTO A DATABASE TABLE:

1 Open the table *The Grande Hotel* in the database *The Willows* in Datasheet view, if necessary.

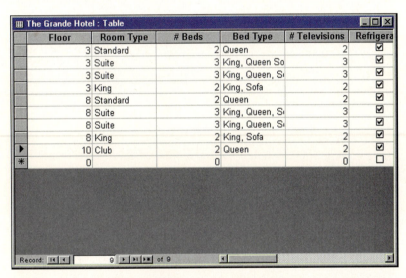

2 Click the New Record navigation button.

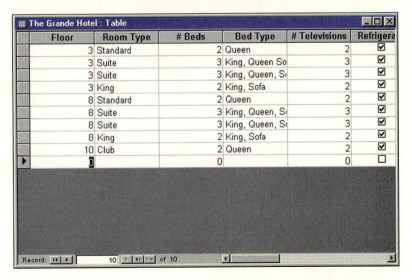

3 Type the following data in fields for the new record, pressing TAB to move from field to field:

loo	Room Typ	# Beds	Bed Type	# Telev	Refrig	Wet Bar	Smokin	Data Port	Coffee	Bath Typ
	3 Accessible	2	Queen	2	☑	☐	☐	☑	☑	Standard

4 Position the pointer on the frame button beside the first record in the table; then click and drag to select four records.

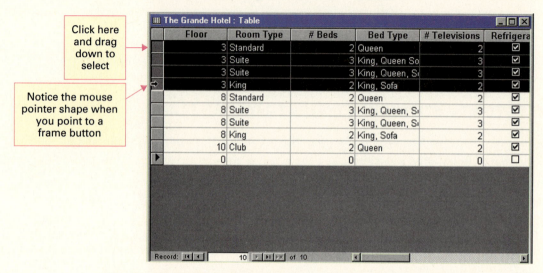

Click here and drag down to select

Notice the mouse pointer shape when you point to a frame button

5 Click the Copy button on the toolbar.
The selected records are copied to the Windows Clipboard.

6 Click
Access positions the insertion point at the bottom of the table and selects a blank row.

7 Click the Paste button on the toolbar.

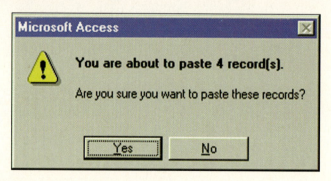

Project 2: Maintaining a Database   ACC-57

8 Click Yes to paste the records.

9 Double-click the Room Type field for each copied record and type **Accessible.**

10 Close the table.

Using the Replace Feature

The Replace feature in Access enables you to find occurrences of words, values, or phrases in a database object and replace the information with new data. You can use the Replace feature to change *Sofa* to *Sofa Sleeper* throughout the table *The Grande Hotel,* as Mr. Gilmore requested.

TASK 4: TO REPLACE EXISTING DATA WITH NEW DATA:

1 Open the table *The Grande Hotel* in the database *The Willows* and display the Datasheet view, if necessary.
The table appears as last edited.

2 Choose Edit, Replace.

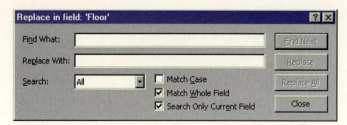

3 Type **Sofa** in the Find What text box, press `TAB`, type **Sofa Sleeper** in the Replace With text box, and if necessary remove the check marks from the Match Whole Field and Search Only Current Field check boxes.

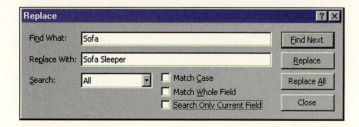

4 Click Find Next.

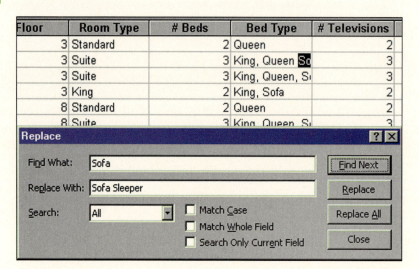

Tip When the Replace dialog box hides the data that Access finds, drag the title bar to move the dialog box to a new location.

Note If your records are in a different order, the record Access finds may differ.

5 Click Replace.
Access makes the substitution and selects the next occurrence of *Sofa*.

Project 2: Maintaining a Database   ACC-59

6 Click Replace All to replace each occurrence of the word *Sofa* with *Sofa Sleeper*.

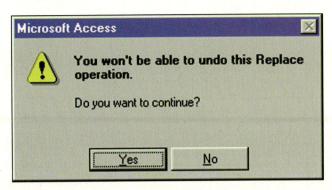

7 Click Yes to acknowledge the Access message.

8 Press ESC to close the Replace dialog box.

Deleting Records

When records become obsolete or outdated, you should remove the records to keep the database current. In Access, you can select individual records or multiple records and delete them at the same time, and you can delete records from the Table Datasheet view or from the Form view.

> **Caution** The Undo feature doesn't restore deleted records, nor does deleting records place them on the Clipboard so that you can paste them back into the database table. As a safety measure, you may want to delete a single record by using the Cut button on the toolbar to place the deleted record on the Clipboard, so you can get it back if necessary. Of course, you can always insert a new record and retype the data if you prefer.

TASK 5: TO DELETE RECORDS FROM A DATABASE TABLE:

1 Click the frame button beside the first record showing Accessible as the Room Type.

> **Tip** To delete records in Form view, click the record selection bar on the left side of the form.

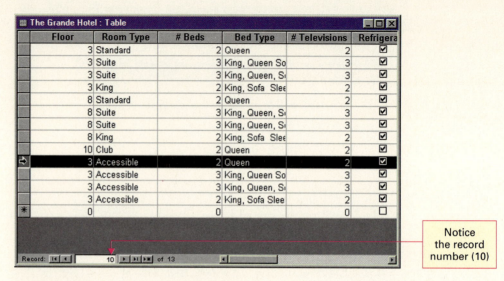

Notice the record number (10)

2 Press DELETE.

3 Click Yes to delete the record.
Records that appear after the deleted record renumber automatically.

Sorting Records

Access enables you to *sort* records in either Datasheet view or Form view on any database field. All you have to do is position the insertion point in the field you want to sort and then click the appropriate Sort button on the toolbar.

TASK 6: TO SORT RECORDS IN A DATABASE TABLE:

1 Click the Room Type field of any record in the table *The Grande Hotel*. Positioning the insertion point in the field that you want to sort makes the field active.

Project 2: Maintaining a Database   ACC-61

2 Click the Sort Ascending button on the toolbar.

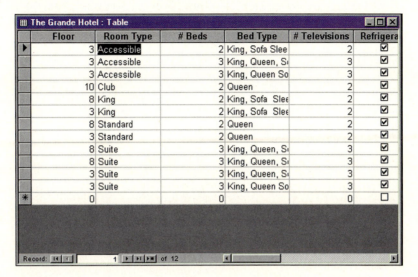

3 Close the table.

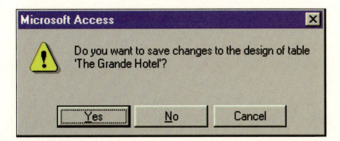

4 Click No to leave data stored in its original order. The database window appears.

5 Open the form *The Grande Hotel*.

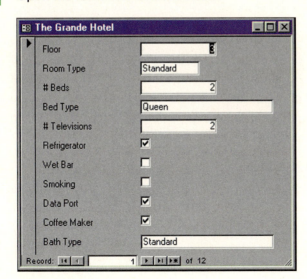

6 Press TAB until the Bed Type field is active.
Pressing TAB to move to a field selects the field contents.

7 Click the Sort Descending button on the toolbar.
Access arranges records with queen-size beds before those with king-size beds.

8 Choose View, Datasheet View to see the results.

9 Close the datasheet for The Grande Hotel without saving.
The form *The Grande Hotel* (which you were using in Datasheet view) closes.

Filtering Records by Selection

With the Access Filter command, you can identify a value in any field and tell Access to select only those records in the table that contain the same value in the selected field.

TASK 7: TO FILTER DATABASE RECORDS BY SELECTION:

1 Open the table *The Grande Hotel* in the database *The Willows*.

2 Position the mouse pointer close to the left border of a cell in the Smoking field that doesn't contain a check mark.

The pointer changes to a hollow plus sign

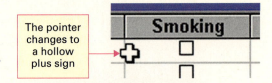

3 Click to select the field.

Selected field

Note If you accidentally click the check box as you select the field, a check mark appears in the check box. When this happens, click the check box again to remove the check mark.

4   Click the Filter by Selection button on the toolbar.

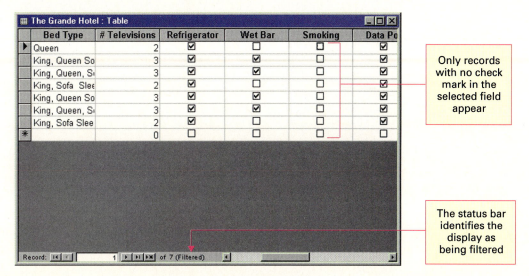

5   Preview and print the datasheet for Mr. Gilmore.

6   Click the Remove Filter button on the toolbar. All table records redisplay.

Filtering Records by Form

When you want to filter by more than one field, you have to open the Filter window to select filter values. You can use the Filter command to display nonsmoking rooms, rooms with king-size beds, and nonsmoking rooms with king-size beds in a datasheet, as Mr. Gilmore requested.

ACC-64

TASK 8: TO FILTER RECORDS BY FORM:

1 Click the Filter by Form button on the toolbar.

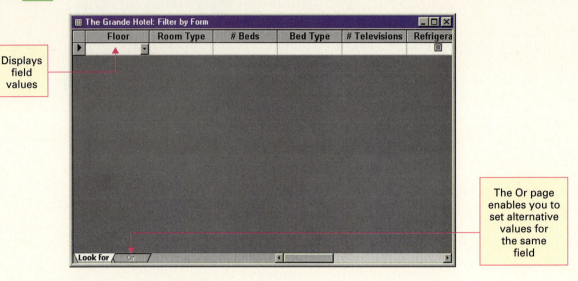

Displays field values

The Or page enables you to set alternative values for the same field

2 Click the Bed Type field.

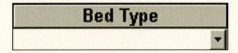

3 Click the arrow button to display valid entries for the Bed Type field.

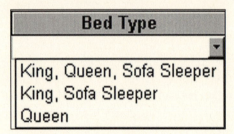

4 Click King, Sofa Sleeper in this list box.

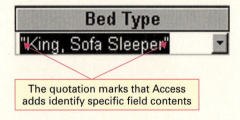

The quotation marks that Access adds identify specific field contents

5 Click the Or tab at the bottom of the window. A blank filter page appears.

6 Click the arrow button for Bed Type, and select King, Queen, Sofa Sleeper in the list box.

7 Click the Apply Filter button on the toolbar.

Floor	Room Type	# Beds	Bed Type	# Televisions
3	Suite	3	King, Queen, Sofa Sleeper	3
3	Suite	3	King, Queen, Sofa Sleeper	3
3	King	2	King, Sofa Sleeper	2
8	Suite	3	King, Queen, Sofa Sleeper	3
8	Suite	3	King, Queen, Sofa Sleeper	3
8	King	2	King, Sofa Sleeper	2
3	Accessible	3	King, Queen, Sofa Sleeper	3
3	Accessible	3	King, Queen, Sofa Sleeper	3
3	Accessible	2	King, Sofa Sleeper	2
	0	0		0

8 Preview and print the list for Mr. Gilmore.

9 Click Remove Filter button to display all records.
All records redisplay in the datasheet.

> **Note** Access remembers the most recent filter values you set. If you want to filter different fields for different values, be sure to remove any filter values previously entered.

10 Click .
The Look For page with previously set filters displays.

11 Click the Smoking field until the check box contains neither shading nor a check mark.

The Smoking check box appears clear

12 Click the Or tab at the bottom of the screen, and then click the Smoking check box until it appears clear.

13 Click .

Bed Type	# Televisions	Refrigerator	Wet Bar	Smoking
King, Queen, Sofa-Sleeper	3	☑	☑	☐
King, Queen, Sofa-Sleeper	3	☑	☑	☐
King, Sofa-Sleeper	2	☑	☐	☐
King, Queen, Sofa-Sleeper	3	☑	☑	☐
King, Queen, Sofa-Sleeper	3	☑	☑	☐
King, Sofa-Sleeper	2	☑	☐	☐
	0	☐	☐	☐

Only nonsmoking rooms with king-size beds appear

14 Print a copy of the list for Mr. Gilmore.

ACC-66

15 Click ▽.
All records in the table redisplay.

16 Close the table *The Grande Hotel,* answer No when prompted to save table changes, and then close the database *The Willows.*
The Access window is blank.

The Conclusion

In the exercises and assignments that follow, you'll continue updating the records in the table *The Grande Hotel* in the database *The Willows*. If you plan to continue working on the exercises and assignments, leave Access running. If you've finished work for the day, close Access, perform the shutdown routine used in your lab, and turn off the computer.

Summary and Exercises

Summary

- You can use the Access Find feature to locate records and the Access Replace feature to update information automatically or to change data.
- Updating data contained in records in a table ensures accuracy of information.
- You can insert and delete records from Form view or Datasheet view and from table objects or form objects. To delete records, be certain that the entire record is selected by clicking the Datasheet view frame button or the Form view record selection bar.
- Records you insert automatically appear at the end of the database table. You can reposition new records by performing a sort routine.
- Sorting enables you to rearrange records by listing them alphabetically or numerically in *ascending* or *descending* order by selected fields.
- Filtering records enables you to select records that contain specific information in selected fields. You can filter on more than one field in a table or select different values for the same field by using the Or tabbed pages in the Filter by Form window.

Key Terms and Operations

Key Terms	Operations
ascending order	delete records
descending order	filter records
filter	find database records
sort	insert records
update	replace database data
	sort records

Study Questions

Multiple Choice

1. To locate a record in a database table quickly, use the
   a. Find feature.
   b. Replace feature.
   c. Datasheet.
   d. Print Preview feature.

2. Updating records includes all the following activities *except*
   a. changing an address.
   b. creating a new database.
   c. inserting new records.
   d. removing obsolete records.

3. To delete a record from a table,
   a. select a field in the table and press Enter.
   b. select a field in a form and press Delete.
   c. click the frame button or record selection bar and press Delete.
   d. select Datasheet View and press Enter.

4. To identify the field you want to use for sorting records,
   a. click the field frame button and press Ctrl+S.
   b. select the complete table.
   c. choose File, New and then select Sort.
   d. position the insertion point in a row in the field column, and click the sort button that you want on the toolbar.

5. Filtering records in a table
   a. contains field entry, properties, and instructions.
   b. selects records containing specific values in specific fields.
   c. sorts the database automatically.
   d. appears in the field description pane only.

6. The easiest way to filter records in a table is to
   a. filter by the value of the active field.
   b. restore data after accidental loss.
   c. delete all records from the table and copy them to the Clipboard.
   d. select an entire record and click the Sort Ascending button.

7. To restore a deleted record,
   a. press Ctrl+Page Down.
   b. close the database without saving and reopen it.
   c. click the Undo button.
   d. retype the record.

8. Options available in the Find dialog box enable you to do all the following *except*
   a. match any part of the field.
   b. move up or down from the active data field.
   c. replace field contents automatically.
   d. search for text with capitalization that exactly matches the text typed.

9. The filter feature that enables you to select records matching data in multiple fields is the
   a. Apply filter feature.
   b. Filter by Form feature.
   c. Filter by Selection feature.
   d. Sort feature.

10. The filter feature that enables you to select records containing the same value as the selected field is the
    a. Apply filter feature.
    b. Filter by Form feature.
    c. Filter by Selection feature.
    d. Sort feature.

Short Answer
1. What's the difference between finding and replacing?
2. What's the difference between sorting and filtering?
3. What's the selection bar on a form and what does it do?
4. How do you select multiple records in the Datasheet view?
5. What's the most efficient way to add new records that closely resemble existing records?
6. What procedure can you use to remove a record from the table to ensure that you can get it back without retyping it?
7. What's the purpose of the Or pages of the filter window?
8. Which filter feature is the most efficient for finding records that contain a value in only one field?
9. Which filter feature is the most efficient for matching records that contain specific values in more than one field?
10. To sort records from highest to lowest based on numeric values in a Number field, which sort button on the toolbar would you use?

For Discussion
1. What influence do the filter features in Access have on the number of tables you need to include in each database?
2. How do you restore records that have been deleted from a database table?
3. Why is it important to maintain consistency in the way you enter data into your database tables?
4. How does table design affect the way you can sort and filter a table?

Review Exercises

1. Sorting Data, Finding and Replacing Data, and Updating a Database Table

The table *The Grande Hotel* in the database *The Willows* needs to contain room descriptions for rooms on floors 4–7, 9, and 11–12. Because the data required for the new records so closely resembles data found in existing records, you can copy the data from existing records and change the floor numbers for the new records. Mr. Gilmore would also like you to change the Room Type descriptions for the Club rooms on the tenth floor to reflect the types of beds they contain. A portion of the completed datasheet appears in Figure 2.2.

Floor	Room Type	# Beds	Bed Type	# Televisions
3	Suite	3	King, Queen, Sofa Sleeper	3
3	Suite	3	King, Queen, Sofa Sleeper	3
3	King	2	King, Sofa Sleeper	2
3	Accessible	3	King, Queen, Sofa Sleeper	3
3	Accessible	3	King, Queen, Sofa Sleeper	3
3	Accessible	2	King, Sofa Sleeper	2
3	Standard	2	Queen	2
4	King	2	King, Sofa Sleeper	2
4	Standard	2	Queen	2
4	Suite	3	King, Queen, Sofa Sleeper	3
4	Suite	3	King, Queen, Sofa Sleeper	3
5	King	2	King, Sofa Sleeper	2
5	Suite	3	King, Queen, Sofa Sleeper	3
5	Suite	3	King, Queen, Sofa Sleeper	3
5	Standard	2	Queen	2
6	Suite	3	King, Queen, Sofa Sleeper	3
6	Suite	3	King, Queen, Sofa Sleeper	3
6	King	2	King, Sofa Sleeper	2
6	Standard	2	Queen	2
7	King	2	King, Sofa Sleeper	2
7	Suite	3	King, Queen, Sofa Sleeper	3
7	Suite	3	King, Queen, Sofa Sleeper	3
7	Standard	2	Queen	2
8	Suite	3	King, Queen, Sofa Sleeper	3
8	Suite	3	King, Queen, Sofa Sleeper	3
8	King	2	King, Sofa Sleeper	2
8	Standard	2	Queen	2
9	Standard	2	Queen	2
9	Suite	3	King, Queen, Sofa Sleeper	3
9	King	2	King, Sofa Sleeper	2
9	Suite	3	King, Queen, Sofa Sleeper	3
10	Club King	2	King, Sofa Sleeper	2
10	Club Reg	2	Queen	2
11	Standard	2	Queen	2
11	Suite	3	King, Queen, Sofa Sleeper	3
11	King	2	King, Sofa Sleeper	2
11	Suite	3	King, Queen, Sofa Sleeper	3
12	King	2	King, Sofa Sleeper	2
12	Standard	2	Queen	2
12	Suite	3	King, Queen, Sofa Sleeper	3
12	Suite	3	King, Queen, Sofa Sleeper	3

Figure 2.2

Refrigerator	Wet Bar	Smoking	Data Port	Coffee Maker	Bath Type
✓	✓	☐	✓	✓	Jacuzzi
✓	✓	☐	✓	✓	Standard
✓	☐	☐	✓	✓	Standard
✓	✓	☐	✓	✓	Jacuzzi
✓	✓	☐	✓	✓	Standard
✓	☐	☐	✓	✓	Standard
✓	☐	☐	✓	✓	Standard
✓	☐	☐	✓	✓	Standard
✓	☐	☐	✓	✓	Standard
✓	✓	☐	✓	✓	Standard
✓	✓	☐	✓	✓	Jacuzzi
✓	☐	☐	✓	✓	Standard
✓	✓	☐	✓	✓	Standard
✓	✓	☐	✓	✓	Jacuzzi
✓	☐	☐	✓	✓	Standard
✓	✓	☐	✓	✓	Jacuzzi
✓	✓	☐	✓	✓	Standard
✓	☐	☐	✓	✓	Standard
✓	☐	☐	✓	✓	Standard
✓	☐	☐	✓	✓	Standard
✓	✓	☐	✓	✓	Standard
✓	✓	☐	✓	✓	Jacuzzi
✓	☐	☐	✓	✓	Standard
✓	✓	✓	✓	✓	Standard
✓	✓	✓	✓	✓	Jacuzzi
✓	☐	✓	✓	✓	Standard
✓	☐	✓	✓	✓	Standard
✓	✓	✓	✓	✓	Jacuzzi
✓	☐	✓	✓	✓	Standard
✓	✓	✓	✓	✓	Standard
✓	✓	✓	✓	✓	Large Standard
✓	✓	✓	✓	✓	Large Standard
✓	☐	✓	✓	✓	Standard
✓	✓	✓	✓	✓	Jacuzzi
✓	☐	✓	✓	✓	Standard
✓	✓	✓	✓	✓	Standard
✓	☐	✓	✓	✓	Standard
✓	☐	✓	✓	✓	Standard
✓	✓	✓	✓	✓	Jacuzzi
✓	✓	✓	✓	✓	Standard

Figure 2.2 *(continued)*

Follow these steps to update the table *The Grande Hotel*:

1. Open the table *The Grande Hotel* in the database *The Willows*.

2. Sort the records in the table on the Floor field in ascending order.

3. Copy four records for third floor rooms (two Suite, one King, and one Standard), and paste them to create four new records. Change the floor number for the new records to 4. Don't copy the accessible rooms.

4. Copy and paste the records again to create four new records for floor 5, four new records for floor 6, and four new records for floor 7.

5. Select the field frame buttons Floor and Room Type, and sort the records in ascending order by both fields by clicking the Sort Ascending button on the toolbar.

6. Copy four records for rooms on floor 8 (two Suites, one King, and one Standard), and paste them to create four new records. Change the floor number for the new records to 9.

7. Copy and paste the records again to create records for rooms on floor 11 and four records for rooms on floor 12. (Tenth floor rooms are Club rooms.)

8. Arrange the records by floor number in ascending order.

9. Add a record for Floor 10 that's the same as the current record for Floor 10. Then change the Room Type to Club King, the # Beds to 2, and Bed Type to King, Sofa Sleeper.

10. Sort the records by floor, and then change the Room Type data for Club rooms with queen-size beds to Club Reg.

When you're finished, you should have 41 records in the table *The Grande Hotel*. Print a copy of the Datasheet view of this table. Save and close the database.

2. Filtering Data in a Database Table

Mr. Gilmore has requested an updated list of room types with specific equipment. Filter the table *The Grande Hotel* in the database *The Willows* to provide the following lists:
- Rooms with Jacuzzi baths
- Smoking rooms with wet bars
- Suites with both king- and queen-size beds
- A complete list of room types on all floors arranged by Room Type

To create these lists, follow these instructions:

1. Open the database *The Willows* and display the table *The Grande Hotel* in datasheet view.

2. Make the Bath Type field for a record which contains *Jacuzzi* active and click the Filter by Selection button.

3. Print a copy of the datasheet and then click the Remove Filter button to display all records.

4. Click the Filter by Form button, click the Smoking and Wet Bar check boxes on the Look for page, and click the Apply Filter button.

5. Print a copy of the datasheet and then click the Remove Filter button to display all records.

6. Click the Filter by Form button, click the Clear Grid button to remove previously set values, select Suite from the Room Type list, and King, Queen, Sofa-Sleeper from the Bed Type list; then click the Apply Filter button.

7. Print a copy of the datasheet and then click the Remove Filter button to display all records.

8. Make the Room Type field active and click the Sort Ascending button to arrange the records by Room Type.

9. Print a copy of the datasheet.

10. Close the database without saving changes.

Print a copy of each datasheet for Mr. Gilmore.

Assignments

1. Sorting, Filtering, Finding, and Updating Database Records

You need to make several changes to other tables in the database *The Willows* as well as to the table in the database *The Willows Personnel*. Use techniques learned in this project to make the following corrections to the tables in your databases:

Database	Table	Find	Replace With
The Willows	The Grande Hotel Rooms	3020–3100; Standard 3120–3200; King	3020–3100; Accessible 3120–3200; Accessible
The Willows Personnel	The Willows Managers	Williams 110 Crozet Street Chuck Mercer Bailey	Wilson 759 Azalea Boulevard Delete the record

Chuck Bailey has been replaced by Simpson Arnold Jackson, who lives at 16903 Summertime Lane, Smithfield, SC 22435. He was hired as Manager of the Willow Pond on 9/15/96 at a salary of $36,000. The business phone number for Mr. Jackson is 803–555–0480, and his home phone number is 803–555–3298. Add a new record for Mr. Jackson.

Mr. Gilmore would like for you to prepare an updated list of all managers at The Willows in alphabetical order by last name. Sort the records in the table *The Willows Managers*, and print a copy of the Datasheet view. Then prepare a list of all managers who live in Willow Grove, and print a copy of the Datasheet view. When you're finished, save and close the database.

2. Updating and Sorting a Database (Optional Assignment)

After you receive your *Competitors* database printout back from Mr. Gilmore (from assignment 2 in Project 1), add the approved records to the database. Then perform another search on the Internet to locate similar resorts on the Pacific and Gulf coasts. Sort the records by location, and print a copy of the datasheet. Then print a list of only those resorts that have golf courses on-site. Save and close the database, and then exit Access.

PROJECT 3
Altering the Table Design

As you become more proficient with using Access and more comfortable storing, searching, sorting, and filtering through data in database tables, you may eventually want to add new fields of data to existing tables and customize the way data appears in the table. In this project, you change the table design, set field properties to control the data in the tables, and rearrange the layout of fields in a table.

Objectives

After completing this project, you will be able to:

- ▶ **Insert table fields**
- ▶ **Rearrange table fields**
- ▶ **Delete table fields**
- ▶ **Create a key field**
- ▶ **Create and save an AutoReport**
- ▶ **Copy a table structure**

The Challenge

After reviewing the printout of the table *The Grande Hotel*, Mr. Gilmore realized that he would need to scan numerous fields to identify room types with features most frequently requested. As a result, he would like to change the design of the table to include a code that identifies room features. In addition, he would like to add price fields to the table to make it easier for reception clerks to determine the cost of rooms when guests check in.

New fields added to the table design

Room Code	Room	#	Bed Type	Low Cost	High Cost	Extension
03ANS	Accessible	2	King, Sofa Sleeper	$85.00	$175.00	30XX
03KNS	King	2	King, Sofa	$95.00	$175.00	30XX
03QNS	Accessible	2	Queen	$85.00	$175.00	30XX
03SNS	Standard	2	Queen	$85.00	$125.00	30XX
03TNJ	Suite	3	King, Queen, Sofa Sleeper	$200.00	$500.00	30XX
03TNS	Suite	3	King, Queen, Sofa Sleeper	$200.00	$500.00	30XX

Format for currency

#	Refrig	Wet Bar	Smokin	Data	Coffe	Bath
2	Yes	No	No	Yes	Yes	Standard
2	Yes	No	No	Yes	Yes	Standard
2	Yes	No	No	Yes	Yes	Standard
2	Yes	No	No	Yes	Yes	Standard
3	Yes	Yes	No	Yes	Yes	Jacuzzi
3	Yes	Yes	No	Yes	Yes	Standard

Figure 3.1

The Solution

As the data-entry specialist at The Willows, you're assigned the task of changing the design of the table *The Grande Hotel* in the database *The Willows* to meet Mr. Gilmore's specifications. You can add a Room Code field and Low Cost and High Cost fields to the table structure, and then add data to the new fields.

The Room Code field presents the greatest challenge because the code must identify rooms by floor and room type, as smoking or non-smoking, and by bath type. Because rooms on the accessible floor contain queen-size beds or king-size beds, accessible rooms with queen-size beds should be coded using a "Q" for the room type, while accessible rooms with king-size beds should be coded with an "A" for accessible. You develop a five-digit code to identify the room types so that each code is different, as Mr. Gilmore requested. Before entering the data in all records of the table, you should complete a sample of the codes for Mr. Gilmore's review and approval.

In addition, Mr. Gilmore would like you to add a field to contain the room telephone extension numbers and would like for you to rearrange fields on the table *The Grande Hotel* and change the format for the Costs fields so that data automatically appears in currency format.

The Setup

So that your screen will match the illustrations and the tasks in this project will function as described, make sure that the following Access 97 settings are selected on your computer:

- View menu: If you don't see the toolbars, choose Toolbars and then click the toolbar listed at the top of the cascading menu.
- Screen settings: Click the Restore button on each object window.
- Tools menu: If you don't see the Status bar, choose Options and then click the View page tab. Click the check box beside Status Bar at the top of the page.

Inserting Table Fields

When you need to add fields to a table, you work in Table Design view.

TASK 1: TO INSERT FIELDS INTO A TABLE AND REMOVE FIELDS FROM A TABLE:

1. Open the database *The Willows* and the table *The Grande Hotel*. The table appears as last edited.
2. Click the View button on the toolbar.

> **Tip** For a list of available views, click the arrow button beside the View button.

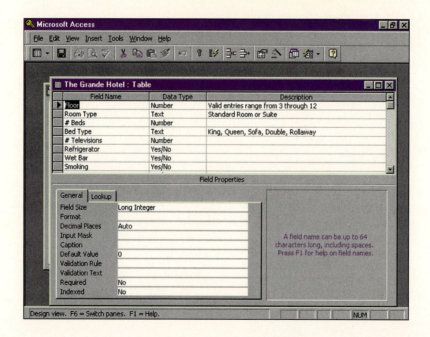

3 Click the frame button for the Floor field.

Field Name	Data Type	Description
Floor	Number	Valid entries range from 3 through 12
Room Type	Text	Standard Room or Suite
# Beds	Number	
Bed Type	Text	King, Queen, Sofa, Double, Rollaway
# Televisions	Number	

4 Click the Insert Rows button on the toolbar.
A blank row appears.

5 Click the Field Name cell, type **Room Code,** and press TAB twice.
The Description cell is active.

6 Type **Floor, Room Type, Smoking Designation, Bath Type.**

Field Name	Data Type	Description
Room Code	Text	Floor, Room Type, Smoking Designation, Bath Type
Floor	Number	Valid entries range from 3 through 12
Room Type	Text	Standard Room or Suite
# Beds	Number	
Bed Type	Text	King, Queen, Sofa, Double, Rollaway

7 Click the frame button for the # Televisions field, and drag to select through the Wet Bar field.

Field Name	Data Type	Description
Room Code	Text	Floor, Room Type, Smoking Designation, Bath Type
Floor	Number	Valid entries range from 3 through 12
Room Type	Text	Standard Room or Suite
# Beds	Number	
Bed Type	Text	King, Queen, Sofa, Double, Rollaway
# Televisions	Number	
Refrigerator	Yes/No	
Wet Bar	Yes/No	

8 Click.
Three blank rows appear.

9 Type three field entries in the blank rows, as in:

Low Cost	Currency	Not less than $85
High Cost	Currency	Not more than $500
Extension	Text	Floor Room Number

10 Click the Save button on the toolbar to save changes to the table design.

11 Click the View button on the toolbar, and maximize the table window.

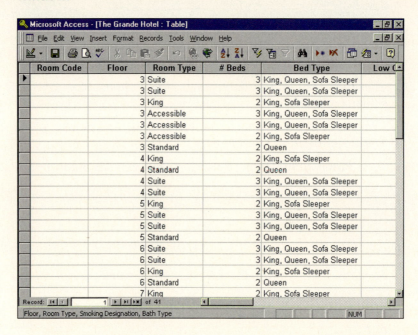

Tip If your records don't appear in the same order as the records shown in the illustration, sort the records by the Floor and Room Type fields.

Rearranging Fields in a Table

Before you delete the Floor field, you need to update each record in the table by entering data for the new fields. You can use the coding scheme identified earlier to update the Room Code field, but because the Smoking and Bath Type fields are off-screen, entering Room Code data could become tedious. By moving the Smoking and Bath Type fields into the table window with the Floor and Room Type fields, you can quickly enter data into the Room Codes field because you can see all fields side-by-side. Rearranging fields in a table doesn't alter the table design.

TASK 2: TO REARRANGE FIELDS IN A TABLE:

1 Click the field frame button for the Smoking field.

Project 3: Altering the Table Design   ACC-79

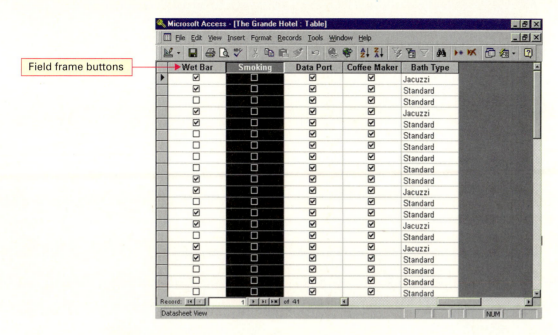

Field frame buttons

2 Position the white pointer arrow on the selected frame button; then click and drag the field to the left.

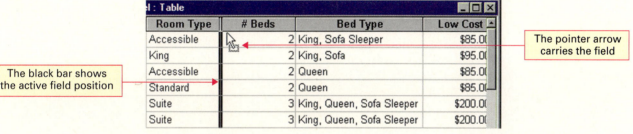

The pointer arrow carries the field

The black bar shows the active field position

3 Position the black bar between the Room Type and # Beds fields, and drop the Smoking field by releasing the mouse button.
The Smoking field appears in the new position.

> **Tip** If you accidentally drop the field in the wrong location, simply pick it up by clicking the frame button again and reposition it, or click Undo and start over.

4 Click the frame button for the Bath Type field, and drag it to a position between the Smoking and # Beds fields.

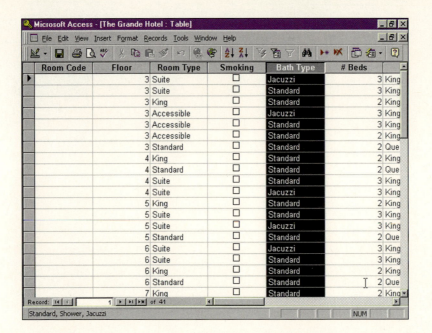

5 Type data into the Room Code field for the third floor rooms, as in:

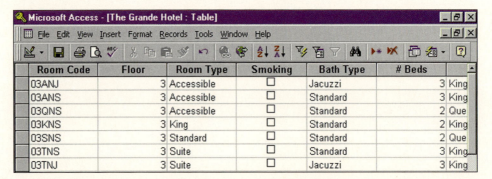

6 Select records for floors 4 through 12 and delete them.
Remember, you want to get Mr. Gilmore's approval before completing the rest of the records.

7 Return the Smoking field to its original position between the Wet Bar and Data Port fields and the Bath Type field to a position after the Coffee Maker field.

8 Use the data in Table 3.1 to enter values into the Low Cost and High Cost fields.

Table 3.1 Low Cost and High Cost Field Data

Room Type	Low Cost	High Cost
Standard	$85	$125
King	$95	$175
Accessible	$85	$175
Suite	$200	$500

9 Type **30xx** into the Extension field for all third-floor records.

Deleting Table Fields

After you add data to the Room Code field in the table *The Grande Hotel*, you can remove the Floor field from the table. Once you delete a field from a table you cannot restore the field by clicking the Undo button, so think before you delete. You wouldn't want to rekey all the information! After you have completed changes to the table structure, you can save the table design.

TASK 3: TO DELETE FIELDS FROM A TABLE:

Field Name	Data Type	Description
Room Code	Text	Floor, Room Type, Smoking Designation, Bath Type
Floor	Number	Valid entries range from 3 through 12
Room Type	Text	Standard Room or Suite
# Beds	Number	
Bed Type	Text	King, Queen, Sofa, Double, Rollaway
Low Cost	Currency	Note less than $85
High Cost	Currency	Not more than $100
Extension	Text	Floor Room Number

1 Click [icon].
The table structure displays in Table Design view.

2 Click the frame button for the Floor field.

3 Press DELETE.

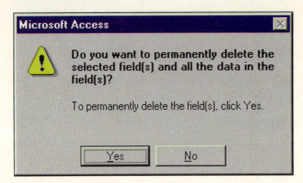

4 Click Yes.
The Floor field is removed from the table design, and other fields move up in the list of fields.

5 Click 💾 and then click 🖽 ▾.

Room Code	Room Type	# Beds	Bed Type	Low Cost	High Cost	Extension	# Telev	Refrige	Wet Bar	Smoking	Data Port	Coffee	Bath
03ANS	Accessible	2	King, Sofa Sleeper	$85.00	$175.00	30XX	2	Yes	No	No	Yes	Yes	Standard
03KNS	King	2	King, Sofa	$95.00	$175.00	30XX	2	Yes	No	No	Yes	Yes	Standard
03QNS	Accessible	2	Queen	$85.00	$175.00	30XX	2	Yes	No	No	Yes	Yes	Standard
03SNS	Standard	2	Queen	$85.00	$125.00	30XX	2	Yes	No	No	Yes	Yes	Standard
03TNJ	Suite	3	King, Queen, Sofa	$200.00	$500.00	30XX	3	Yes	Yes	No	Yes	Yes	Jacuzzi
03TNS	Suite	3	King, Queen, Sofa	$200.00	$500.00	30XX	3	Yes	Yes	No	Yes	Yes	Standard

Creating a Key Field

You may have noticed that the records in your table rearrange themselves each time you switch to a different view. Because the table doesn't contain a *key field,* Access isn't quite certain how you want to arrange records, so it automatically chooses the first field in the table and arranges records by that field. When you perform a sort on a different field or filter records based on data in another field, Access appears to arrange your records randomly. Assigning a key field tells Access which field you want to use as the primary field for organizing your records. A key field ensures that your records are arranged or sorted on that field each time you change views. A key field must contain data that's different (unique) for each record. For the table *The Grande Hotel,* you can use the Room Code field as a key field.

TASK 4: TO CREATE A KEY FIELD:

1 Click 📝 ▾.
The table displays in Table Design view.

2 Click the frame button for the Room Code field.

Project 3: Altering the Table Design ACC-83

3 Click the Primary Key button on the toolbar.

A key appears in the frame button for key fields →

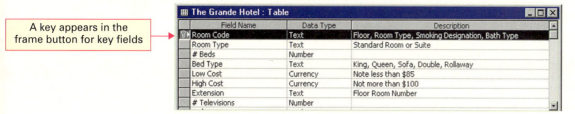

4 Click 💾 and then click 📊 ▼.
Access displays the table in Datasheet view.

> **Note** If Access determines that data in the key field contains duplicates, a warning message advises you that the key field assignment couldn't be saved. To correct the error, review field values, make the necessary corrections, and then repeat steps 1–4 to assign the key field.

Creating and Saving an AutoReport

Forms you create are designed primarily for on-screen viewing. Reports are database objects designed to print summarized data from database tables on paper. You can design reports using fields in one database table or fields from multiple tables using a query. In this task, you learn how to create, modify, and print **AutoReports.** You can create and save an AutoReport using the same techniques you used to create and save forms. The fields displayed on an AutoReport are the same fields contained in the table on which you base the report.

TASK 5: TO CREATE AND SAVE AN AUTOREPORT:

1 Click the arrow button beside the New Object: AutoForm button on the toolbar.

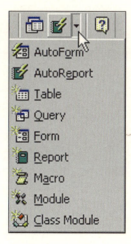

ACC-84

2 Select AutoReport.

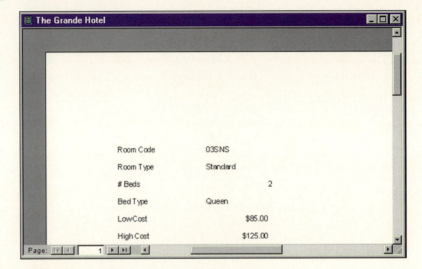

3 Choose File, Save to save the report.

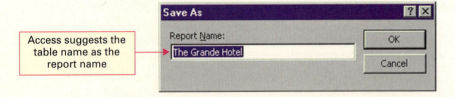

Access suggests the table name as the report name

4 Type **The Grande Hotel** in the Report Name text box and press (ENTER).
The report name appears in the title bar.

5 Click the Close ⊠ button on the report window, and then click ⊠ on the table window.
The new report name appears alphabetically in the Reports page of the database dialog box.

Copying a Table Structure

When an existing table contains basically the same fields and field structure that you need for a new table, you can copy the structure of the existing table to create the new table.

TASK 6: TO COPY A TABLE STRUCTURE:

1 Click the Tables tab of the database window for *The Willows,* and select the table *The Grande Hotel*—but don't open it.
The table is selected.

2 Click the Copy 🗎 button on the toolbar.
Access stores the table on the Clipboard.

3 Click the Paste button on the toolbar.

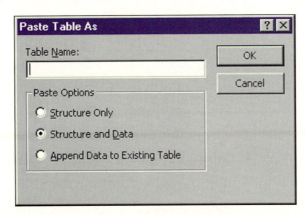

4 Type **The Willows Beach Cottages** in the Table Name text box, and click the Structure Only radio button.

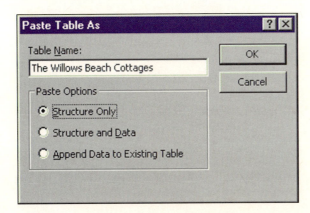

5 Click OK.
The new table name appears in the list of tables on the Tables tab.

After you copy the table, you can open the new table and add records to the table, using the same procedures you used to add records to other tables.

The Conclusion

Because you specified a key field, records rearrange automatically in the correct order each time you open your table. If you plan to continue working on the exercises and assignments, leave Access open and continue after you finish updating the table. If you're finished working in Access, exit Access properly by clicking the Close button on the application window.

Summary and Exercises

Summary

- To change the structure of a table, you must work in Table Design view.
- You can rearrange the display of fields in a table in Datasheet view without affecting the underlying structure of the table.
- When you delete a field, you can't restore it by using the Undo feature; you must insert a new field.
- A key field identifies the primary field you want Access to use to arrange records in a table.
- Reports are database objects designed to print summarized data from database tables on paper. AutoReports create simple report formats using the fields contained in the table you select.
- Access enables you to copy the structure of an existing table to create a new table, using the Copy and Paste technique.

Key Terms and Operations

Key Terms	Operations
AutoReport	add fields to tables
key field	copy a table structure
primary key	create an AutoReport
	designate a field as a key field
	edit fields in tables
	remove fields from tables

Study Questions

Multiple Choice

1. The view you use to insert fields in a table is
    a. Table Design view.
    b. Datasheet view.
    c. Form view.
    d. Table view.

2. A warning appears when you
    a. insert a field.
    b. delete a field.
    c. edit field data.
    d. change fields.

3. The Undo feature can't reverse
    a. inserting a field.
    b. editing a field.
    c. deleting a field.
    d. rearranging fields.

4. For a list of available views,
    a. click the field frame button.
    b. select the complete table.
    c. click the View button.
    d. click the arrow button beside the View button on the toolbar.

5. To select a field in Table Design view,
    a. click the Field Entry, Properties, and Instructions text boxes.
    b. click the field frame button.
    c. insert a new field.
    d. enter new properties in the Field Description pane.

6. To insert new fields in a database table,
    a. select the field that follows the new field, and click the Insert Rows button on the toolbar.
    b. select the field that follows the new field, and press Insert.
    c. select a record in the table, and press Enter.
    d. select the field that follows the new field, and choose File, Insert New Record.

7. To move a field in the Datasheet view,
    a. select the field frame button, and press Ctrl+Page Down.
    b. select the field frame button, and press Insert.
    c. select the field frame button, and press the arrow key that represents the direction the field needs to move.
    d. click the field frame button, and drag the field to a new position.

8. AutoReports format and arrange table records for output to the
    a. screen.
    b. database.
    c. printer
    d. form.

9. To sort a table on the same field each time you switch views or open a table,
    a. save the table after you sort on the field.
    b. make the field a primary key field.
    c. filter the field.
    d. make the field a required field.

10. Key fields must contain
    a. filtered data.
    b. default values.
    c. unique data.
    d. presorted information.

Short Answer
1. What effect does rearranging fields in Datasheet view have on the table structure?
2. How does inserting fields in Table Design view affect the Datasheet view?
3. What's a field frame button?
4. How do you format data to appear with dollar signs?

5. What's a key field?
6. What's the quickest type of report format to create?
7. What fields does Access place in an AutoReport?
8. Can you make a field a key field after you have added data to a table?
9. What button on the toolbar do you use to switch from Datasheet view to Table Design view and back?
10. When you change the table structure, what must you do before returning to Datasheet view?

For Discussion
1. What's the difference between moving fields in Datasheet view and adding fields in Table Design view?
2. How many fields can be identified as primary key fields? Why?
3. What's the difference between key fields and sorted fields?
4. What procedure would you follow if you deleted the wrong field in Table Design view and needed to restore it?
5. Why would you want to copy the structure of a table to create a new table, and when would you want to copy both the structure and data of an existing table to create a new table?

Review Exercises

1. Insert and Delete Fields, Assign a Key Field, and Update a Table

Mr. Gilmore wants you to revise the table *The Willows Managers* in the database *The Willows Personnel.* Because the table title reflects the positions of the people listed in the table, you can delete the Positions field from the table. In addition, Mr. Gilmore would like to add a field for managers' Social Security numbers. Because each person has a different Social Security number, you can make the field a primary key field. Mr. Gilmore would also like to include a field that contains the number of assistant managers assigned to each manager, a field for Termination Date, and a field for Comments/Reason. To make the changes to the database table, follow these instructions:

1. Open the table *The Willows Managers* in the database *The Willows Personnel.*
2. Display the table in Table Design view.
3. Insert the SSN# field as the first field in the table; position the Asst. Mgr. field just after the Salary field.
4. Insert Termination Date as a date field and Comments/Reason as a memo field at the end of the table.
5. Delete the Position field from the table.
   After you finish making changes to the table structure, add the data shown in Table 3.2 to the SSN# field and Asst. Mgr. field.

Table 3.2 Social Security Numbers and Number of Assistant Managers

Manager's Last Name	SSN#	Asst. Mgr.
Gilmore	334–85–1263	10
Jackson, R.	452–47–5920	5
Lindsey	441–34–8840	10
Taylor	441–31–8418	3
Atkinson	452–55–2817	7
Holmes	441–81–8405	2
Bradbury	326–93–1254	2
Cho	541–32–7749	4
Wilson	342–36–0354	3
Carr	331–84–4523	2
Davis	343–44–4675	2
Jackson, S.	548–85–3206	3
Sanchez	338–45–9468	3

6. Make the SSN# field a required key field.
   Print a copy of the table in Datasheet view. Save and close the database.

2. Rearranging Fields in a Table and Creating an AutoReport

Mr. Gilmore would like a report format that lists managers in chronological order with the names of those who have been with The Willows longest at the top and those who have been with The Willows the shortest amount of time at the bottom of the list. He would also like for you to change the Salary data type to Currency so that it displays entries as dollar values. In addition, he would like the list arranged so that the order of fields left to right appears as follows: SSN#, Date Employed, Last Name, First Name, Middle Name, Salary, Asst. Mgr., Department, Business Phone, Home Phone, Street, City, State, ZIP, Termination Date, and Comments/Reasons.

Follow these steps to complete these requests:

1. Open the table *The Willows Managers* in the database *The Willows Personnel*.
2. Sort the table on the Date Employed field, and then display the Table Design view.
3. Change the Data Type for the Salary field to Currency, and save the changes to the table design.
4. Return to Datasheet view, and drag fields to position the fields in the order specified by Mr. Gilmore.
5. Create an AutoReport named *Managers* based on the revised table structure.

Print a copy of the AutoReport.

Assignments

1. Insert Fields, Delete Fields, Set Key Field, and Set Field Properties

For this exercise, ask your instructor for the database *The Willows Updated*, and review the structure of each table in the database. Then add the following fields to the end of the table *The Grande Hotel Rooms:* View, Check-In Date, Scheduled Check-Out, Check-Out Date, Peak Rate, and Off-Season Rate. Make the Room Number field the key field. Suites and Club rooms are Ocean view rooms; Standard and Accessible rooms are Resort view rooms. King rooms with lower numbers on each floor are Ocean view, and King rooms with higher numbers on each floor are Resort view rooms. Enter views for each of the rooms in the table *The Grande Hotel Rooms*.

Print a copy of the Datasheet view for the table *The Grande Hotel Rooms*.

2. Editing and Copying the Structure of a Database Table

You need to add a new table to the database *The Willows Personnel* to hold the information about assistant managers. You can use the structure of the table *The Willows Managers* to create the new table. Name the table *The Willows Assistant Managers*. Then delete the Asst. Mgr., Termination Date, Comments/Reasons, and Salary fields from the new table, and add a Supervisor field to the end of the table. Change the name of the Date Employed field to Date Hired. In Datasheet view, move the Department field to just before the Supervisor field, move the Business Phone field between the Home Phone field and the Department field, and move the Last Name field to the left of the First Name field. Then enter the records shown in Figure 3.3 for the table.

Print a copy of the datasheet for the new table. Save and close the database; then exit Access if you have finished your work.

SSN#	Last Name	First Name	Middle Name	Street	City	State	ZIP	Date Hired	Home Phone	Business	Department	Supervisor
130-50-3005	Lavatto	Marietta	Walana	7302 Centerville Rd.	Ridgelake	SC	22454	4/28/96	803-555-2831	803-555-0855	Willows Beach Cottages	Jackson, R.
138-75-0573	Lancaster	Jodi	Kathleen	2501 N. Century	Willow Grove	SC	22345	5/22/94	803-555-2832	803-555-1011	Victorian Tea Room	Lindsey
141-57-7461	McGrath	Gary	Donald	146 Burges Lane	Smithfield	SC	22435	11/12/87	803-555-4005	803-555-0805	Red Rocker Restaurant	Cho
212-13-1540	Park	William	Prince	1123 North Lake Road	Ridgelake	SC	22454	7/16/72	803-555-2420	803-555-1201	The Grande Hotel	Gilmore
212-19-2016	York	Dennis	Millard	1883 Jones Creek Rd.	Smithfield	SC	22435	5/7/96	803-555-8318	803-555-0850	The Willow Top	Atkinson
212-24-6404	Thibodeaux	Lena	Baugh	3502 West Rockville	Altamont	SC	22234	3/31/86	803-555-2440	803-555-1013	Cherry Street Market	Lindsey
212-26-5436	Warren	Edward	Dwayne	307 Oregon Ridge	Willow Grove	SC	22345	9/11/83	803-555-8095	803-555-1016	Creative Cutlery	Lindsey
212-29-2129	Ritchie	Anna	Jane	16782 Central Ave.	Ridgelake	SC	22454	6/12/70	803-555-1619	803-555-1204	The Grande Hotel	Gilmore
212-40-2875	Lanham	Kevin	Marc	3478 W. Bladen, #15	Smithfield	SC	22435	5/3/91	803-555-5045	803-555-0852	Willows Beach Cottages	Jackson, R.
216-15-6616	Sparks	Robin	Parkton	2095 Oak Street	Smithfield	SC	22435	5/28/89	803-555-2931	803-555-0520	Wind in the Willows	Bradbury
217-17-7124	Lambrusco	Heather	Marie	112 East Ocean Drive,	Willow Grove	SC	22345	6/10/88	803-555-0626	803-555-0362	Willows Water Park	Sanchez
225-26-9555	Oxley	Gray	Wilbur	2180 N. Century	Altamont	SC	22234	9/26/87	803-555-1521	803-555-0652	The Atrium Grill	Taylor
226-23-2559	Baker	Janet	Burton	3604 Oceanview Dr.	Willow Grove	SC	22345	11/15/94	803-555-1980	803-555-0302	Miniature Golf Courses	Davis
231-98-1535	Fleming	Sherman		726 Hov Drive	Ridgelake	SC	22454	2/5/87	803-555-4621	803-555-0854	Willows Beach Cottages	Jackson, R.
232-35-0252	Pargo	Carlos	Reme	3457 Hereford Dr.	Willow Grove	SC	24354	3/18/90	803-555-2313	803-555-0702	The 18th Hole	Holmes
240-10-6109	Oconnell	Barre	Charles	112 Shoe House Rd.	Willow Grove	SC	22345	2/5/87	803-555-4025	803-555-0482	Bike Rentals	Jackson, S.
252-23-2325	Ashby	Virginia	Lane	2953 Ocean Drive	Willow Grove	SC	22345	6/26/74	803-555-4832	803-555-0751	Game Set Match	Williams
252-72-8419	Knox	Tina	Beth	736 Telegraph Road	Smithfield	SC	22435	6/1/89	803-555-1592	803-555-1210	The Willow Top	Gilmore
256-74-2114	Sparks	Mary	Denise	8308 Highway 173	Willow Grove	SC	24354	9/2/93	803-555-2530	803-555-1014	Victorian Tea Room	Lindsey
260-21-1296	Bridges	Andrew	Steel	1507 Allentown Rd.	Willow Grove	SC	22345	4/2/94	803-555-7986	803-555-0820	The Willow Top	Atkinson
261-34-1869	Gadsby	Alexander	Edward	6132 Telegraph Road	Smithfield	SC	22435	10/11/72	803-555-1769	803-555-0810	The Willow Top	Atkinson
263-44-2523	Washington	Mary	Renee	16944 Old Mill Road	Willow Grove	SC	22345	1/2/81	803-555-8599	803-555-1019	Weeping Willows Gallery	Lindsey
274-06-2744	Suitland	Marley	Green	5670 Millage Circle,	James Way	SC	24354	8/13/93	803-555-5478	803-555-0361	Willows Water Park	Sanchez
290-23-2318	Sires	Mayra	Lucille	7414 Millage Circle #5	Willow Grove	SC	22345	6/1/89	803-555-3021	803-555-0483	Riding Stables	Jackson, S.
305-57-0214	Herbert	Benjamin	James	2462 Wrightsville	Ridgelake	SC	22454	7/11/92	803-555-2412	803-555-0870	The Willow Top	Atkinson
311-41-2461	Wilkins	Travis	Edmond	274 Frederick Road	Willow Grove	SC	22454	2/22/92	803-555-3650	803-555-0840	The Willow Top	Atkinson
312-49-3501	Canton	Cally	Riley	831 Plymouth Point	Willow Grove	SC	22345	11/14/86	803-555-5350	803-555-0653	The Atrium Grill	Taylor
313-71-7589	Wright	Douglas	Michael	4981 Walnut Street	Willow Grove	SC	22345	8/23/96	803-555-5180	803-555-1012	Appalachian Crafts	Lindsey
314-35-9401	Towson	Kathleen	Louise	77 East Ocean Drive	Willow Grove	SC	22345	1/3/92	803-555-6170	803-555-0481	Riding Stables	Jackson, S.
322-10-3320	Boudreau	Jonathan	Earl	72 Shoe House Road	James Way	SC	24354	2/28/90	803-555-7867	803-555-0363	Willows Water Park	Sanchez
331-34-4391	Bitts	Lori	Michelle	3638 Bel Air Dr.	Smithfield	SC	22435	1/6/97	803-555-4854	803-555-0802	Willow Green	Cho
334-10-6951	Temple	Henson	Thomas	5509 Outer Loop	Willow Grove	SC	22454	9/7/85	803-555-1251	803-555-0752	Black Mountain Tavern	Williams
337-13-1248	Adams	Valerie	Kay	304 Windy Hill Road	Willow Grove	SC	22345	10/14/90	803-555-0895	803-555-0803	The Cola Shop	Cho
341-21-8195	Canton	Albert	Joseph	831 Plymouth Point	Willow Grove	SC	22345	11/14/86	803-555-5350	803-555-0853	Willows Beach Cottages	Jackson, R.
347-41-1269	Pohick	Gunston	Lee	3691 Hov Drive	Ridgelake	SC	22454	4/3/88	803-555-2411	803-555-0851	Willows Beach Cottages	Jackson, R.
355-89-1019	Pena	Ernest	Toro	1568 Strayer Lane	Altamont	SC	22234	11/27/82	803-555-9309	803-555-0860	The Willow Top	Atkinson
365-86-8365	Springfield	Frank	Dulles	395 W. Rockville	Altamont	SC	22234	4/5/92	803-555-9549	803-555-0651	The Atrium Grill	Taylor
371-92-4247	Smith	Emery	David	5902 Hereford Dr.	James Way	SC	24354	8/19/91	803-555-6524	803-555-0301	Little Tree Playground	Davis
391-16-1716	Concorde	Charles	Edward	1612 Second Street	Willow Grove	SC	22345	10/30/88	803-555-6017	803-555-1207	The Grande Hotel	Gilmore
394-92-4549	Jessup	Glen	Albert	173 New York Ave.	Smithfield	SC	22435	12/14/92	803-555-5402	803-555-0830	The Willow Top	Atkinson
401-20-0324	Forest	Vernon	John	592 Indian Head	James Way	SC	24354	11/12/96	803-555-7791	803-555-1018	Live Oak Gifts	Lindsey
401-22-6849	Marlow	Lesa	Walton	1471 Barnabas Street	Ridgelake	SC	22454	2/12/84	803-555-5095	803-555-1203	The Grande Hotel	Gilmore
403-55-9145	VanDorn	Ginger	Mae	1096 Strayer Lane	Altamont	SC	22234	5/30/81	803-555-9968	803-555-1202	The Grande Hotel	Gilmore
414-30-7612	Butler	Parker	William	6371 Mt. Vernon Dr.	Ridgelake	SC	22454	12/23/95	803-555-8442	803-555-1208	The Grande Hotel	Gilmore
414-80-6206	Randal	George	Grayton	4143 North South Blvd	Smithfield	SC	22435	10/9/75	803-555-9252	803-555-0753	The Pro Shop	Williams
419-39-4315	Ho	Chen	Lee	4717 Columbia Pike	Ridgelake	SC	22454	12/7/76	803-555-3018	803-555-0503	Exercise/Aerobic Facility	Carr
423-21-2195	Higgins	Carl	Deaton	136 Silver Circle #10	Altamont	SC	22234	2/4/87	803-555-7295	803-555-1205	Grey Fox Deli	Gilmore
441-35-5441	McGrath	Myra	Ellen	146 Burges Lane	Smithfield	SC	22435	2/5/87	803-555-4005	803-555-0804	The Grande Hotel	Cho
462-81-8180	Anthony	Mark	Edward	538 S. George Street	Ridgelake	SC	22454	7/18/94	803-555-8331	803-555-1209	The Grande Hotel	Gilmore
462-92-3842	Green	Marcia	Rose	980 South Maryland	James Way	SC	24354	11/10/78	803-555-4945	803-555-0502	The Health Bar	Carr
466-93-5350	Timmons	Catherine	Marie	8382 Shawan Road	Altamont	SC	22234	4/15/87	803-555-8131	803-555-1015	Ken's Kids	Lindsey
526-16-7017	Newington	Rocky	James	6495 Baltimore Lane	Willow Grove	SC	22345	12/5/73	803-555-2234	803-555-1020	Newsstand	Lindsey
554-83-2613	Park	Laurel	Kay	4865 First Street	Willow Grove	SC	24354	7/24/95	803-555-5820	803-555-0510	Wind in the Willows	Bradbury
645-55-7821	Rich	Howard	Dean	972 Highway 173	James Way	SC	22345	3/6/95	803-555-5198	803-555-1017	Sindy's Sun Closet	Lindsey
725-77-7355	King	Jose	Filipe	7813 Silver Fox	Altamont	SC	22234	3/10/80	803-555-1769	803-555-0701	The 18th Hole	Holmes
820-53-1289	Skaggs	Elliot	Camp	3525 Tunnel Road	Willow Grove	SC	22345	7/10/96	803-555-2269	803-555-1206	The Grande Hotel	Gilmore

Figure 3.3

PROJECT 4

Creating Queries

The primary objective of a database management system is to enable you to provide meaningful information in a timely manner. You build database tables to include the information you need and then sort, filter, and rearrange the display of *all* fields of table data. Using queries, you can display specific table fields and select records based on conditions. You design and save queries as objects of the database. In this project, you build, save, and run simple queries, and learn how to set query criteria.

Objectives

After completing this project, you will be able to:

- ▶ Create a new query
- ▶ Add fields to the query grid
- ▶ Run a query
- ▶ Save and close a query
- ▶ Open and run a query
- ▶ Set query sort order and criteria
- ▶ Edit a query

The Challenge

Mr. Gilmore often requests lists that show only specific fields of data contained in tables of the database *The Willows*. He would also like for reception clerks to be able to quickly display a list of rooms available to meet guest requests—to prevent double-booking of rooms and to distribute guests appropriately throughout the hotel.

The Solution

As the data-entry specialist, you are asked to create and save queries to display the fields Mr. Gilmore requests. Figure 4.1 displays two examples of Datasheet views that are the results of queries Mr. Gilmore wants.

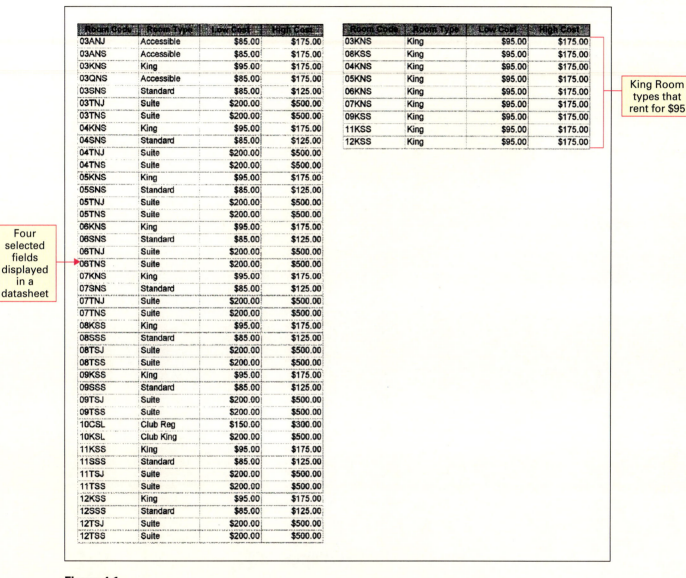

Figure 4.1

The Setup

So that your screen will match the illustrations and the tasks in this project will function as described, make sure that the Access 97 settings listed below are selected on your computer:

- View menu: If you don't see the toolbars, choose Toolbars and then click the toolbar listed at the top of the cascading menu.
- Screen settings: Click the Restore button on each object window.
- Tools menu: If you don't see a status bar, choose Options and then click the View page tab. Click the check box beside Status Bar at the top of the page.

You use the database *The Willows Updated* for activities in this Project. If you have not yet downloaded the database, do so before starting these activities or check with your instructor about how to proceed.

Creating a New Query

You create *queries* using the same basic procedures you use to create tables and other database objects. Because queries use data and information stored in database tables, you select the table (or tables) containing fields you want to display in a datasheet and use the table(s) as you create the query. The *select query* is the most common type of query and can be used to display selected fields of data in Datasheet view to make updating easier.

TASK 1: TO CREATE A NEW SELECT QUERY:

1. Open the database *The Willows Updated* and click the Queries tab.

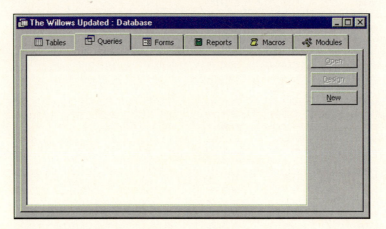

2. Click the New button.

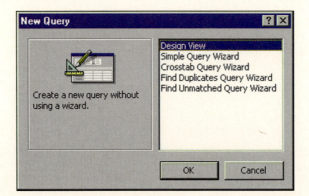

3. Select Design View and click OK.

Project 4: Creating Queries   ACC-95

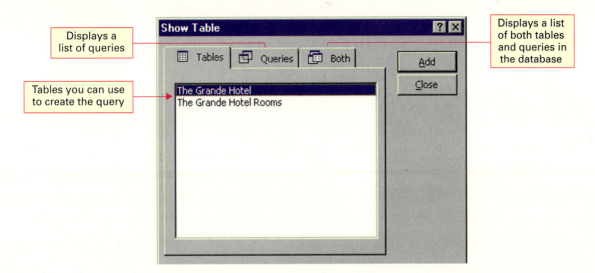

4 Select the table *The Grande Hotel,* click the Add button, and then click the Close button.
The query window shown in Figure 4.2 displays.

> **Tip** If you already have a table open and want to create a query based on fields contained in the open table, click the New Object button and select Query from the drop-down list; then select Design View. Access automatically adds the active table to the query window.

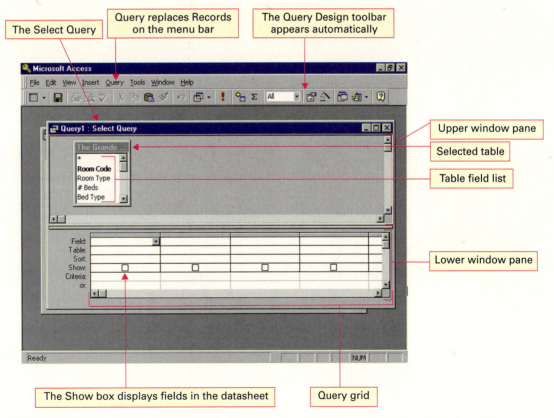

Figure 4.2

The query window shown in Figure 4.2 is divided into two panes. The upper pane lists fields contained in tables you add to the query, and the lower pane provides a grid where you tell Access which fields you want to use in the query. You select fields you want to display in the datasheet, identify the table that contains the field, set a sort order (if you want), and tell Access to show the field by clicking the Show box. You also use the grid to set conditions, called *criteria,* to limit the information displayed in the datasheet.

Adding Fields to the Query Grid

You can select the fields to add to a query from the table field list in the upper pane of the query window or from the drop-down list in the Field row of the *query grid.* Only one field appears in each column of the query grid.

TASK 2: TO ADD FIELDS TO THE QUERY GRID:

1 Click the arrow button beside Field in the first column of the query grid.

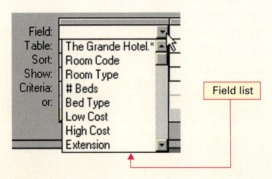

2 Click Room Code.

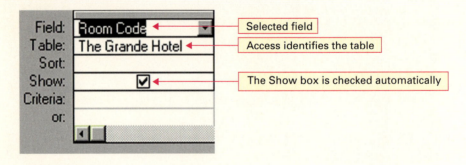

Project 4: Creating Queries   ACC-97

3 Double-click Room Type in the table field list in the upper pane.

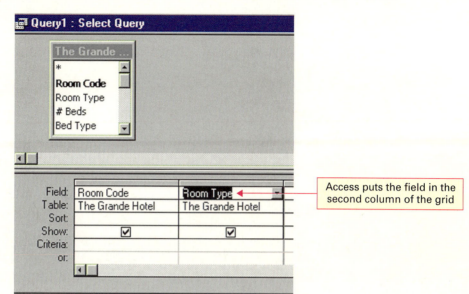

Access puts the field in the second column of the grid

4 Add Low Cost and High Cost to the grid, using the method you prefer.

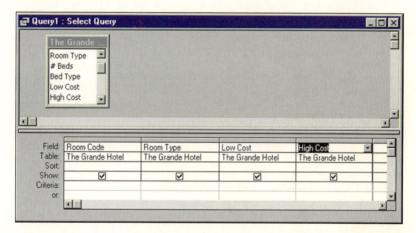

Running a Query

Running the query tells Access to display a datasheet that contains only those fields you've added to the query grid.

ACC-98

TASK 3: TO RUN A QUERY:

1 Click the Run button on the Query design toolbar.

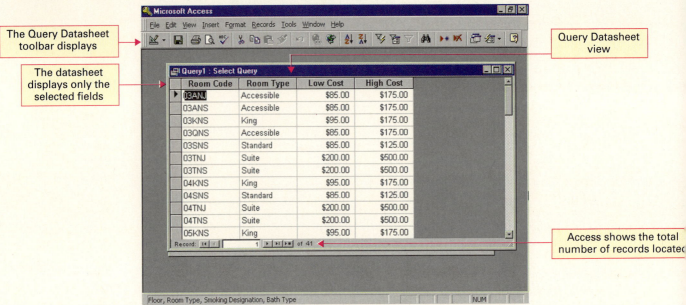

- The Query Datasheet toolbar displays
- The datasheet displays only the selected fields
- Query Datasheet view
- Access shows the total number of records located

2 Click the View button to return to the Query Design window. The Query Design view redisplays.

> **Note** Running a query displays data in a table-like format. You can print the results of a query using the same techniques you use to print a table.

Saving and Closing a Query

Often you'll create a query to use one time; other times you'll find that you use a query frequently. When you create a query that you plan to use again, save the query as an object in the database so that it's available the next time you want to use it. You can save a query from either the Query Datasheet view or the Query Design view. After you save a query, you can close it. Access displays a list of queries on the Queries page tab of the database window.

TASK 4: TO SAVE AND CLOSE A QUERY:

1 Click the Save button to save the query.

Project 4: Creating Queries   ACC-99

2 Type **Room Type and Price** in the Query Name text box.

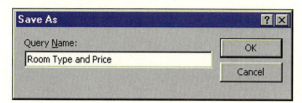

> **Tip** Because you frequently create more than one query for each table in a database, choose a query name that describes the information or fields included in the query.

3 Click OK and then click the Close ⊠ button for the query window.

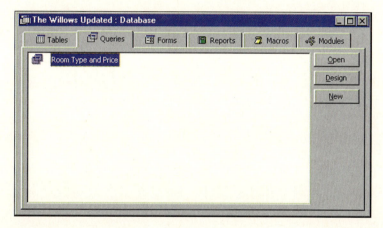

Opening and Running a Query

Saving queries you use frequently eliminates the time required to reconstruct the query the next time you need to view the same fields. Access runs the query when you open it.

TASK 5: TO OPEN AND RUN A QUERY:

1 If necessary, display the database window for the database *The Willows Updated* and click the Queries tab.

ACC-100

2 Select the Room Type and Price query and click Open.

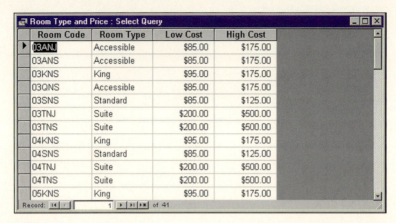

3 Close the query.

Setting Query Sort Order and Criteria

When you want Access to run a query and sort records based on data contained in a field at the same time, you can select a sort order for the field in Query Design view. When you want to limit the records displayed to those that contain certain values in specific fields, you can set criteria for the fields in the query grid. Fields you use to set criteria and fields you sort don't have to appear in the Query datasheet. They do, however, need to appear in the query grid. Figure 4.3 displays sample criteria in the query grid.

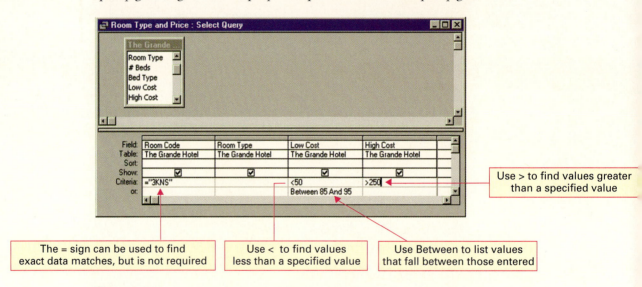

Figure 4.3

Tip In addition to the comparison operators identified in Figure 4.3, you can use <> to find values not equal to the value entered, >= to locate values greater than or equal to the value entered, and <= to find values less than or equal to the value entered. When you use the comparison operators to locate alphanumeric data, > and < locate data that alphabetically follow or come before the value entered.

Project 4: Creating Queries   ACC-101

TASK 6: TO SET CRITERIA AND SORT USING A QUERY:

1 Open the Room Type and Price query.

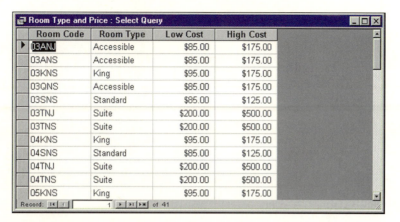

2 Click 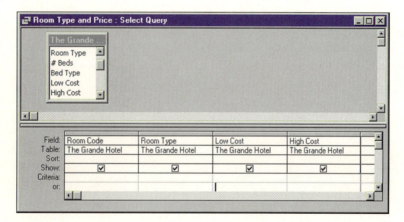.

3 Click the Criteria row for the Low Cost field and type **<100**.

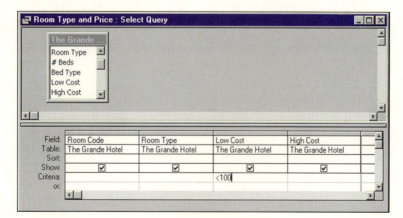

4 Click ▣.

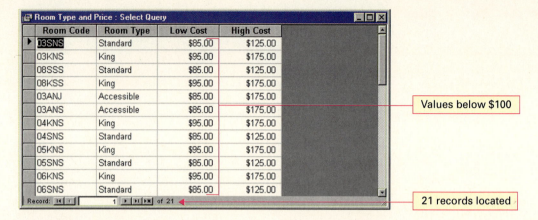

5 Click ▣.
The Query Design view displays.

6 Type **>100** in the Criteria row for the Low Cost field and click ▣.

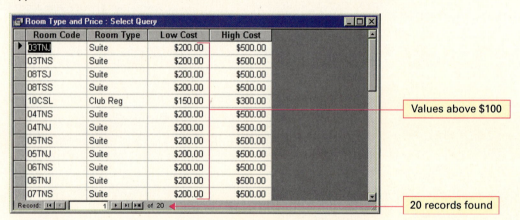

7 Click ▣, type **95** in the Criteria row for the Low Cost field, and click ▣.

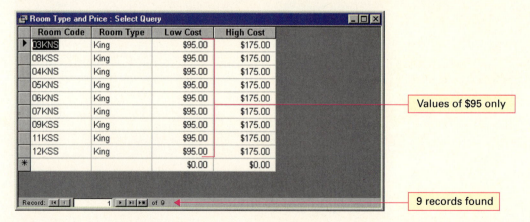

Project 4: Creating Queries ACC-103

8 Click ⌨️, click the Show box for the Low Cost and High Cost fields to remove the check mark, and then click ❗.

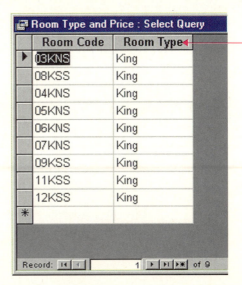

The records are the same, but only two fields appear in the datasheet

Note Access remembers the last query grid settings you ran; be sure to restore or delete those you no longer need before running the next query.

9 Click ⌨️, delete **95** from the Criteria row, select Ascending from the Sort row for the Room Type field, and click ❗.

Alphabetic listing of Room Types

10 Click ❌ on the query window, and click No when asked to save changes to the query.
Because you want to leave the query in its original format, don't save changes to the query.

Tip To search for data contained in a field when you aren't certain of the exact data contents, use the asterisk (*) wildcard before and after your query criteria. Placing an asterisk in front of and after the value you're trying to match tells Access to find records where the value you enter appears within the field data.

Editing a Query

You can edit the queries you save by adding fields to the query, removing fields from the query, and adding tables to access new fields using the query. You can then discard the changes to the query when you close it, or save the new query using a different query name.

TASK 7: TO EDIT A QUERY:

1 Open the Room Type and Price query.

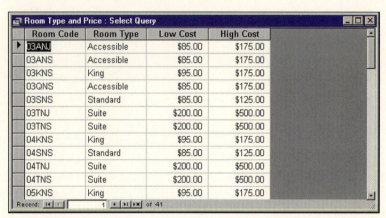

2 Click .

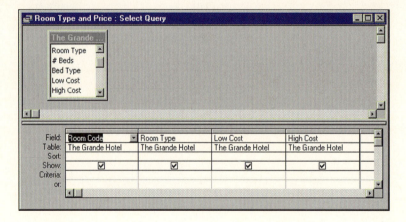

3 Click the frame button for the Low Cost field, and drag across to select the High Cost field.

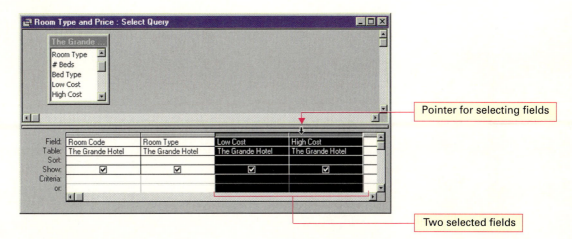

Pointer for selecting fields

Two selected fields

4 Press (DELETE) to clear the fields.

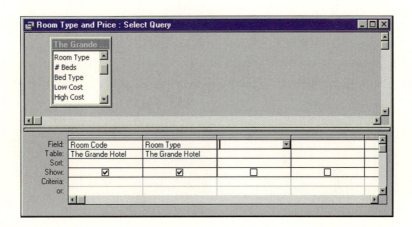

5 Add the Bed Type field to the third column of the query grid, and then run the query

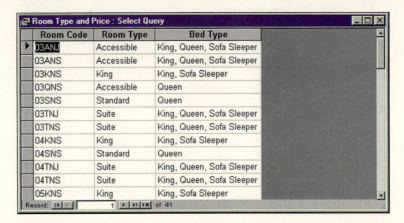

6 Display Query Design view and click the Show Table button on the toolbar.

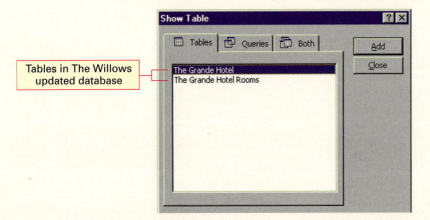

Tables in The Willows updated database

7 Click the table *The Grande Hotel Rooms,* click the Add button, and then click the Close button.

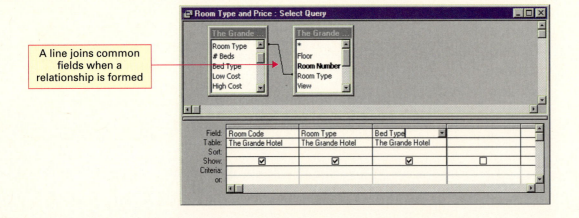

A line joins common fields when a relationship is formed

Project 4: Creating Queries   ACC-107

> **Note** Access tries to establish a connection between fields of tables added to a query window. These connections are sometimes called relationships and are used in advanced database applications.

8 Add the View field from the table *The Grande Hotel Rooms* to the query grid.

9 Run the query.
Access has combined each record in the first table with every record in the second table! This shows you that just because two tables have the same field doesn't mean you can combine the tables in a meaningful way.

10 Click the View button.

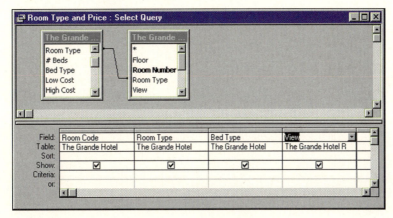

11 Right-click the title bar of The Grand Hotel Rooms list of fields.

12 Click Remove Table. The list is deleted.

13 Close the query.
A meassage displays asking if you want to save changes.

14 Click No.
The database window displays.

The Conclusion

You can create and save additional queries from scratch or edit existing queries to create new queries. After you have completed your work, close the database *The Willows Updated* and exit Access. If you plan to continue working on the exercises and assignments, leave Access open and continue.

Summary and Exercises

Summary

- Queries enable you to select specific fields of a table and display them in a datasheet.
- Queries enable you to sort, filter, and select the fields of a table that you want to display.
- You can select fields from more than one table and display them together on a datasheet by using queries.
- Queries are objects that you can save as part of a database to use again.
- You can set criteria for Access to use to select specific records and display them in a datasheet.

Key Terms and Operations

Key Terms
criteria
query
query grid
relationships
select query

Operations
add fields to a query grid
add tables to queries
create a query
edit queries
run a query
save, close, and open a query

Study Questions

Multiple Choice

1. To display specific fields on a datasheet, create a
    a. table.
    b. form.
    c. query.
    d. module.

2. The query window displays table field lists in
    a. front of other windows.
    b. the upper pane of the query window.
    c. the lower pane of the query window.
    d. another window.

3. The query grid appears in
    a. front of other windows.
    b. the upper pane of the query window.
    c. the lower pane of the query window.
    d. another window.

4. To add fields to a query grid,
    a. double-click the field in the table field list.
    b. select the field from the list in the Field row of the grid.

ACC-109

ACC-110

   c. press Enter.
   d. double-click the field in the table field list, or select the field from the list in the Field row of the grid.

5. To display records in a datasheet that meet query criteria,
   a. run the query.
   b. choose File, Display.
   c. choose Records, View.
   d. close the query window.

6. To find records with values greater than the value entered in the Criteria row of the query grid, which symbol do you type before the value in the query grid?
   a. <
   b. >
   c. <>
   d. >=

7. To locate records with dates that fall in October and November of the year 1997, type
   a. **> October** in the Criteria row for the field.
   b. **< November** in the Criteria row for the field.
   c. **between 09/30/97 and 12/01/97** in the Criteria row for the field.
   d. **October** in the first Criteria row and **November** in the second Criteria row.

8. To use a field to set criteria but not display the field in the datasheet,
   a. click the Show box in the grid to remove the check mark.
   b. type **don't show** in the Criteria row for the field.
   c. enter criteria in the Criteria row without adding the field to the grid.
   d. run the query and delete the field from the datasheet.

9. To add a field from a different table to the query grid,
   a. add the field to the table already contained in the query.
   b. create a new query using the table and combine both queries.
   c. copy the field from the table and paste it into the grid.
   d. add the table containing the field to the query and then add the field to the grid.

10. To edit a query,
    a. run the query and edit the data.
    b. open the Query Design view and change fields, criteria, or Show boxes.
    c. delete the existing query and create a new query using the new fields and criteria.
    d. edit the table contained in the query.

Short Answer

1. What's the difference between filtering and creating a query?

2. How do you sort records in a query?

3. When you edit a query, should you save the changes to the query?

4. What fields can you display in a datasheet?

5. What are the comparison operators Access recognizes for comparing field values?

6. What are the two parts of the Query Design view window, and what does each part contain?
7. How do you add a new table to the Query Design view?
8. What's the purpose of the Show box in the query grid?
9. What fields can you use to set criteria in the query grid?
10. Do you have to display fields in the datasheet that you use to set criteria?

For Discussion
1. What's the advantage to creating a query instead of simply filtering records?
2. Why would you want to add additional tables to the same query?
3. How do you save a query?
4. What procedures can be used to run a query? What's the result of running a query?

Review Exercises

1. Creating and Saving a Simple Query
Create two query designs that display the information shown in Figure 4.4. One query should create a phone list of managers, and the second query should create a phone list of assistant managers for The Willows.

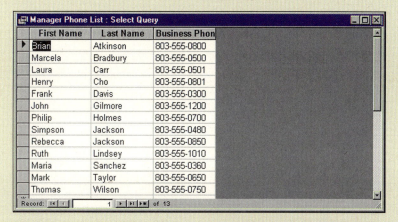

Figure 4.4

Follow these steps to create the queries that generate the lists:

1. Open the database *The Willows Personnel* and create a new query.
2. Add the table *The Willows Managers* to the query design.
3. Add the First Name, Last Name, and Business Phone fields to the query grid.
4. Select Ascending from the Last Name Sort row drop-down list.
5. Run the query and compare the format of your data display with the one shown in Figure 4.4.
6. Print a copy of the Managers phone list.
7. Save the query using the query name *Manager Phone List,* and close the query.
8. Repeat Steps 1–7 using the table *The Willows Assistant Managers* and name the query *Assistant Managers Phone List.*
9. Save and close the database.

2. Creating, Running, Saving, Editing, and Using Criteria in a Multi-Table Query

At the next staff meeting, Mr. Gilmore would like to present awards to the assistant managers who have reached milestones in their employment at The Willows. He needs copies of the lists displayed in Figure 4.5 by the first of next week so that he can prepare the awards.

First Name	Last Name	Date Hired
Kathleen	Towson	1/3/92
Frank	Springfield	4/5/92
Benjamin	Herbert	7/11/92
Travis	Wilkins	2/22/92
Glen	Jessup	12/14/92

← Five-year employees in 1997

First Name	Last Name	Date Hired
Barre	Oconnell	2/5/87
Myra	McGrath	2/5/87
Catherine	Timmons	4/15/87
Gary	McGrath	11/12/87
Gray	Oxley	9/26/87
Carl	Higgins	2/4/87
Sherman	Fleming	2/5/87

← Ten-year employees in 1997

First Name	Last Name	Date Hired
Ernest	Pena	11/27/82

← Fifteen-year employees in 1997

First Name	Last Name	Date Hired
William	Park	7/16/72
Alexander	Gadsby	10/11/72

← Twenty-five-year employees in 1997

Figure 4.5

Set up a query that displays the names and hire dates of assistant managers, sorted by department. Save the query using the query name *Employment Anniversaries*. Use the query and set query criteria to print separate lists of the managers and assistant managers who have worked for The Willows for the following lengths of time:

- 5 years
- 10 years
- 15 years
- 25 years

Follow these guidelines to complete this exercise:

1. Open the database *The Willows Personnel*.
2. Create a new query and add the Assistant Managers table to the query.
3. Add the following field names to the query grid: First Name, Last Name, Date Hired, and Department.
4. Click the Show box for Department so that it doesn't appear in the datasheet display when you run the query; select Ascending from the Sort row for the Department field in the grid.
5. Save the query using the name *Employment Anniversaries*.
6. Run the query to verify that the query sorts on the Department field but displays the other three fields.
7. Set criteria in the Date Hired field using the format **Between 12/31/91 and 1/1/93** (for those who have worked for The Willows for five years) and run the query. Print a copy of the datasheet display.
8. Return to Query Design view and use the criteria example in Step 7 to edit the data in the criteria row to generate a list of those who have worked for 10, 15, and 25 years. Print a copy of each datasheet.
9. Save and close the query.

Assignments

1. Creating a Query; Saving, Editing, Opening, and Running a Query

To make locating rooms with specific views easier when guests check into The Grande Hotel, create and save the following queries using the tables in the database *The Willows Updated:*

ACC-114

Query	Description
Ocean View Query	Display Room Number, View, and Check-In Date fields from the table *The Grande Hotel Rooms* for those rooms with an ocean view. Print a copy of the datasheet. Save the query using the name *Ocean View Query*.
Resort View Query	Display Room Number, View, and Check-In Date fields from the table *The Grande Hotel Rooms* for those rooms with a resort view. Print a copy of the query datasheet. Save the query using the name *Resort View Query*.
Vacant Rooms	Display Room Number, View, Check-In Date, and Scheduled Check-Out fields from the table *The Grande Hotel Rooms* for rooms with no value in the Check-In Date field. Save the query using the name *Vacant Rooms*.

Desk clerks will be able to use the queries you set up when guests check into the hotel and ask for specific types of rooms. Running the *Vacant Rooms* query now would display all records because there are no dates entered in the Check-In Date field. Save and close the database.

2. Creating Queries from Data on the World Wide Web

Ask your instructor how to obtain a database called *Tunes of the Century*. (If you have access to the Internet, you can download the database from the Addison-Wesley site on the World Wide Web.) This database contains a table named *Popular Tunes* that includes a variety of song titles, artists, and song types. Update the list by adding records for your favorite pop, country, jazz, rock, and blues titles.

After you update the database table, create queries to display the title and recording artist for each of the following song categories: Pop, Country, Jazz, Rock, and Blues. Run each query and print a copy of the datasheet. Save each query using the song category as the name of the query. Close all queries and the database, and then exit Access.

PROJECT 5

Creating and Modifying Forms

In Project 1, you learned how to create a simple form using the AutoForm feature in Access. Using forms, you can display individual records on-screen and present the data in a more aesthetically pleasing format. Because you may often want to display data from more than one table in a form, Access enables you to create forms based on fields contained in a table or fields contained in a query. In this project, you learn how to create a new form and modify the layout of fields on a form, using Form Design view.

Objectives

After completing this project, you will be able to:

➤ Create a new form and identify Form Design view features
➤ Select and remove fields from a form
➤ Rearrange fields on a form
➤ Save a form
➤ Align fields on a form
➤ Change form field labels
➤ Adjust field length on a form
➤ Add a title as a form header

The Challenge

Mr. Gilmore would like for you to create a form called *The Grande Hotel* that desk clerks can use to assign rooms as guests check in. He has sketched out the general layout of the form he would like for you to develop and asks you to create the form and design it using the sketch as a guide.

The Solution

After you review the design of the form requested, follow the steps in the tasks shown in this project to create the form. Mr. Gilmore would like for the form to appear as shown in Figure 5.1.

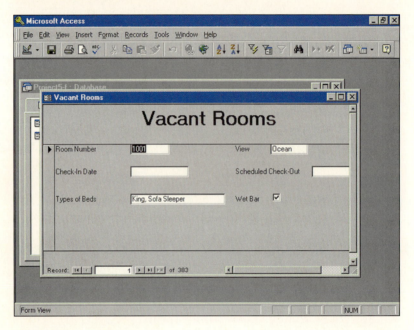

Figure 5.1

The Setup

So that your computer screen will match the illustrations and the tasks in this project will function as described, make sure that the Access 97 settings listed below are selected on the computer:

- View menu: If you don't see toolbars, choose Toolbars and then click the toolbar listed at the top of the cascading menu.
- Screen settings: Click the Restore button on each object window.
- Tools menu: If you don't see the status bar, choose Options and then click the View page tab. Click the check box beside Status Bar at the top of the page.

Project 5: Creating and Modifying Forms   ACC-117

Creating a New Form and Displaying Form Design View

The fields you need to add to the form shown in Figure 5.1 come from two separate tables: *The Grande Hotel* and *The Grande Hotel Rooms*. Both tables appear in the database *The Willows Updated,* and you used both tables to create a query in Project 4. As a result, you need to create a new form using fields contained in the *Vacant Rooms* query. The easiest way to create a form using most of the fields contained in a table or query is to use the AutoForm feature and then reposition fields the way you want them. To arrange fields the way you want them to appear on the form, you must use Form Design view.

TASK 1: TO CREATE A NEW FORM AND DISPLAY FORM DESIGN VIEW:

1 Open the database *The Willows Updated* and then open the *Vacant Rooms* query.

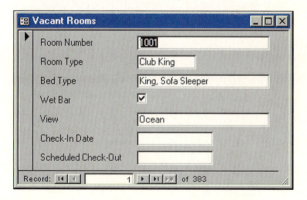

2 Click the New Object: AutoForm button on the toolbar.

3 Click the View button on the toolbar.
The form displays in Form Design view.

As you study Figure 5.2, notice that each field on the form appears twice. Each field displayed in Form Design view is considered a **field control** and consists of two parts:

- *Field labels* identify the data when you display records in the Form view.
- *Field data boxes* hold the actual table data when you display records in Form view.

As you work with Form Design view, you'll also notice different pointer shapes. Each of these shapes has a distinctive purpose, as shown in Table 5.1.

Table 5.1 Pointer Shapes

Mouse Shape	Description
	Selects field controls
	Moves selected label or data box separately
	Moves selected label and data box together
	Sizes selected field label or data box

Identifying Form Design View Features

Form Design view, shown in Figure 5.2, contains a number of new features.

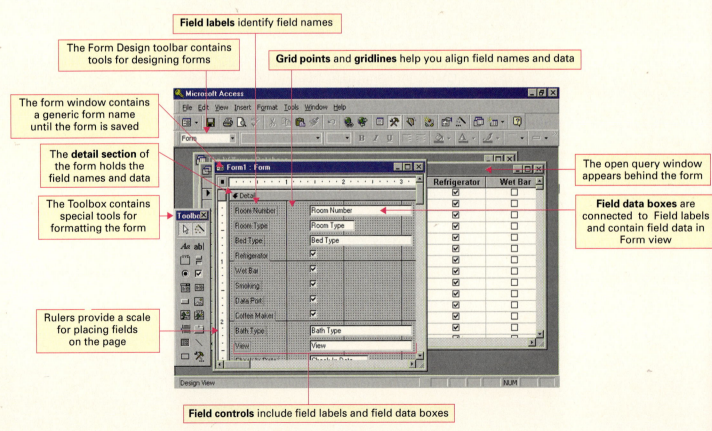

Figure 5.2

Project 5: Creating and Modifying Forms   ACC-119

TASK 2: TO DISPLAY MOUSE POINTER SHAPES:

1 Click the Room Type field data box.

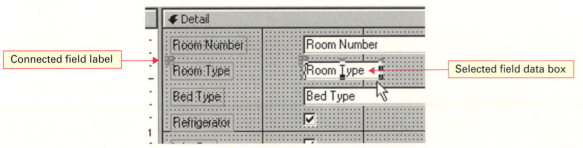

2 Point to a border of the selected data box away from a handle until you see a flat hand, but don't click.

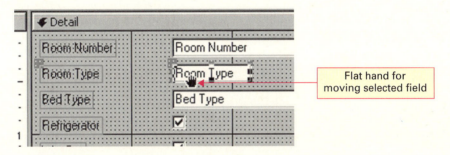

3 Point to the handle in the upper-left corner of the connected field label to see a pointing hand, but don't click.

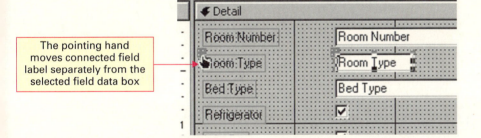

Selecting and Removing Fields from a Form

In Form Design view, you can quickly and easily select fields you don't need and remove them from the form.

ACC-120

TASK 3: TO SELECT AND DELETE FIELDS FROM A FORM:

1 Click the Room Type field label.

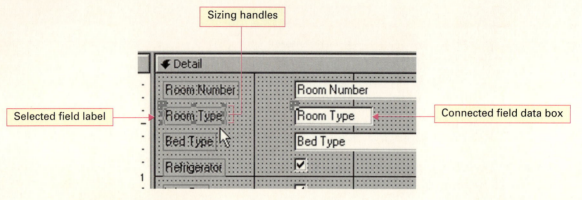

2 Press DELETE.
Both parts of the field control are removed from the form.

> **Tip** If you accidentally delete a field in error, reverse the action by using the Undo feature.

Rearranging Fields on a Form

After you delete the unnecessary fields from the new form, you can reposition the remaining fields as you need them. Use Form Design view to rearrange fields on the form. To allow more working room and to see more of the form page, maximize the form window.

TASK 4: TO REARRANGE FIELDS ON A FORM:

1 Select the field data box for the Room Number field.

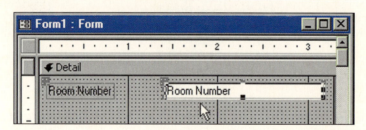

2 Point to the top or bottom border of the selected field data box until you see a flat hand; then click and drag the field until the label bumps against the left side of the form and the top of the box is aligned at the top of the screen.

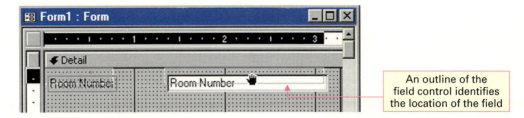

An outline of the field control identifies the location of the field

> **Tip** You can close the Toolbox or drag it out of the way to see the area of the screen you need to access.

3 Point to the View field data box, and drag it to position the field at the top of the form next to the Room Number field. The left edge of the field name should be aligned at about the 3-inch mark on the horizontal ruler at the top of the page.

4 Click the large box in the upper-left corner of the View field data box until the pointer changes into a pointing hand; then click and drag the data box closer to the View field label, positioning the left edge of the data box at the 3.75-inch mark on the horizontal ruler.

5 Continue to drag field data boxes and labels to position them approximately as in:

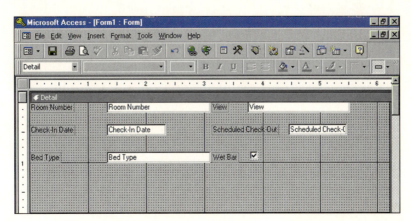

Tip To move more than one field at a time, press Shift to select all field data boxes, and then position the pointer on the border of one selected field data box. Next, click and drag the fields to a general area of the form. Then select each field separately to position it more precisely.

Note You learn how to align field labels and data boxes later in this project.

Saving a Form

Because forms are objects in a database, you save them using the same techniques you use to save tables and queries.

TASK 5: TO SAVE A FORM:

1. Click the Save button to save the form design. The Save Form dialog box displays.

2. Type **Vacant Rooms** in the Form Name text box and press ENTER. The form name appears in the title bar of the window.

3. Close the form by clicking the Close button on the form window, and click the Forms page tab of the database window.

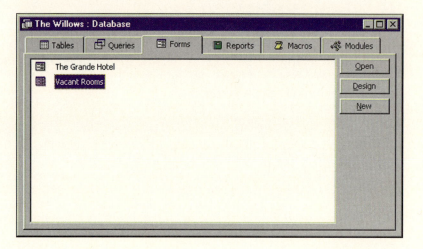

Aligning Fields on a Form

When you need to line up field names or data boxes more precisely than you can place them manually, you can use the Align options to position selected fields.

TASK 6: TO ALIGN SELECTED FIELDS:

1. Open the *Vacant Rooms* form and maximize the form window.

2. Click .

Project 5: Creating and Modifying Forms   ACC-123

3 Press SHIFT and click to select the Check-In Date and Scheduled Check-Out field labels.

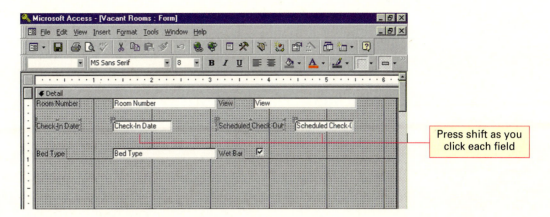

Press shift as you click each field

4 Choose Format, Align.

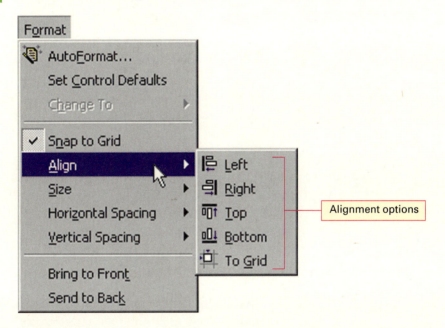

Alignment options

5 Select Top.

> **Tip** If a field label becomes misaligned from its data box, press Shift and click both the field label and the field data box before aligning the objects.

Changing Form Field Labels

When you created the tables to contain the data for the database, you abbreviated some of the field names. When you use the field names on forms, you need to expand or change the labels to make them more descriptive and self-explanatory. Changing the labels on a form doesn't change the field names in database tables; labels on forms simply make identifying the data presented easier.

TASK 7: TO CHANGE A FORM FIELD LABEL:

1 Click to select the Bed Type field label.

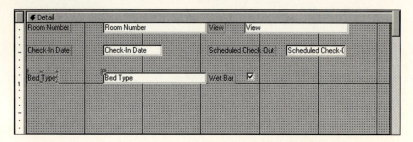

2 Position the pointer on the selected field label until it changes to an I-beam and then click.

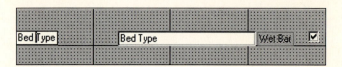

3 Click and drag to select the label text, type **Types of Beds,** and press ENTER.

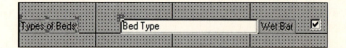

> **Tip** Use the same techniques to select field label text that you use to select text in Access tables: double-click to select a word, Shift+arrow key to select characters, and so forth.

Adjusting Field Length on a Form

When you need to adjust the size of the field data box to accommodate data on a form, you can change the size of the field data box without affecting the structure of the table.

> **Note** Adjusting the field length for Yes/No data types doesn't change the size of the check box.

Project 5: Creating and Modifying Forms   ACC-125

TASK 8: TO ADJUST FIELD DATA LENGTH ON A FORM:

1. Display the form in Form Design view.
2. Click to select the field data box for Room Number.

3. Position the pointer on the center handle on the right side of the data box so that the pointer appears as a two-headed arrow.

4. Drag the right border of the data box to about the 2-inch mark on the horizontal ruler.
5. Use the techniques presented in steps 2–4 to adjust the size of the View and Bed Type fields, and position them as in:

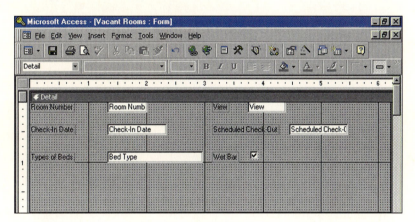

6. Click to save changes to the form.

Adding Titles to Forms

After you complete the Detail section of a form, you can add a title to the form that describes the purpose of or information contained on the form. You could add the form title to the Detail Section of the form so that the title would appear on-screen as each record is displayed. When the form title appears in the Detail section, the title would print multiple times on each printed page — once for each form on the page. If you type the form title into the header area of the form, the title appears on-screen for each record you display and only once at the top of each printed page.

> **Note** Displaying the header section of a form also places the footer section of the form at the bottom of the window. Scroll to see the footer section on the form. Information you add to the footer section prints at the bottom of every printed page in Access just as it does on Word documents.

ACC-126

TASK 9: TO ADD A TITLE TO THE HEADER SECTION OF A FORM:

1 Display the form in Form Design view.

2 Choose View.

3 Click Form Header/Footer.

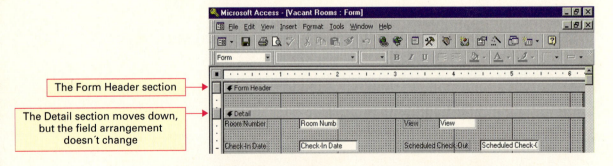

The Form Header section

The Detail section moves down, but the field arrangement doesn't change

4 Click the Label `Aa` tool on the Toolbox palette.
The pointer appears as a crosshair carrying an *A*.

Project 5: Creating and Modifying Forms ACC-127

> **Note** If the Toolbox palette is nowhere to be seen, click the Toolbox button to display it.

5 Position the crosshair at the top of the Form Header area close to the 2-inch mark; then click and drag diagonally to the 3-inch mark to form a box.

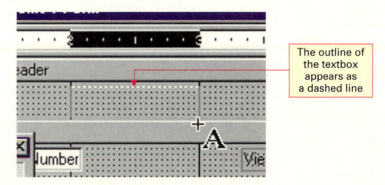

The outline of the textbox appears as a dashed line

6 Type **Vacant Rooms** in the label box.

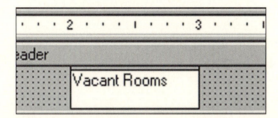

7 Click an area outside the label box, and then click to select the label control.

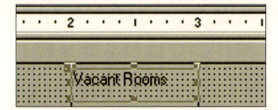

8 Click the Bold **B** button on the Formatting toolbar.
The text appears in bold print.

9 Click the arrow button beside the Font Size box on the Formatting toolbar, and select 24.

ACC-128

10 Size the box by dragging a corner handle until the complete title is visible, and then position the title in the approximate center of the form.

11 Click 💾 to save the changes to the form.

The Conclusion

After you finish designing and saving the form, you're ready to use it to display data, edit records, and add new records to the database. Simply click the View button to return to Form view, and use the techniques described in Project 1 to view individual records. To print a single record form, display the form in Form view and click the Selected Record(s) option in the Print dialog box.

Summary and Exercises

Summary

- You can create a form using fields from tables and queries.
- The easiest type of form to create is the AutoForm.
- To modify a form layout, you must use Form Design view.
- Fields are called *controls* in Form Design view. Controls consist of field labels and field data boxes.
- Form Design view displays rulers, grid points, and gridlines that you can use to position fields.
- Changing field labels and field data box size on a form doesn't change the structure of the field in the table or query.
- Field controls appear in the Detail section of a form.
- To add a title to a form, you can place it at the top of the Detail section or in the Form Header section of the form. To view the header, choose View, Form Header/Footer.

Key Terms and Operations

Key Terms	Operations
control	create an AutoForm
Detail section	edit field labels and field data boxes
field label	move and align field controls
field data box	save a form
grid points	select field controls
gridlines	
header/footer	

Study Questions

Multiple Choice

1. To arrange selected fields on-screen so that records appear individually, create a
   a. table.
   b. form.
   c. query.
   d. module.

2. The easiest way to create a form is to
   a. use Design view and add only the fields you want to include on the form.
   b. create an AutoForm and remove fields you don't want to include on the form.
   c. create a new database to hold the form.
   d. create a report.

3. You can create an AutoForm based on
   a. table fields.
   b. query fields.
   c. table or query fields.
   d. other forms.

4. Fields on a form are called
    a. controls.
    b. objects.
    c. fields.
    d. titles.

 5. To remove a field from a form,
    a. double-click the field in the table field list.
    b. select the field control and type **REMOVE.**
    c. select the field and press Enter.
    d. select the field control and press Delete.

 6. Field controls on forms are made up of
    a. field labels.
    b. field data.
    c. field labels and data.
    d. field names.

 7. Field labels
    a. can be changed without affecting the field structure.
    b. pull data from the table or query.
    c. must be aligned with the field data.
    d. can't be changed on forms.

 8. Field data boxes
    a. can be changed without affecting the field structure.
    b. pull data from the table or query.
    c. must be aligned with the field label.
    d. can't be moved on forms.

 9. To move a field control on a form, the pointer should appear as
    a.
    b.
    c.
    d.

 10. To edit a form layout,
     a. display the form and press Page Down or Page Up.
     b. open the form in Design view, select the field control(s) you want to move, and drag the field control(s) to a new position.
     c. delete the existing form and create a new form using new fields.
     d. edit the table or query used in the form.

Short Answer

 1. What's the main purpose of a form?

 2. What are the three main parts of a form displayed in Form Design view, and what does each part of the form contain?

 3. What screen features appear in Form Design view that don't appear in Form view?

 4. What are the two parts of a field control, and what does each part control?

5. When do you use a query instead of a table as the basis for a form?
6. How do you add a title to a form?
7. What features are available in Form Design view to help you adjust the placement of fields on the form?
8. How do you save a form?
9. How are form names arranged in the database window?
10. How do you adjust the size of field data length on a form, and what effect does changing the field data length on a form have on the field structure in the table or query?

For Discussion

1. What's the advantage to creating a form based on fields in a query instead of fields in a table?
2. How do the header/footer sections of a form compare to the header/footer sections of a document?
3. How do the procedures for saving and naming a form differ from the procedures used to save tables and queries?
4. How would you limit the records that appear as you browse through records in Form view?

Review Exercises

1. Creating a New Form, Rearranging Fields, and Saving a Form

Create a new form named *Rooms With A View* for the database *The Willows Updated*, based on the *Room, Bed, and View Types* query. Arrange the fields and information on the form so that they appear as shown in Figure 5.3.

Figure 5.3

Follow these instructions to complete the form:

1. Open the *Room, Bed, and View Types* query and create a new AutoForm.
2. Display the new form in Form Design view.
3. Select and drag the field labels to the locations shown in Figure 5.3.
4. Choose Format, Align and use the ruler to position the fields.
5. Select fields not shown and delete them from the form.
6. Save the form by entering the form name **Rooms With A View.**
7. Print a copy of the form design.
8. Close the database and exit Access after you have completed your work.

2. Editing Field Labels, Adjusting Field Length, and Adding a Form Title

Figure 5.4 displays the edited *Rooms With A View* form. Follow these instructions to edit the form:

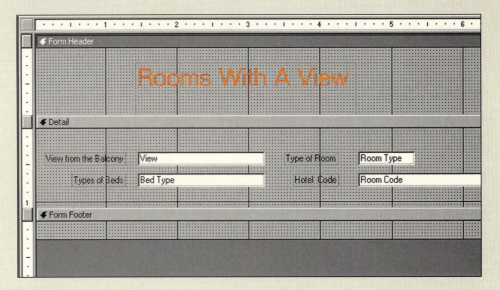

Figure 5.4

1. Display the header/footer sections in Form Design view, and use the Toolbox Label tool to add the title shown in Figure 5.4.
2. Change the field labels to those shown in Figure 5.4.
3. Select and size the field data box, adjusting the length to display the field data more appropriately.
4. Save the changes to the form, and print a copy of the form design.
5. Close the database and exit Access after you've completed your work.

Assignments

1. Creating a Form: Rearranging Fields, Removing Fields, Changing Field Labels, Adjusting Field Length, Adding a Title, and Saving

Open the *Assistant Managers* table in the database *The Willows Personnel*, and create an AutoForm layout to make it easier to enter the names and data for new employees. Group similar fields together on-screen, and format the layout so that all fields are visible on-screen. Adjust the field length of all fields so that data contained in the fields fits the data box more appropriately, and edit the field labels to identify field contents more appropriately. Add a title to the header section of the form, and save the design as a new form by entering the form name *The Willows Assistant Managers*. Print a copy of the form design.

Then open the *Managers* report you created in Project 3, and apply the techniques learned in this project to change the report layout so that it displays the information more attractively. Save changes to the report design, and print a copy of the report. Close the database and exit Access.

2. Locating Forms on the Internet

If you have access to the Web, search the Internet to locate form designs that you might use for each of the following:

- Registering guests at resorts
- Ordering hand-crafted items from specialty shops
- College applications or job applications

Download two examples of each type of form and print a copy of each example.

6 PROJECT

Customizing AutoReports

Forms you create are designed primarily for on-screen viewing. Reports are database objects designed to print summarized data from database tables on paper. You can design reports using fields in one database table or fields from multiple tables using a query. In this project, you learn to open, modify, and print AutoReports.

Objectives

After completing this project, you will be able to:

➤ **Open a report and identify Report Design screen features**
➤ **Select and remove fields from a report**
➤ **Save and view reports**
➤ **Modify a report design**
➤ **Print reports**

The Challenge

Mr. Gilmore wants a report similar to the one pictured in Figure 6.1 for a meeting of The Willows Board of Directors. Because the information he needs to include in the report is currently stored in The Willows Updated database tables, he asks you to design a report in The Willows Updated database to provide the information in the right format.

The Solution

As data-entry specialist at The Willows, you have been asked to design the report Mr. Gilmore wants. Follow the steps in the tasks in this project to make the report look like the one in Figure 6.1.

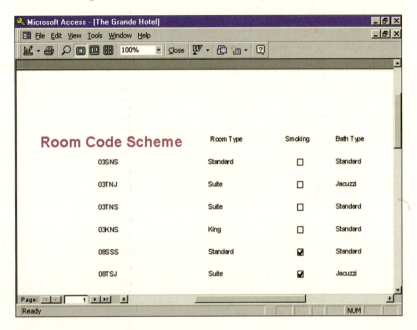

Figure 6.1

The Setup

So that your computer screen will match the illustrations in this project, make sure that the Access 97 settings listed in Table 6.1 are selected on the computer:

Table 6.1 Access Settings

View Menu	Select Toolbars if they are not displayed and then click the toolbar listed at the top of the cascading menu.
Screen Settings	Click the restore icon on each maximized object window.
Tools Menu	If you don't see the Status Bar, select Options and then click the View tab. Click the check box beside "Status Bar" at the top of the page.

Opening a Report and Identifying Report Design Screen Features

In Project 3, you created an AutoReport for The Willows Updated database and saved the report as an object in the database. A list of reports stored as part of the database appears on the Reports page of the Database window. Opening the report places the report in a preview window so that you can view the data. To create reports that display information the way you want them to, you must use Report Design view. Many of the features displayed in the Report Design window shown in Figure 6.2 are the same as those used in Form Design view.

TASK 1: TO OPEN A REPORT:

1. Open *The Willows Updated* database and click the Reports tab of the Database window.

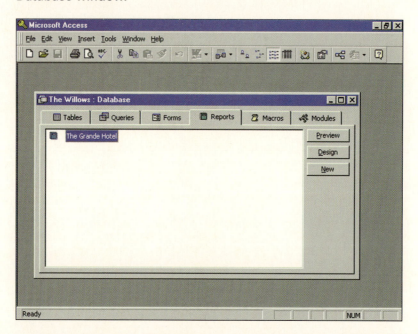

2. Select The Grande Hotel report name and then click Preview.

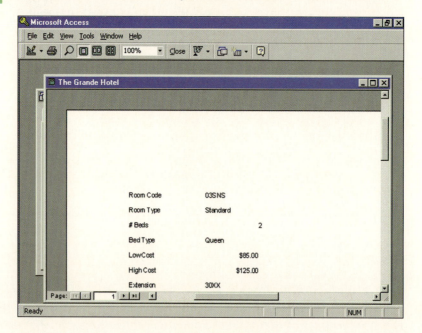

3 Click the toolbar View button.

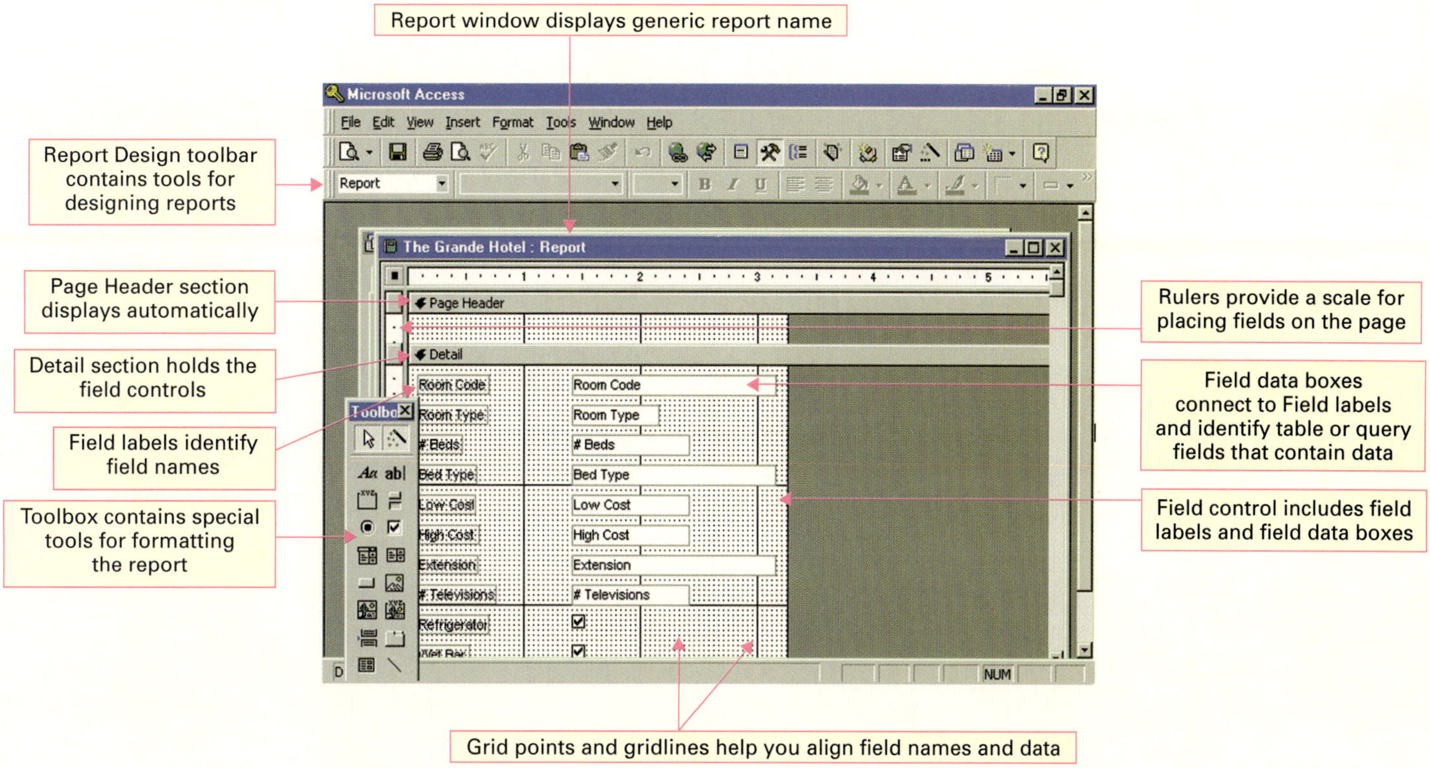

Figure 6.2

Callouts in figure:
- Report window displays generic report name
- Report Design toolbar contains tools for designing reports
- Page Header section displays automatically
- Detail section holds the field controls
- Field labels identify field names
- Toolbox contains special tools for formatting the report
- Rulers provide a scale for placing fields on the page
- Field data boxes connect to Field labels and identify table or query fields that contain data
- Field control includes field labels and field data boxes
- Grid points and gridlines help you align field names and data

Note The Page Footer section appears off-screen at the bottom of the report window. Use the scroll bars to view the page footer.

Selecting and Removing Fields from a Report

When you create an AutoReport based on fields contained in a table or query, Access automatically places all fields displayed in the Datasheet view on the report page. You can use the same techniques to remove unnecessary fields from the report page that you used to remove fields from a form. Because reports often display field data without field labels, you need to select the field data box to remove both parts of the field control. Selecting the field label removes the field label and leaves the field data box.

ACC-138

TASK 2: TO SELECT AND DELETE FIELDS FROM A REPORT:

1 Click the # Beds field data box.

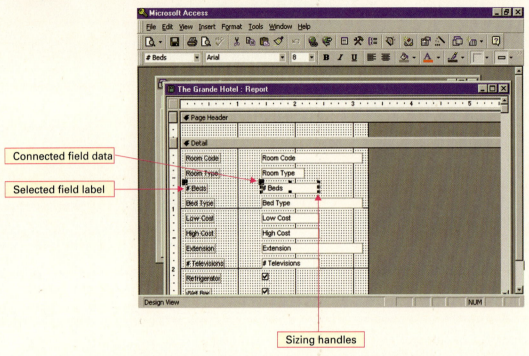

2 Press SHIFT and click to select the field data boxes for all fields *except* Room Code, Room Type, Smoking, and Bath Type fields.
Mr. Gilmore does not want to show the selected fields on the report.

3 Press DELETE.

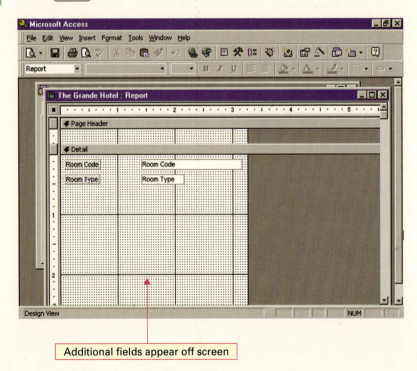

> **Tip** If you accidentally delete a field in error, reverse the action using the Undo feature. In Design view, Access permits you to reverse only the last action.

Saving and Viewing Reports

You need to save reports that you design or modify so that you can use them again. Because reports are objects in a database, you save them using the same techniques you use to save tables, forms, and queries.

Access provides three views for displaying reports: Design view for arranging field controls on the page, Print Preview to display the design with all the data in place as it will print, and *Layout Preview* which displays data from only a few records so that you can check the layout and then make adjustments before printing.

TASK 3: TO SAVE AND VIEW A REPORT:

1. Click 🖫 to save changes to the report design.
2. Click the drop-down list arrow beside the View button on the Report Design toolbar.

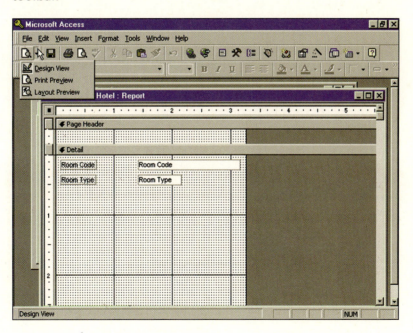

3 Click Layout Preview.

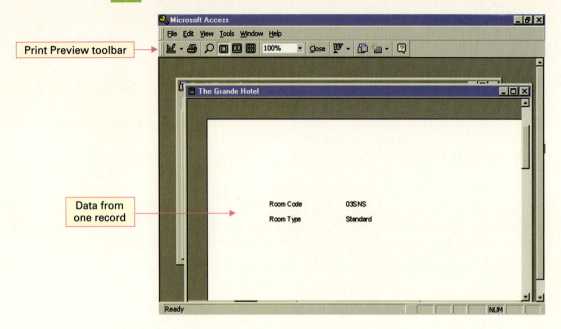

4 Click the toolbar Close ☒ button.
The report appears in Design view again.

Modify a Report Design

After removing unwanted fields from the report design, you need to reposition the remaining fields, move field labels to the *Page Header* section, and reduce the size of the report's Detail section. Maximize the report window so that you have more working area and can see the full width of the report page.

Project 6: Creating AutoReports   ACC-141

TASK 4: TO MODIFY A REPORT DESIGN:

1 Select the label for the Room Code field, and press DELETE.

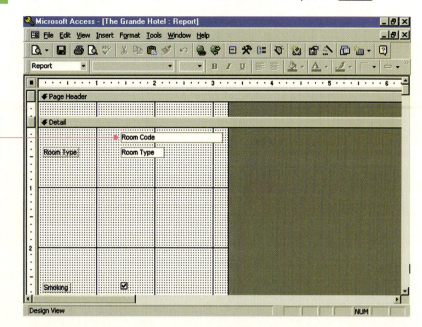

Field data box remains after the label is deleted

2 Select the field data box for the Room Code field, and drag the field data box until the right edge is aligned with the 2-inch mark on the horizontal ruler and the top of the box is aligned at the top of the Detail section.

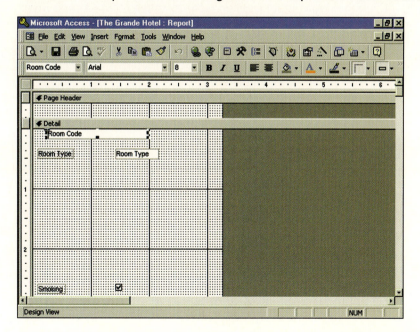

Tip To drag a field data box without deleting the field label, point to the large square in the upper left corner of the field data box until the mouse pointer changes to a pointing hand. Then click and drag the field data box, leaving the field label in its original position.

ACC-142

3 Drag the field data boxes for additional fields until they are positioned as shown here:

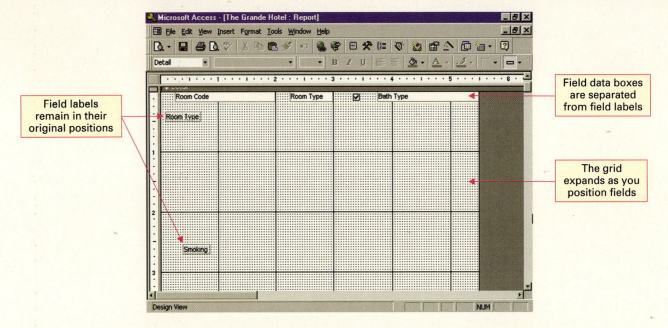

4 Click the field label for the Room Type control, and click the Cut button. The field label no longer appears on the report Detail section but is available on the Clipboard.

5 Click the Page Header section bar to make the section active.

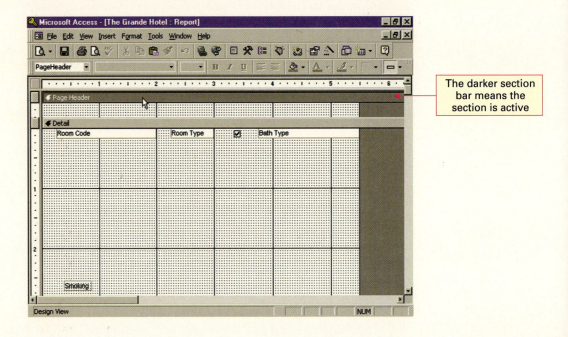

Project 6: Creating AutoReports   ACC-143

6 Click the Paste button.

The field label appears in the upper left corner of the Page Header section

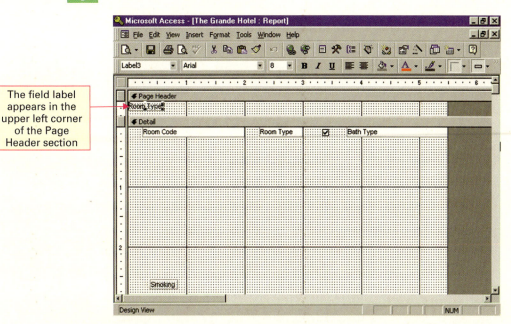

7 Drag the label and position it in the Page Header section centered above the Room Type data box.

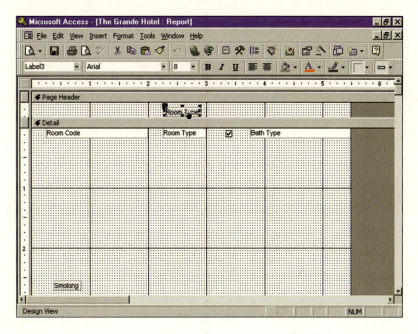

ACC-144

8. Select the field label for the Smoking field, click [icon], click the Page Header section bar, click [icon], and then drag the field label to center it above the Smoking data check box.

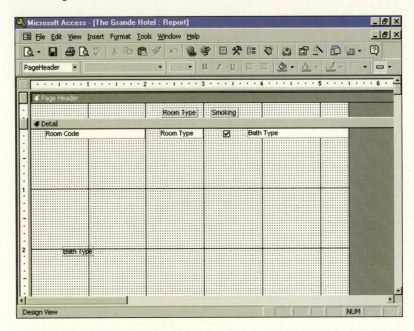

Tip Use the techniques you learned for aligning field controls on Forms to align field controls on reports.

9. Cut and Paste the Bath Type field label in the Page Header above the Bath Type field data box.

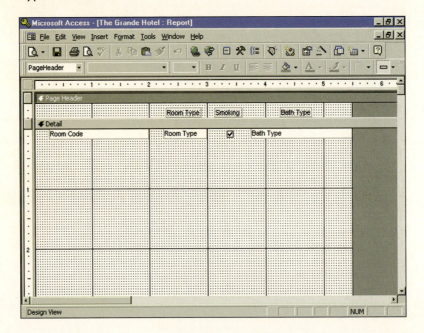

Project 6: Creating AutoReports   ACC-145

10 Preview the printout of the report by clicking the Print Preview button, and then click the Zoom button on the Print Preview toolbar.

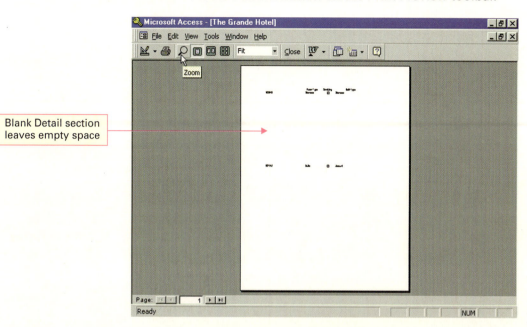

Blank Detail section leaves empty space

11 Click the toolbar Close button to return to Design view, and then scroll to display the bottom of the report design.
The Page Footer area of the report displays at the bottom of the report.

12 Position the pointer on the top edge of the Page Footer section bar until the mouse pointer turns into a ✢.

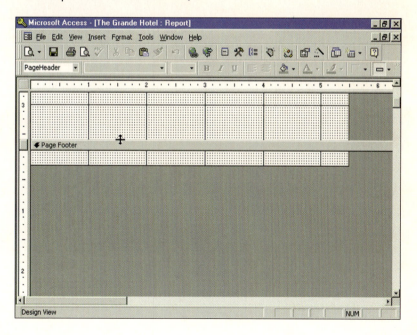

ACC-146

13 Click and drag the Page Footer section bar toward the top of the report to reduce the size of the Detail section.

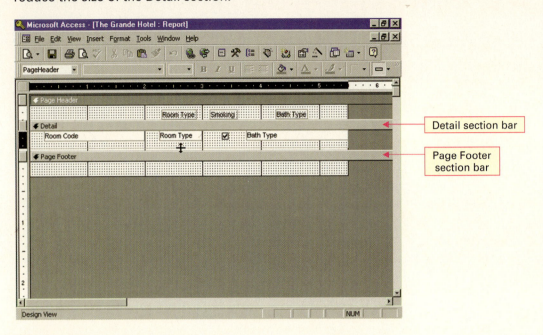

14 Preview the report again.

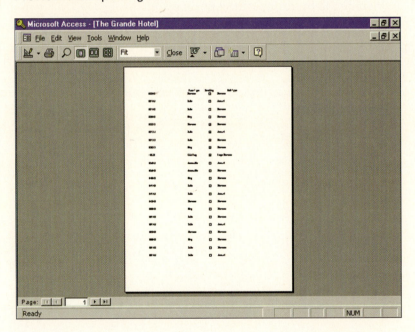

Project 6: Creating AutoReports ACC-147

15 Return to Design view, and adjust the size and position of the field control data boxes so that the data appears centered below the field control labels and at the horizontal positions shown here:

Note that the position is different from the previous screen shots

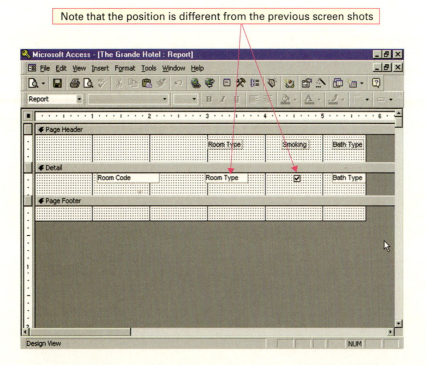

16 Add the report title displayed here using the Label tool from the Report Toolbox and the same techniques you used to add a title to a form in Project 5.

> **Note** If the Toolbox is not displayed on the screen, click the Toolbox button on the Standard toolbar.

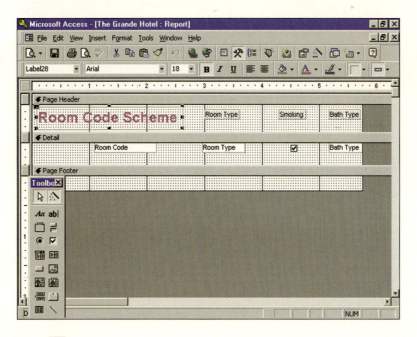

17 Click 🖫 to save the changes to the report.

ACC-148

Printing Reports

The report design serves as a shell that Access uses to display data contained in the fields of a table or query datasheet. After you have the report designed to display the data in the format you want, you can print the report on paper.

> **Tip** To print a report that was based on a query containing data for records which meet certain criteria, run the query to select those records, and save changes to the query before printing the report.

TASK 5: TO PRINT A REPORT:

1 Click to ensure the report appears as you want it.

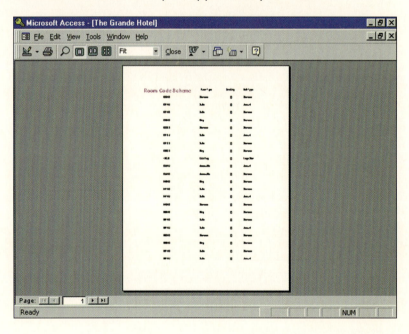

2 Click the Two Pages button.

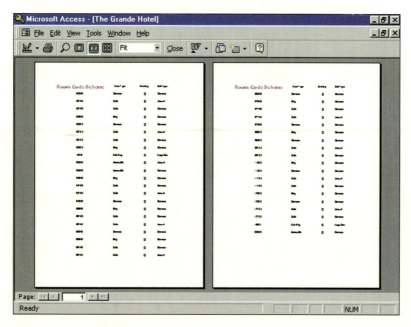

3 Click the Print button to print the report.

The Conclusion

Before closing the report, make final adjustments to the report design to line up the column heading properly, and then print a copy of the report. Save changes to the report design, and then close the report and exit Access if you have finished working.

Summary and Exercises

Summary

- Reports are database objects designed to print summarized data from database tables on paper. You can design reports by using fields in a table or fields in queries.
- You can use a variety of different techniques to create a new report; the easiest type of report to create is the AutoReport.
- To modify a report layout, you must use Report Design view.
- Field controls on reports consist of field labels and field data boxes; you can delete a field label without removing the field data box; deleting the field data box removes the field label attached to it.
- Report Design view displays rulers, grid points, and gridlines you can use to position fields.
- Changing field labels and field data box sizes on a report does not change the structure of the field in the table or query.
- Field controls appear in the Detail section of an AutoReport.
- The Page Header and Page Footer sections appear automatically in Report Design view.
- To change the size of the Detail section of a report, drag the section bar of the Page Footer section up or down.
- To change the size of the Page Header section, drag the Detail section bar up or down.

Key Terms and Operations

Key Terms
Layout Preview
Page Header/Footer

Operations
Create and save an AutoReport
Select, move, cut, paste, and size field controls in Report Design view
Print reports

Study Questions

Multiple Choice

1. To arrange selected fields on-screen so that information from multiple records appears on the same page, create a
   a. table.
   b. form.
   c. query.
   d. report.

2. The easiest way to create a report is to
   a. use Design view and add only the fields you want to include on the report.
   b. create an AutoReport and remove fields you don't want to include on the report.
   c. create a new form and then base the report on form data.
   d. create a new table and base the report on the new table.

3. Creating a report uses many of the same techniques used to create a
   a. form.
   b. query.
   c. table.
   d. database.

4. To arrange fields on a report layout, you must
   a. use controls.
   b. use Form Design view.
   c. display Report Design view.
   d. use Headers and Footers.

5. When you want to place a field label as a column heading,
   a. cut the label from the Detail section, click the Header section bar, and then paste and drag the field label into position.
   b. select the field label and type the column heading.
   c. select the field label and press (DELETE).
   d. drag the field label to the top of the Detail section.

6. To eliminate blank space between records on a report,
   a. drag the column headings closer together.
   b. add multiple field data boxes to the Detail section.
   c. drag the Footer section bar toward the top of the report to reduce the size of the Detail section.
   d. drag the Detail section bar toward the bottom of the report to reduce the size of the Detail section.

7. Reports are designed to
   a. display database data on paper.
   b. pull data from the table or query and print one record per page.
   c. present data on-screen.
   d. summarize data and print totals only.

8. Data entered in the Header section of a report
   a. appears before data from each record.
   b. pulls data from the table or query.
   c. must be aligned across the Header section.
   d. prints at the top of each report page.

9. Reports can be viewed using
   a. two views.
   b. three views.
   c. one view.
   d. four views.

10. Layout view
    a. displays the report with grid points and gridlines.
    b. displays only a sample of data from a few records.
    c. displays all data as it will print on paper.
    d. is unavailable for reports.

Short Answer
1. What is the main purpose of a report?
2. What are the three main parts of a report displayed in Design view, and what does each part of the report contain?
3. What screen features appear in Report Design view that do not appear in other views?
4. How do the two parts of a field control in Report Design differ from the two parts of a field control in Form Design?
5. When do you use a query instead of a table as the basis for a report?
6. How do you move field labels from the Detail section to the Header section of Report Design view?
7. How do the techniques for aligning fields in Report Design view differ from the techniques used to align fields in Form Design view?
8. How do you save a report?
9. What are the views used to display reports, and how do they differ?
10. What view is available for reports that is not available for any other database object?

For Discussion
1. What is the advantage to creating a report based on fields in a query instead of fields in a table?
2. What is the advantage of displaying reports in Layout view rather than Print Preview?
3. What should you consider when determining a report naming scheme?
4. How do you reduce the blank space on each page of a report?

Review Exercises

1. Creating a new AutoReport, rearranging fields, and saving a report
Figure 6.3 shows a confirmation certificate for The Willows Grande Hotel. Create an AutoReport named *Confirmation Certificate* based on The Grande Hotel Rooms table in The Willows Updated database so that reservationists can send it as the confirmation report.

Figure 6.3

Follow these instructions to complete the report:

1. Open The Willows Updated database, display the Vacant Rooms query, and create an AutoReport.
2. Remove all fields except those shown in Figure 6.3.
3. Rearrange remaining fields so that they appear as shown in Figure 6.3.
4. Save the report using the report name *Confirmation Certificate*.
5. Print a copy of the report design.
6. Close the report and the database, and exit Access after you have completed your work.

2. Editing field labels, adjusting field length, and adding a report title

Figure 6.4 displays the edited Confirmation Certificate report. Follow these instructions to edit the report:

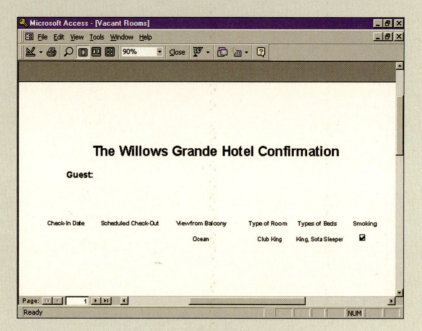

Figure 6.4

1. Add the title shown in Figure 6.4 to the Page Header section of the report.
2. Adjust the space for the Page Header section to allow room for the recipient's address on blank lines after "Guest:"
3. Set the Footer Section bar so that only two records appear on each page of the report.
4. Change field labels to those shown in Figure 6.4.
5. Adjust the field length of all fields to display data appropriately.
6. Save the changes to the Confirmation Certificate report.
7. Print a copy of pages 1 and 2 of the report.
8. Close the report and the database, and exit Access after you have completed your work.

Assignments

1. Creating a new query to use for creating, designing, modifying, and saving a report

Guests at The Grande Hotel call the front desk to report problems with their rooms. Mr. Gilmore has asked that receptionists report electrical, mechanical, and temperature problems to the Engineering department immediately and record the problems in the Comments field of The Grande Hotel Rooms table of The Willows Updated database. From the table, he wants you to generate a report similar to the one shown in Figure 6.5.

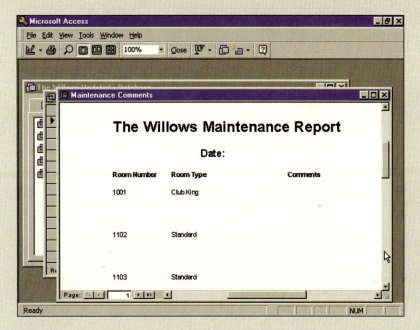

Figure 6.5

Add a Comments field as a text field containing 100 characters to The Grande Hotel Rooms table. Then create a new query for The Willows Updated database that contains the fields shown on the report and selects only those rooms with comments in the Comments field. Use the Help feature in Access to learn how to identify those records with a value in a query field. Save the query using the query name *Maintenance Comments*.

Design and save a report titled *Maintenance Report* using fields contained in the *Maintenance Comments* query. Print a copy of the first page of the report.

Close the report and the database, and exit Access after you have completed your work.

2. Locating report layouts on the Internet

Search the Internet to locate sample report designs for each of the following:

- Company profit/loss statement
- Company annual reports
- Top money winners on the PGA tour

Download examples of each report, and print a copy of each example.

Notes

Notes

Notes

Beyond the Basics: Exploring the Power of Microsoft Access

Projects 1 through 6 introduced you to the basics of database management. You are now able to build a database and add database objects such as tables, queries, custom forms, and custom reports. In addition, you know how to import Microsoft Excel data into an Access table and merge data from Access with Microsoft Word.

The projects that follow will challenge you as you learn more about the relational database model. You will notice some differences in the level of detail and complexity. Access is extremely powerful as a relational database management tool. From this point on, we assume that you are able to create and modify database objects, and copy an Access database file as a method for backing up your work. Here is a summary of what you will learn in the next six projects.

In Project 7 you will learn more about the relational database model. In addition to reviewing a simple database design process, you will learn how to conceptualize the structure of a relational database using Entity-Relationship diagrams. You will also learn how a simple data dictionary simplifies the database design process.

In Project 8 you will learn how to implement a relational database by creating additional database table objects and specifying relationships among tables. In addition, you will learn why the cardinality of relationships is important in maintaining data integrity, and how a detailed Entity-Relationship diagram assists in the database design process as relationships are established.

Project 9 will introduce you to advanced query features as you interact with data from three Access tables. You will learn how the AutoLookup feature of Access assists in viewing data in a query, and how calculated fields provide you with information from your database without creating additional data fields. You will also learn how Visual Basic controls add functionality to Access forms.

In Project 10 you will learn how to create Access forms based upon more than one table. In addition to creating a form based upon two tables, you will learn how a Subform can be added to a Main form to add power to your database.

Microsoft Access includes many capabilities for creating complex database systems, but from a user perspective, database objects are difficult to work with. In Project 11 you will learn how to create a database application that includes more sophisticated reporting and data entry capabilities. In addition to exploring the capabilities of Visual Basic controls in more detail, you will learn how a macro can be used to control the behavior of a form. You will also learn how to create a Startup form that can be used as a menu for interacting with the database.

Although Microsoft Access is powerful as a relational database management system, you can increase the usefulness of an Access database by sharing Access data and objects with other applications. In Project 12 you will learn how to create HTML documents from Access, so that table or query data can be published on the World Wide Web or within a corporate Intranet. In addition, you will learn how to create a Microsoft Visual Basic application that uses data from an Access database. By creating an executable application, you can install and use your database on computers that do not have Microsoft Access.

These projects will help you to extend your basic knowledge of database management by introducing you to the database design process, database normalization, and strategies for making your data accessible to others. After completing Project 12, we encourage you to develop additional databases for exploring Access in even more detail.

PROJECT 7

Designing a Relational Database

In the general Overview to *Microsoft Access 97* you learned that Microsoft Access is a relational database management system (RDBMS). The database objects you have created thus far—tables, queries, forms, and reports—are the basic tools for managing data using an RDBMS. Microsoft Access includes a number of tools for creating and modifying these objects. In this project you will learn how to design a relational database that minimizes data redundancy, and can easily be converted into a database application.

Objectives

After completing this project, you will be able to:

▶ Describe the database design process

▶ Explain the role of an entity-relationship diagram in database design

▶ Design a simple data dictionary

▶ Create a Microsoft Access database

▶ Import an ASCII-delimited file into a Microsoft Access database as a table object

▶ Modify the structure of a database table

The Challenge

Resort Sales Incorporated is a company that franchises gift shops in resorts throughout the United States. The company recently began a mail-order operation that has been very profitable. In fact, sales have been so strong that the current computer system for processing orders is inadequate. You have been charged with designing a Microsoft Access sales transaction database that can store and manipulate product, customer, and sales transaction data.

The Solution

To successfully design the sales transaction database, you will need to follow a ***database design process***. During the analysis and design phases, the overall needs and structure of a database are determined. You will conclude these phases by creating a simple entity-relationship diagram showing the overall database structure, and a data dictionary that lists the characteristics of all relations. Finally, you will ***migrate*** (convert) the current customer data from the old database to the new one.

Before creating your database, it is important to understand the characteristics of RDBMSs. The relational database model was designed specifically to address specific problems associated with storing information on computers. By understanding the strengths of the relational model, you will be equipped to design more efficient databases.

The Setup

Microsoft Access is a complex application that can be installed with a number of additional tools and features. Once you launch Microsoft Access, click the Cancel button to close the Microsoft Access dialog box. Your screen should look like Figure 7.1.

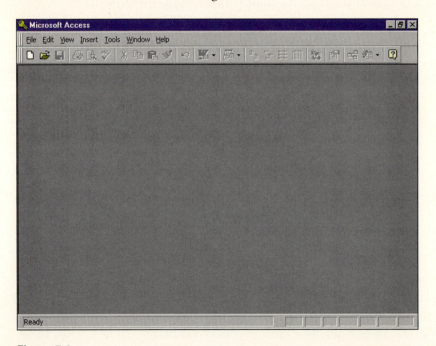

Figure 7.1

If you do not see a toolbar on the screen when you launch Access, choose View, Toolbars and click the Database toolbar option. If additional toolbars are visible, close them.

Most of the figures in this project will display the database window and other Access dialog boxes in a restored state. You may resize any dialog boxes by clicking the Restore button in each dialog box.

Close the Microsoft Office Shortcut Bar. In this Project, you will not need to launch any additional applications.

File Processing Systems

In many organizations, the traditional approach to designing information systems focuses on the data processing needs of individual departments within the organization. A *file processing system* is an application or program designed for individual use, often without regard to the information resources that exist throughout an organization. Although file processing systems automate certain procedures, they have serious limitations. Many companies use databases or other information processing applications such as electronic spreadsheets to automate and organize redundant tasks, but these applications lack a coherent method for tying together all of an organization's data resources. Therefore, the computerized systems are merely replicating the manual file systems on which they are based. The proliferation of file processing systems within organizations has become a serious issue.[1] Uncontrolled data redundancy leads to inconsistent data, inflexible programs with private files limit data sharing, poor enforcement standards such as using two different terms for the same data item, all characterize file processing systems. The database approach seeks to eliminate these problems.

The Database Approach

It is important to understand databases in the broader context of how and why an organization values data and information. There are different ways of describing the relationship between data and information, but in general, *data* is unevaluated facts and figures, and *information* is data that makes sense in a specific context and for a specific purpose. "In today's highly competitive global economy, managers are increasingly aware that their data resources are essential to the survival of their organizations."[2] Thus, data is a valuable commodity that a company must carefully acquire, manage, and protect.

---

[1] F. R. McFadden and J. A. Hoffer (1994), *Modern Database Management,* 4th ed. (Redwood City, Calif.: Benjamin/Cummings), p. 16.
[2] Ibid., p. 5.

As you learned in the Overview, a ***database management system (DBMS)*** is a software application that manages databases stored on a computer. Many businesses today, to conduct their daily business operations, use databases designed according to the relational database model. As more and more organizations convert their databases to microcomputers or to client-server systems on micro- mini-, and mainframe computers, the relational model has become the dominant logical model. A DBMS that manages a relational database is a ***relational database management system (RDBMS)***. Most DBMSs for microcomputers are RDBMSs.

Microsoft Access is a software tool for creating databases in which the information can easily be shared among users to fulfill a variety of business functions. Based on E. F. Codd's ***relational model***, Access allows database designers to create efficient databases, those that minimize data redundancy, which is information stored in more than one location and therefore increase data integrity, or the accuracy of information. You will now learn how efficient databases are designed, created, and maintained.

The Database Design Process

The database approach emphasizes data integration and data sharing throughout an enterprise. Conceptually, the database approach is easy to understand—in the Overview you read about a simple database design process. In the real world, however, organizations are often slow to implement databases that truly integrate and share data.[3] This may be due to the complexity (and therefore the cost) of designing a relational database. At a minimum, the database design process for organizations developing a database for the entire enterprise involves the phases shown in Figure 7.2.

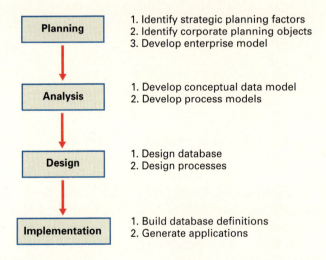

Figure 7.2

Although these phases appear simple, they are actually rather complex. Most of the terms introduced here will be defined in later sections.

[3] Ibid., p. 20.

The Planning Phase

The planning phase focuses on understanding the information needs of the organization, including the factors contributing to the organizations' success, and the organizational units and functions of the enterprise. During this phase, analysts develop the ***enterprise data model***, which is a high-level model displaying the relationships among the entities in an enterprise. *The enterprise data model emphasizes data, not processes.*

The Analysis Phase

In the analysis phase, database developers examine the flow of information within an organization and the business rules that govern information processes in order to develop an overall structure for the organization's data. This ***conceptual data model*** is independent of any specific DBMS and includes a description of the attributes defining each entity. The analysis phase also involves identifying the processes affecting the flow of information. The result of this phase is often a detailed entity-relationship (E-R) diagram.

The Design Phase

It is during the design phase that database developers design the database according to a specific RDBMS. There are two specific tasks. First, database designers translate the conceptual data model to specific structures in the database system. This includes normalizing the database, which is a process of designing the most efficient combination of relations (database tables). In the second step, database designers complete the process design. This includes understanding the logic for each process and designing the user interface elements (such as forms and reports) that support use of the database.

The Implementation Phase

During the implementation phase, programmers install the database on the computer system. This includes creating database definitions and writing program code for the database system. Migrating the data from the old system to the new, and developing training materials and documentation are necessary before the database application can be used.

Reading about the database design process may tempt you to give up on database management and revert to the file processing approach! A description of this process has been included here to give you an appreciation for its complexity as a field. Designing a relational database is a costly and time-consuming task. However, organizations adopting the RDBMS approach know that the time and cost are worthwhile because the database will be serviceable and operational for a longer period of time than a non-relational database. As with other things, you get what you pay for.

In this project, we will focus on the enterprise model and a simple data dictionary. A ***data dictionary*** is a set of specifications for how to design the database tables. The data dictionary is designed according to the detailed E-R diagram.

Using the Entity-Relationship Model in Database Design

In 1976 Peter P. Chen introduced the entity-relationship approach to systems analysis and design.[4] His approach is well suited to database design because it allows developers to more easily convert the enterprise data model into a specific database design during the design phase.

Entities and Relations

The entity-relationship approach develops a data model concerning an organization's *entities*, the things it desires to keep data about. An example of an entity for a retail sales organization is the customer. Assuming that a business services more than one customer, the company needs a way of distinguishing each *instance* of the customer entity, in this case one customer from another. A database with address information for 500 customers thus contains 500 instances of the customer entity.

Entities often relate to other entities within an enterprise. The relational database model stores the data describing entities in *relations*, which are two-dimensional, named tables containing data. Microsoft Access stores data this way (see Table O.2 of the Overview).

> **Note** All relations are tables, but not all tables are relations. A table is a relation only if each cell contains exactly one value, and each row of data is unique. This is accomplished through the process of database normalization, which we will cover in more detail in Project 8. From this point on, "table" and "relation" will be used interchangeably.

Attributes

Entities are identified by their attributes. An *attribute* is a characteristic that helps to distinguish one instance of an entity from another. For example, Last Name, First Name, and Address are three attributes that help distinguish one customer from another in a customer relation. Most likely, no two customers will be represented in the database by exactly the same values of all three attributes, so this combination of attributes will adequately identify each customer in most databases. In Microsoft Access, attributes such as Last Name are the field data that describe each instance of an entity. For example, Mary Smith is one instance of the customer entity in the organization's database.

Keys

In a relational database, each entity must have a *candidate key* in order to establish relationships among tables. A single attribute or combination of attributes that uniquely identifies each instance of an entity is a candidate key. A *simple key* is based on only one attribute, a *compound key* on two or more. In some situations, more than one candidate key may exist. For

---

[4] P. P. Chen, (1976), The entity-relationship model: Toward a unified view of data. *ACM Trans. on Database Systems* 1, 1 (March 1976): 9–37.

example, a database containing Last Name, First Name, Address, Phone Number, and Social Security Number will include more than one candidate key. The database designer could use the combination of Last Name, First Name, Address, and Phone Number to uniquely identify each customer. Or, the designer could use the Social Security Number attribute as the key. In general, a simple key is preferred to a compound key (this is why many schools use Social Security Number as a Student Number). A *primary key* is the candidate key selected to be the unique identifier for an entity. Developers usually determine the keys of a database when creating its structure during the design phase. When selecting a candidate key for a relation, certain considerations are important: the values of the key should (1) not change over time, and (2) never include the null (empty) value. And (3), for the sake of simplicity, a simple key is preferable to a compound one, which is a key that is comprised of more than one attribute. As noted above, a student's Social Security Number is often selected as a primary key precisely because it fulfills each consideration listed here.

The Entity-Relationship Diagrams

In an RDBMS, relationships are established among entities in order to make the database efficient, or to reduce it to the minimum number of relations required to minimize redundant data. An *entity-relationship (E-R) diagram* represents these relationships. For example, in order for customers to place an order with the company, information is required about at least three things: the customer, the product, and the specific order. Figure 7.3 is an E-R diagram for these entities.

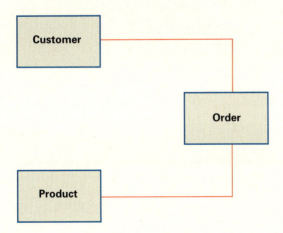

Figure 7.3

The rectangular boxes identify the entities, while the lines between the entities indicate that some relationship exists between them.[5] This E-R diagram is high-level, since it does not specify any information about entity attributes or exactly how the entities interrelate. You will develop a more detailed E-R diagram in Project 8.

---

[5] Some E-R diagrams represent relationships with a diamond symbol. To simplify the concept of entities and attributes, lines are used here instead.

What information is usually required to identify customers? Most of the information listed in the left column of Table O.3 of the Overview will suffice to uniquely identify each customer in the database. Recall that the term *attribute* refers to the field data in a Microsoft Access data table. The E-R diagram shows attributes as ellipses, with the primary key attribute underlined. Figure 7.4 displays the updated E-R diagram with the attributes for the Customer entity.

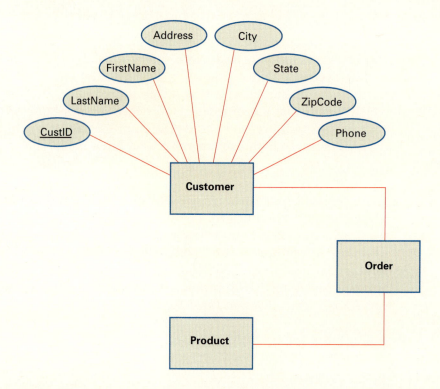

Figure 7.4

Designing a Simple Data Dictionary

When designing relational databases, you will find creating a simple data dictionary useful for documenting your design should you or someone else modify the database at a later date. The data dictionary is a paper document that lists all the database entities and their attributes. Figure 7.5 shows the data dictionary for some of the information documenting the database you will create, in particular, for the Customer entity.

Field Name	Field Size	Data Type	Field Description
CustID	Auto	AutoNumber	Primary key; format to 4 digits using \0000
LastName	25	Text	Last name of customer
FirstName	20	Text	First name of customer
Address	35	Text	Street address or post office box
City	20	Text	Customer's city of residence
State	2	Text	State; input mask force to upper case, required >LL
ZipCode	10	Text	Zip code with optional extension; input mask
HomePhone	14	Text	Customer's phone; input mask

Figure 7.5

Later the *Customers* data table will be filled in with the name and address information for each customer who orders products from Resort Sales Incorporated. We will update this dictionary to display information about each table, as additional tables are added to the database.

Creating a Microsoft Access Database

Some of the data your database will need to contain already exists in computer format, so you can import it into a Microsoft Access table object. As you learned in the Overview, a database file must be defined before you can create any database.

TASK 1: TO CREATE A MICROSOFT ACCESS DATABASE:

1. Launch Microsoft Access
2. Select New Database from the File menu.
3. By default, the General tab should be active, and the Blank Database icon selected. Click OK, as shown in Figure 7.6.

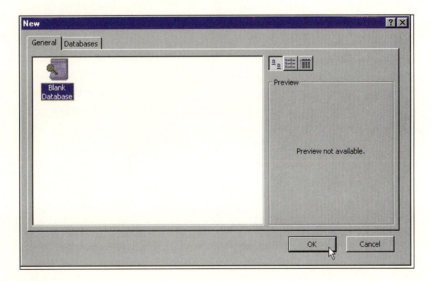

Figure 7.6

4. Create a database entitled *Resort Sales (Resort Sales.mdb* on your floppy diskette), as shown in Figure 7.7.

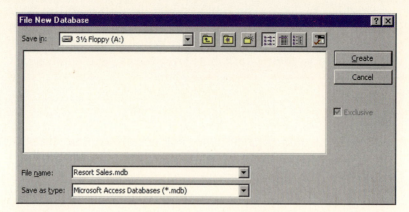

Figure 7.7

5 Click the Create button to create a blank database.

Creating a Table Object by Importing Data

Most microcomputer database systems support importing and exporting text data from and to a variety of sources. This is because microcomputer database systems are used in client/server environments that may include mini- or mainframe computer database files. Data about Resort Sales Incorporated customers has been exported from another computer application as ASCII text. Data stored in *ASCII text* format contains only letters, numbers, and symbols and is not formatted in any way. ASCII text files allow computers to share data among computers with differing operating systems. In addition, virtually all microcomputer applications can read ASCII data.

ASCII text files imported into database applications often store data in a specific format. Each row of data in an ASCII file usually constitutes one database record. Recall that a *record* is all the information about an instance of an entity, such as a customer, that is kept in the database, while *field* data (or attributes of an entity) are the categories of information defining each entity.

ASCII files are often *delimited* in order to separate the attributes included in the file. To delimit means to fix the limits of or specify a boundary for something. ASCII delimited files delimit field data with one or more characters. The *delimiting character* or *delimiter* is the specific ASCII character used to separate field data. Figure 7.8 displays an ASCII-delimited text file opened with the Microsoft Windows 95 Notepad application.

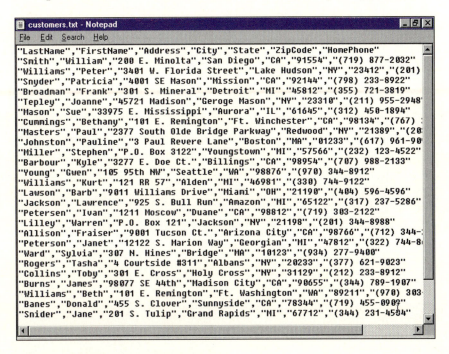

Figure 7.8 ASCII-delimited text file

This file uses both the comma character as a delimiter, and the double quote character as a text qualifier. The text qualifier encloses each data attribute. ASCII-delimited files can easily be imported into Microsoft Access. The delimiter and text qualifier will differentiate the field data as Access builds a table from the file.

TASK 2: TO CREATE A TABLE FROM AN ASCII FILE:

 Select Get External Data, Import . . . from the File menu, as shown in Figure 7.9.

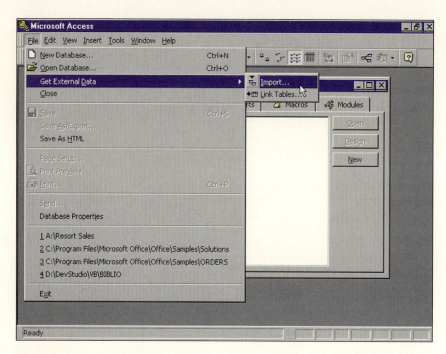

Figure 7.9

2 In the Import dialog box, select the 3½-inch floppy diskette, and Text Files in the Files of Type list, as shown in Figure 7.10.

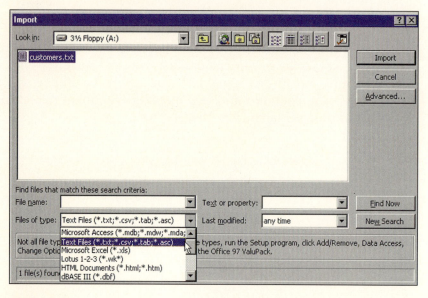

Figure 7.10

Troubleshooting If you do not see the Text Files option, then not all import filters have been installed. Inform your instructor, and open the *Resort Sales.mdb* file from the Files folder on your floppy diskette.

3 Select the customers.txt icon, and click the Import button. Access now invokes the Import Text Wizard.

Project 7: Designing a Relational Database   ACC-173

4 In the Import Text Wizard, select the Delimited option button, which should appear as the default. Click the Next button, as shown in Figure 7.11.

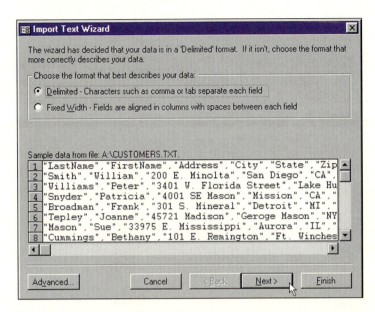

Figure 7.11

5 The Comma delimiter option button should be selected by default. Check the checkbox for First Row Contains Field Names. When the dialog box settings match those in Figure 7.12, click Next.

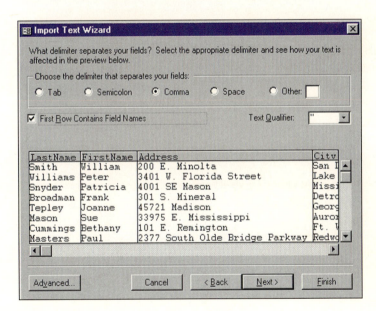

Figure 7.12

6 Select In a New Table, the default option to store the data in a new table, as shown in Figure 7.13. Click Next.

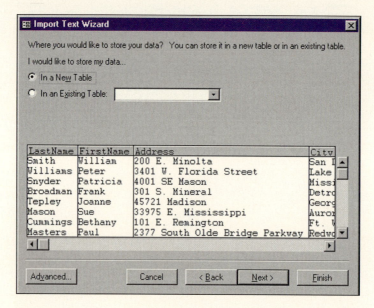

Figure 7.13

7 Access will now verify the field name and data type for the first attribute, and will automatically name the field LastName, since this is included in the first row of data. Retain the default field name LastName, and the default data type Text. Click Next, as shown in Figure 7.14.

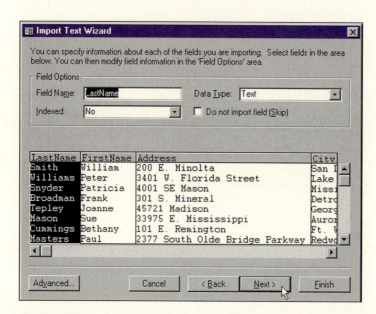

Figure 7.14

Tip Although Microsoft Access table objects can contain spaces in the field names, it is a good idea to name the fields without spaces or special characters, in the event that the database will be used in conjunction with other applications that do not support spaces in the field names.

8 The Access Import Text Wizard will recommend that you add a primary field to the table. Select the option button for Access to add a primary key. When your settings match those in Figure 7.15, click Next.

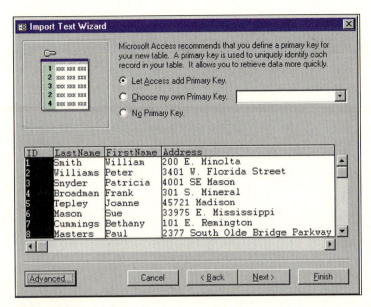

Figure 7.15

9 The final step of the Import Text Wizard allows you to name the database table object. By default, Access uses the name of the text file as the table name. Select the default name for the table as shown in Figure 7.16, and click the Finish button.

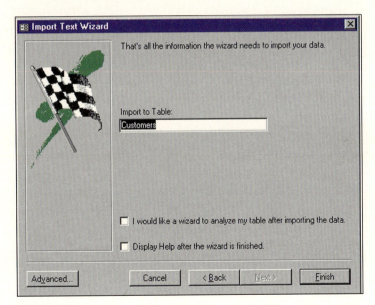

Figure 7.16

10 The Text Import Wizard will indicate that the file has successfully been imported, as shown in Figure 7.17. Click the OK button. Notice the Table Object icon that now appears in the database window, along with the table name.

ACC-176

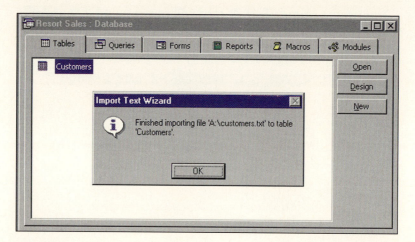

Figure 7.17

Modifying the Design of the *Customers* Table

When you import ASCII text files into a Microsoft Access table, Access applies the default size for text fields. Depending on how Access was installed on your computer or network, the field size may be as large as 255 characters. Access will reserve the number of characters specified in the field size for each database record. Since unnecessarily large field sizes use up a lot of memory, you will alter the table design to reflect the field size more closely. In addition, you will modify the State field so that it will display any values entered in uppercase. Finally, you will add an input mask to the ZipCode and HomePhone fields. An *input mask* is a series of characters that controls how data is entered in a field. Input masks are useful for simplifying data entry and for requiring data in certain fields.

TASK 3: TO MODIFY THE TABLE DESIGN:

1. Select the Tables tab in the Database window, if it is not currently active.
2. With the *Customers* table selected, click the Design button, as shown in Figure 7.18.

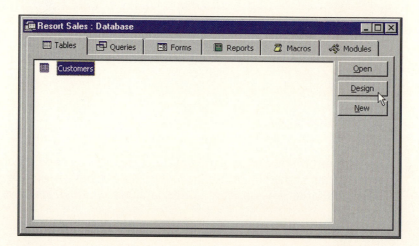

Figure 7.18

3 In the Design View grid of the *Customers* Table window, change the field name ID to CustID. In the Field Properties window below the design grid, with the General tab active, change the Format pane to read \0000. This format will display all the field data in a four-digit format for consistency: each customer number should appear in the same format, whether we are talking about customer 0001 or customer 1231. In the Description column of the design grid, type **Primary Key; format to 4 digits using \0000**, as shown in Figure 7.19.

> **Tip** By entering the Description data from the data dictionary in the table design grid, you ensure that internal database documentation is included in the database file.

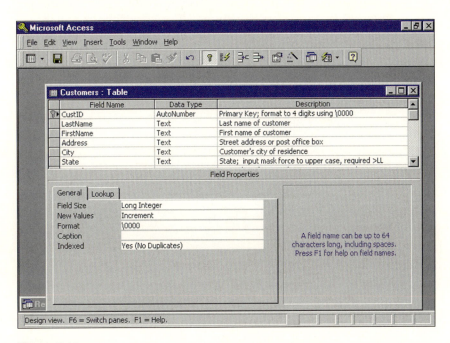

Figure 7.19

4 Change the field size property of all fields to match the data dictionary shown in Figure 7.5. Add the appropriate field description data into the Description column of the table design grid.

5 Save the database. Since the field widths have been changed, the dialog box shown in Figure 7.20 will appear. Select Yes.

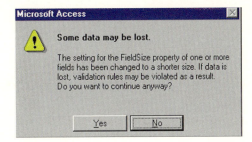

Figure 7.20

ACC-178

> **Caution** When modifying the database structure, make sure that the field size for each field is sufficient to contain any existing data. If not, field data will be truncated (part of it cut off).

6 Select the State field in the design grid. Place the insertion point in the Input Mask pane in the Field Properties window (with General tab active). Type **>LL**, and press (ENTER). This input mask will force lowercase values to be displayed as uppercase. The > symbol indicates that the entry should be displayed as uppercase, while "L" indicates that a character entry is required.

7 Select the ZipCode field in the design grid and type **00000\-9999;0;** in the Input Mask pane. The zeros in the mask indicate required entries, the nines indicate that the data is optional. The backslash character will display the hyphen as a literal character, and the semicolons separate the sections of the input mask placeholders.

8 Select the HomePhone field in the design grid, and type **!\(000") "000/-0000;0;_** in the Input Mask pane below. The zeros specify that the entry is required.

The table design grid should now look like Figure 7.21.

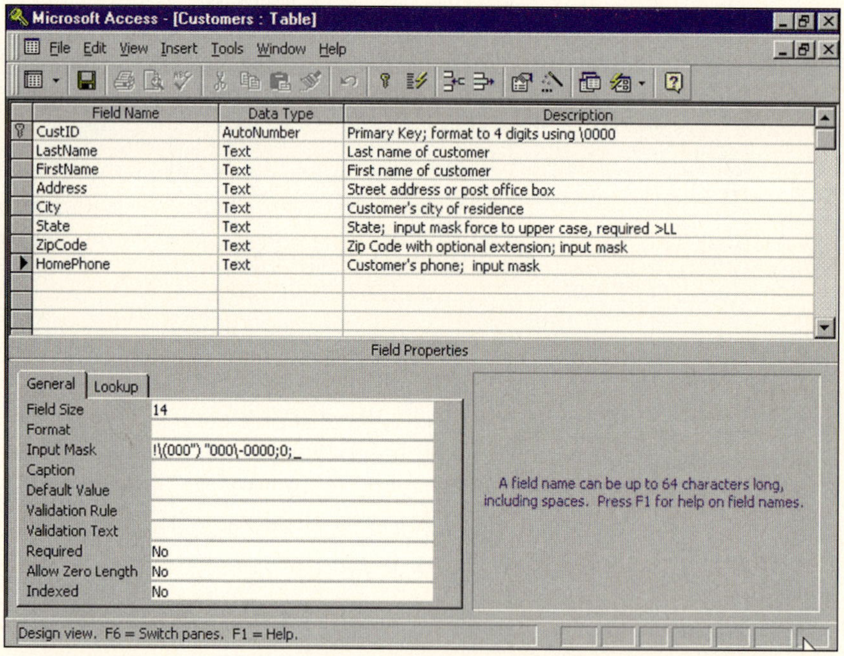

Figure 7.21

Select Datasheet View from the View menu. Since you have made changes to the table design, Access will verify that you want to update the database by displaying the dialog box shown in Figure 7.22.

Figure 7.22

Click Yes. The completed data table will appear as shown in Figure 7.23.

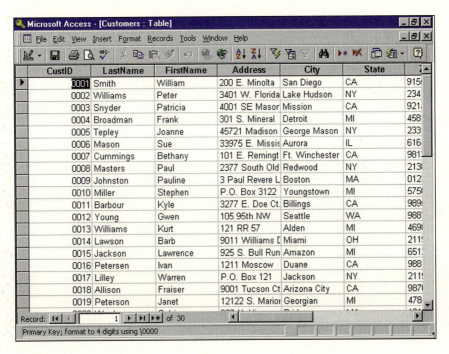

Figure 7.23

The Conclusion

The Customers table is now complete. You see how easy it is to import existing data into Microsoft Access. In the next project you will learn about the relational capabilities of Microsoft Access by creating two additional tables to your database, and establishing relationships between all three tables.

Summary and Exercises

Summary

- Relational database management systems (RDBMSs) can minimize redundant and inaccurate data.
- File processing systems have inherent weaknesses that the database approach can correct.
- Efficient databases are built according to a specific design process.
- During the planning phase, database designers construct an enterprise data model.
- The analysis phase usually produces a high-level entity-relationship (E-R) diagram.
- A database is normalized during the design phase.
- A database is fully constructed during the implementation phase.
- A data dictionary contains documentation about the database design.
- A relation is a two-dimensional, named table containing data.
- An entity is anything an organization desires to keep data about, for example, customers.
- An instance of an entity is one representation of it in the database; for example, a particular customer could be an instance of the entity Customers.
- An attribute is a characteristic of an entity.
- Keys are used to identify instances of an entity.
- ASCII text is a common format for storing data.
- An input mask is used to simplify data entry in a database.

Key Terms and Operations

Key Terms

ASCII text
attribute
candidate key
compound key
conceptual data model
data
database design process
database management system (DBMS)
data dictionary
delimited text
delimiting character (delimiter)
enterprise data model
entity
entity-relationship (E-R) diagram
field
information
file processing systems
input mask
instance
migrate data

primary key
record
relation
relational model
relational database management system (RDBMS)
simple key

Operations

interpret an entity-relationship diagram
create a database
design a data dictionary
create a table by importing ASCII data
add a primary key field
modify field sizes
add input masks

Study Questions

Multiple Choice

1. Which Microsoft Access object can be created from ASCII data?
   a. table
   b. query
   c. form
   d. report
   e. module

2. Which database design phase includes designing the user interface?
   a. planning
   b. analysis
   c. design
   d. implementation

3. What term is used to describe unevaluated facts and figures?
   a. table
   b. information
   c. data
   d. entity
   e. relation

4. What term best describes the process of designing an efficient relational database?
   a. entity
   b. attribute
   c. relation
   d. input mask
   e. normalization

5. Which of the following is the formal name for a table?
   a. entity
   b. instance
   c. attribute
   d. relation
   e. normalization

6. Which term is the formal name for a field?
   a. entity
   b. instance
   c. attribute
   d. relation
   e. normalization

7. Which of the following describes a combination of fields that uniquely identifies each record in a table?
   a. instance
   b. compound key
   c. primary key
   d. candidate key
   e. attribute

8. What is used to differentiate field data in an ASCII data file?
   a. compound key
   b. E-R diagram
   c. instance

       d. input mask
       e. delimiter

9. Which character in an input mask identifies data that is required?
    a. 0 (zero)
    b. L
    c. > (greater than)
    d. , (comma)
    e. answers a and b above

10. Which of the following is considered a weakness of file processing systems?
    a. redundant data
    b. normalized relations
    c. the presence of compound keys
    d. the ability to establish relationships between relations
    e. the ability to distinguish instances of an entity

Short Answer

1. What does a detailed E-R diagram include that a high-level E-R diagram does not?
2. What information is included in a data dictionary?
3. What character is commonly used to delimit ASCII data?
4. Which phase of the database design process results in a detailed E-R diagram?
5. Microsoft Access is based upon which logical database model?
6. What is used to differentiate instances of an entity?
7. What is a more common term for a relation?
8. What is the name of a field that uniquely identifies each instance of a relation?
9. What is the more common term for an attribute?
10. What is often added to the fields in a table to simplify data entry?

For Discussion

1. What are the limitations of file processing systems? Why is the database approach deemed superior?
2. What steps are included in the database design process?
3. Explain the difference between entities, relations, instances, and attributes.
4. How do input masks simplify entering data into an Access table?

Review Exercises

1. Creating an Employee Database

Ms. Perkins has asked you to create an Employee database that will store information about each employee at Roaring Fork Sports Incorporated. Your first task will be to create a table similar to the one you created in Project 1, although the data for this table will be stored in an ASCII-delimited text file. Follow these steps to create the database:

Project 7: Designing a Relational Database ACC-183

1. Create a blank database named *Employees* (*Employees.mdb*) on your floppy diskette.
2. Select Get External Data from the File menu.
3. Select Import. When the Import Text wizard appears, import the employees.txt ASCII file into the database.
4. Specify that the file is delimited.
5. Indicate that the delimiting character is a comma and that the first row contains field names.
6. Change the data type of the DateHired field to Date/Time.
7. Change the data type of the PayRate field to Currency.
8. Do not set a primary key.
9. Name the table *Employees*.

Your table should appear similar to the one shown in Figure 7.24.

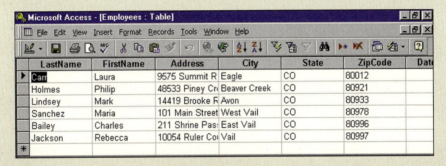

Figure 7.24

10. Close the table and the database.

2. Adding a Primary Key and Input Mask to a Table Design

You will need to add a customer identification number to the *Employees* table in the *Employees* database. Since a primary key needs to uniquely identify each record, use the employee's Social Security Number. Follow these steps to add a primary key to the *Employees* table:

1. Open the database *Employees*.
2. Click the Tables tab to make Tables the active window.
3. Click the Design button.
4. Select Rows from the Insert menu to add a blank field row to the database design.
5. Type **EmpID** as the field name for the blank row.
6. Set the Field Size in the Field Properties window to 11 characters.
7. Type **000\-00\-0000;;_** in the Input Mask pane.
8. Type **Social Security Number** as a caption for this field. The Field Properties window should now look like the one shown in Figure 7.25.

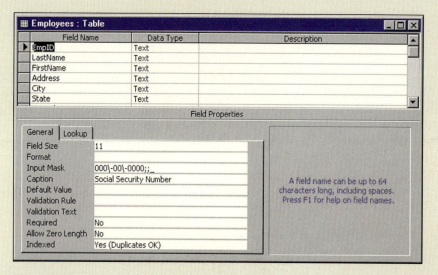

Figure 7.25

9. Select Datasheet View from the View menu.
10. Save your changes to the table design.
11. Enter the data shown in Table 7.1 into the database.
12. Select Design View from the View menu.
13. Set EmpID as the primary key.
14. Close the table and save the Changes to the table design.
15. Close the database.

Table 7.1 Employee Identification Data

Record Number	EmpID
1	123-45-6789
2	322-11-2333
3	477-10-3908
4	421-90-5969
5	334-27-1672
6	765-21-3829

Assignments

1. Creating a Student File
Create a blank database named *Students*. Using the Text Import wizard, create a table from the *Students.txt* file that is available on your data diskette. Set the StudentID field as the primary key. Name the table *Students*. Change the width of all fields to an appropriate number. Save all changes to the table design, and close the database.

2. Finding Information on the Internet (Optional Assignment)
In order to develop a database of restaurants in the Vail area, search the Internet for the term "Vail." Visit the home page for the town of Vail, Colorado. Create an Access database consisting of the names, addresses, and cuisine for five of Vail's eating establishments.

8 PROJECT

Creating Additional Tables and Establishing Relationships

In Project 7 you began constructing a relational database using Microsoft Access. At this point your database contains only one table. To be relational a database needs two or more tables (relations). Normalization is the process of determining the optimum number of relations to include in a database. The process involves converting complex data structures into a simple form, by considering the attributes necessary to identify each instance of an entity and the kinds of relationships that must exist between entities. In this project you will create two additional tables in your database, learn about cardinality, and normalize the database.

Objectives

After completing this project, you will be able to:

➤ **Define cardinality**

➤ **Interpret a detailed entity-relationship (E-R) diagram**

➤ **Create a table containing text, currency, and numeric data types from ASCII data**

➤ **Create a table containing text and numeric data types using the Table Design View grid**

➤ **Add tables to the Relationships window, and create one-to-many relationships**

Project 8: Creating Additional Tables and Establishing Relationships ACC-187

The Challenge

You are off to a good start in designing the *Resort Sales Incorporated* database. You have represented data about current customers, and are able to uniquely identify each customer using the customer identification number. You need to represent data concerning the Resort Sales Incorporated products, and design a method for storing and viewing customer orders.

The Solution

To represent and store the data required in the Challenge, you will need to create two new tables. One will list product information, and the other will contain information about specific orders. Once you have created these tables, you can establish relationships between them. In Microsoft Access, the relationships will appear in the Relationships window, as shown in Figure 8.1.

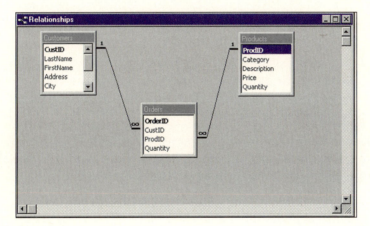

Figure 8.1

The Setup

In Microsoft Access there is no method for saving a copy of a database file from within Access. Therefore, to create a back-up copy of a database file you must physically make a copy of the file using the Windows operating system. To complete the steps in this project, you will first make a copy of the *Resort Sales* database:

TASK 1: TO MAKE A COPY OF THE ACCESS DATABASE FILE:

1. Minimize Microsoft Access.
2. Click My Computer on the Desktop.

3. Place your data diskette in the computer's floppy disk drive.
4. Click the floppy diskette icon.
5. Select the *Resort sales.mdb* file icon by clicking it once with the left mouse button.
6. Select Copy from the Edit menu in the 3-1/2 Floppy (A) window.
7. Select Paste from the Edit menu in the 3-1/2 Floppy (A) window.
8. Place the insertion point over the icon or description of the file *Copy of Resort Sales.mdb* and click the right mouse button.
9. Select Rename from the right-click menu.
10. Enter *Resort Sales 2.mdb* as the new filename, and press ENTER.
11. Restore Access and open the *Resort Sales 2.mdb* database.

> **Troubleshooting** If you are having trouble copying and renaming this file, ask your instructor for assistance.

To complete this project, make sure you do the following in Access:

▶ **If you do not see a toolbar on the screen after launching Access, choose View, Toolbars, and click the Database toolbar option. If additional toolbars are visible, close them.**

▶ **Most of the figures in this project will display the Database window and other Access dialog boxes in a restored state. You may resize any dialog boxes by clicking the Restore button in each dialog box.**

▶ **Close the Microsoft Office Shortcut bar. In this project, you will not need to launch any additional applications.**

Understanding Relationships

As you learned in Project 7, a relational database management system (RDBMS) often establishes relationships between relations. Entities and their relationships are often graphically represented using E-R diagrams. Figure 8.2 shows a high-level E-R diagram for the three tables your database will contain.

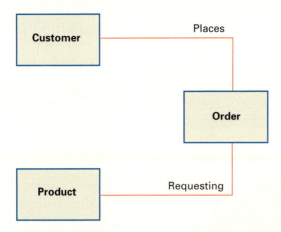

Figure 8.2

Read this diagram as follows: "A customer places an order requesting a product."

Kinds of Cardinalities

What happens when a customer places multiple orders? In a relational database, not only are relationships important, but the cardinality is as well. *Cardinality* is the number of instances of one entity that can or must be associated with instances of a second entity.

One characteristic of relationships between entities is whether they are optional or mandatory. ***Mandatory cardinality*** occurs when each instance of one entity *must* relate to one or more instances of a second entity, while ***optional cardinality*** occurs when one or more instances of one entity may relate to *no* instances of the second entity. We shall see examples of both kinds shortly.

Another characteristic of cardinality is to specify the minimum and maximum number of cardinalities that may or must exist between two entities The two most common of these types of relationships are one-to-one and one-to-many. Many-to-many relationships are possible, but they rare in a well-designed RDBMS. A ***one-to-one relationship*** specifies that for a record in one table, one and only one record in a second table can relate to it. An example would be a grade received by a student in a particular course. Assuming that class data and student data are contained in two separate tables, only one grade can be assigned to each student per class. A ***one-to-many relationship*** specifies that for each record in a particular table, one or more records in another table may relate to it. In the database you are currently constructing, for any customer there will be zero, one, or more related records in the *Orders* table. How can this be true? If a business buys a mailing list with information about potential customers in it, the database will most likely contain records for customers who have not (yet) placed any orders. Thus the cardinality between customers and orders is optional zero, one or many.

Reading Cardinalities in E-R Diagrams

Cardinalities are represented in E-R diagrams using specific notation. Figure 8.3 displays four common ways to represent one, many, optional, and mandatory E-R cardinalities.

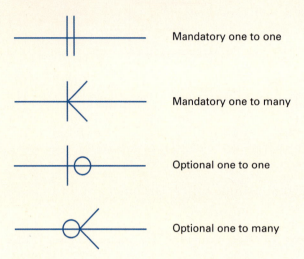

Figure 8.3

Comment There is no consistent standard for representing cardinalities in E-R diagrams. Some diagrams use the symbolic approach shown here, while others use text representations such as (1:1) for one-to-one and (1:n) for one-to-many.

Cardinalities are sometimes difficult to read in E-R diagrams. Look at the expanded E-R diagram shown in Figure 8.4.

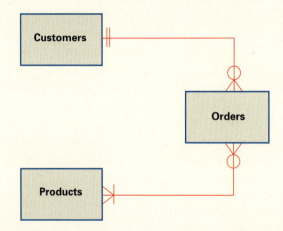

Figure 8.4

You read an E-R diagram such as this in two directions to determine the cardinalities between entities. For example, there is an optional cardinality between a customer entity and an order entity because there may be a customer instance with no corresponding order instance in the database. This could happen if the name of a customer was added to the database by referral or from a purchased mailing list, but he or she has never (or not yet) placed an order.

Now let's consider the relationship in the reverse direction, reading from an order entity to a customer entity. Notice the mandatory "one-to-one" symbol is next to the Customers entity in Figure 8.4. Whenever a customer places an order, the cardinality between the order and that customer is one-to-one, since one and only one customer places any order, and an Order entity instance cannot exist without a corresponding customer who placed the order.

In a similar fashion, consider the cardinalities involving products and orders. There is an optional cardinality between product and order because a company may have database records for a new product that has not sold yet. Once an order is placed, there is a mandatory one-to-many relationship between order and product, since each order must consist of at least one instance of a product entity, but any given order may be for more than one product.

Figure 8.5 shows a detailed E-R diagram for the completed database table structure. This logical data model includes all the information required to complete a data dictionary for the sales data database.

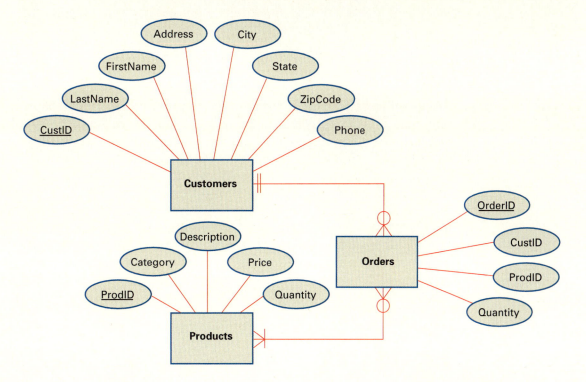

Figure 8.5

The Updated Data Dictionary

We can now update the data dictionary according to the detailed E-R diagram shown in Figure 8.5. Recall that the purpose of the data dictionary is to assist in developing the database and to provide documentation for subsequent updates. With the information presented in the detailed E-R diagram, the database dictionary can be modified as shown in Figure 8.6.

Customers Table	Products Table	Orders Table	Field Name	Field Size	Data Type	Field Description
X		X	CustID	Long Integer	AutoNumber	Primary key; format to 4 digits using \0000; nonkey in Orders Table
X			LastName	25	Text	Last name of customer
X			FirstName	20	Text	First name of customer
X			Address	35	Text	Street address or post office box
X			City	20	Text	Customer's city of residence
X			State	2	Text	State; input mask force to upper case, required >LL
X			ZipCode	10	Text	Zip code with optional extension; input mask
X			HomePhone	14	Text	Customer's phone; input mask
	X	X	ProdID	8	Text	Product ID; primary key in Product Table, nonkey in Orders Table (Text, size of 8)
	X		Category	15	Text	The product's category; used for sorting
	X		Description	45	Text	Description of the product
	X		Price	Auto	Currency	The current price for the product
	X	X	Quantity	Long Integer	Number	Units in stock in Product Table; units ordered in Orders Table
		X	OrderID	Long Integer	AutoNumber	The primary key in the Orders table; format to \90000

Figure 8.6

The data dictionary now has three additional columns and eight additional rows. The three left-most columns indicate the three tables (relations) in the database. The rows indicate the attributes for each relation. The Field Name, Field Size, and Data Type columns are helpful for designing the table objects. The right-most column contains additional information about the fields. Later in this project you will create two additional tables, but first you will see why this database design is efficient.

Database Normalization

As mentioned in Project 7, it is important to make a relational database as efficient as possible, and normalization is the process for doing this. During *normalization* you convert complex data structures into simple and stable data ones, in order to maximize the integrity of data while at the same time reducing data redundancy. Database normalization is based on the concept of functional dependency, which is a particular relationship between two attributes. For relation R, attribute B is *functionally dependent* upon attribute A if the value of A uniquely determines each valid instance of attribute B. The notation $A \rightarrow B$ is used to represent a functional dependency, where the first entity, here attribute A, is called the *determinant*. For example, in Figure 8.5, a customer's last name, first name, and address are functionally dependent upon his or her customer number.

Normalization is usually accomplished in stages, where each stage introduces simple rules concerning dependencies between entities and their relationships. In Codd's relational model, each stage of the process corresponds to a *normal form*. We introduce four normal forms here—first, second, third, and Boyce-Codd—and relations must be converted to each form in that order during normalization. Although Codd's model includes additional normal forms, databases normalized to either the third normal form or the Boyce-Codd normal form are considered efficient.[1]

The normal forms have been designed to remove anomalies from a database when data is updated. Anomalies are of three types. An *insertion anomaly* occurs when data is inserted. A *deletion anomaly* occurs when data is deleted. A *modification anomaly* occurs when records are changed.

The First Normal Form (1NF)

The first stage of normalization is to get each relation into the *first normal form*, which means it contains no multivalued attributes or repeating groups. A *multivalued attribute* can assume multiple values for a given database record. An example is an employee's skill. Since a given employee has more than one skill, the structure of the database should avoid fields that can assume more than one value per record. Repeating groups are similar to multivalued attributes. An example of a *repeating group* would be two sales items corresponding to a single customer and price, as shown in Figure 8.7.

CustName	Product	Price
Jones, Sally	Stationery set	$9.95
	Mechanical pencil and lead	
Williams, Peter	Long-sleeve T-shirt	$19.95
Smith, Bill	CD Collection	$29.95

Figure 8.7

Thus, to put a table into first normal form, you must select the attributes defining a relation so as to avoid multivalued attributes and repeating groups. Changing the table as shown in Figure 8.8 by adding a second record for Sally Jones eliminates the repeating group, and the relation is now normalized to the first normal form.

CustName	Product	Price
Jones, Sally	Stationery set	$9.95
Jones, Sally	Mechanical pencil and lead	$9.95
Williams, Peter	Long-sleeve T-shirt	$19.95
Smith, Bill	CD Collection	$29.95

Figure 8.8

The Second Normal Form (2NF)

A relation is in the *second normal form* if it is in the first normal form and in addition, there are no partial dependencies. A *partial dependency* occurs when one or more nonkey attributes are not fully functionally dependent on the entire primary key but are dependent on only part of it. Consider the relation shown in Figure 8.9.

---

[1] For a detailed discussion of database normalization, see F. R. McFadden and J. A. Hoffer (1994), *Modern Database Management*, 4th ed. (Redwood City, Calif.: Benjamin/Cummings), pp. 209–225.

CustName	SaleDate	ProdID	Product	Price
Jones, Sally	2/1/98	A11609	Stationery set	$9.95
Jones, Sally	3/2/98	B27010	Mechanical pencil and lead	$9.95
Williams, Peter	2/17/98	X45661	Long-sleeve T-shirt	$19.95
Smith, Bill	2/21/98	R10211	CD Collection	$29.95

Figure 8.9

This relation is in the first normal form since it avoids repeating groups, but it is not in the second normal form because there are partial dependencies. Why? To uniquely identify each transaction in this table requires a compound primary key. If the key consists of customer name, sale date, and product number, then the two nonkey attributes—product description and price—are not fully dependent on the primary key. For example, if a new product is added to the database, both a customer name and sale data will have to be added as well to uniquely identify the new product. This is an update anomaly. Also note that if a product needs to be deleted from the database, information about one or more orders will be lost as well, which is an example of a deletion anomaly. Finally, if Sally Jones changes her last name the data must be updated in multiple rows, which is an example of a modification anomaly.

A relation is in the second normal form when certain conditions are met. A relation with a simple primary key (a key consisting of a single attribute) is always in the second normal form. A relation is also in the second normal form if every nonkey attribute is functionally dependent upon the entire primary key. The relation shown in Figure 8.9 can be normalized to the second normal by decomposing it into two relations, one consisting of customer name, sale data, and product number, second of product number, product name, and price, as Figure 8.10 shows. The upper relation in the figure meets the second condition, while the lower relation meets the first condition. The Product ID field can then be used to relate data between the two tables.

CustName	SaleDate	ProdID
Jones, Sally	2/1/98	A11609
Jones, Sally	3/2/98	B27010
Williams, Peter	2/17/98	X45661
Smith, Bill	2/21/98	R10211

ProdID	Product	Price
A11609	Stationery set	$9.95
B27010	Mechanical pencil and lead	$9.95
X45661	Long-sleeve T-shirt	$19.95
R10211	CD Collection	$29.95

Figure 8.10

The Third Normal Form (3NF)

A relation is in the **third normal form** if it is in the second normal form and no transitive dependencies exist. A **transitive dependency** is a functional dependency between two or more nonkey attributes. Transitive dependencies can result in anomalies, and therefore must be removed. Consider the relation shown in Figure 8.11.

OrderID	CustName	SaleDate	ProdID	UnitsSold	NumInStock
1001	Jones, Sally	2/1/98	A11609	2	87
1002	Jones, Sally	3/2/98	B27010	1	121
1003	Williams, Peter	2/17/98	X45661	4	312
1004	Smith, Bill	2/21/98	R10211	2	46

Figure 8.11

The relation is in the second normal form because all nonkey attributes are fully dependent on the primary key (OrderID). However there is a transitive dependency: the number in stock entity is functionally dependent on product number, and product number is functionally dependent on OrderID. If any order is deleted from the database, information about the remaining quantity in stock will be lost, since this is the only place in the database where the current stock is recorded. This situation can be corrected by decomposing the relation into two distinct relations: *Orders* (containing the attributes Order number, customer name, sale data, and units sold) and *Products* (with the attributes, product number, and number in stock).

The Boyce-Codd Normal Form (BCNF)

Conceptually, normalization is a difficult concept, and bringing a database to the third normal form is often a challenge. The **Boyce-Codd normal form (BCNF)** is a stronger version of the third normal form and easier to understand. A relation is in the Boyce-Codd normal form if and only if every determinant is a candidate key.

Review again the high-level E-R diagram (Figure 8.5) and data dictionary (Figure 8.6) for the database you will now create. Each relation—*Customers*, *Orders*, and *Products*—is normalized to the second normal form, since each has a primary key consisting of one attribute. In addition, the relations have been decomposed so that no transitive dependencies exist, and the primary key for each relation is a determinant for all nonkey attributes. Therefore, the database has been normalized to both the 3NF and the Boyce-Codd normal form. In some circumstances, a database may be normalized to the 3NF but not the BCNF. Since this database is normalized to both, you are now ready to proceed with the database design.

Designing the Database

Creating the Products Table

Before customers can place orders, data representing products must first be added to the database. Since the product data is stored in an ASCII-delimited file, it can easily be imported into the existing database.

TASK 2: TO CREATE THE PRODUCTS TABLE:

1 Select Get External Data and Import from the File menu.

2 Select Text in the Files of Type drop-down list box, and highlight the *Products.txt* file on your data diskette.

3 Click the Import button in the Import dialog box.

4 Select the option button for a delimited file, and click Next.

5 Select the Comma option button as the delimiter, and check the box indicating that field names appear in the first row. Click Next.

6 Select the option to store the data in a new table, and click the Next button.

7 Using the horizontal scroll bar near the bottom of the Text Import Wizard, scroll to the right until the Price field is visible. Click anywhere within the field data to select the entire field.

8 Change the data type of the Price field to Currency, as shown in Figure 8.12.

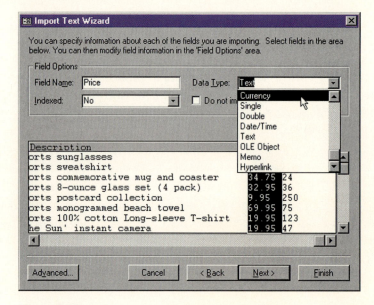

Figure 8.12

9 Change the data type for the Quantity field to Long Integer.

10 Click Next.

11 Select the option button to choose your own primary key. Verify that ProdID will be the primary key field, and click Next.

12 Type **Products** as the table name, and click the Finish button. When a message appears indicating that Access is finished importing the file, choose OK. The Database window should now display two table objects, as shown in Figure 8.13.

Project 8: Creating Additional Tables and Establishing Relationships   ACC-197

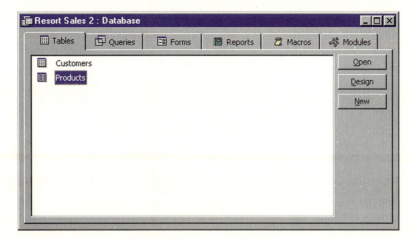

Figure 8.13

Creating the *Orders* Table

Although sales transaction data does not yet exist, you need to create the *Orders* table in order to complete the database design by establishing relationship between tables. You can use the Table Design View grid for this task.

TASK 3: TO CREATE THE *Orders* TABLE:

1. Verify that the Tables tab is selected in the Database window.
2. Click the New button.
3. Select Design View in the New Table dialog box, then click OK, as shown in Figure 8.14.

Figure 8.14

4. Use the information from your data dictionary shown in Figure 8.15 to create the *Orders* table.

Field Name	Field Size	Data Type	Description
OrderID	Auto	AutoNumber	The primary key; format to \90000
CustID	Long Integer	Number	Used to relate information in the Customers Table
ProdID	8	Text	Used to relate information in the Products Table
Quantity	Long Integer	Number	Units ordered

Figure 8.15

5 Figure 8.16 shows how the fields and properties should appear when the table is complete.

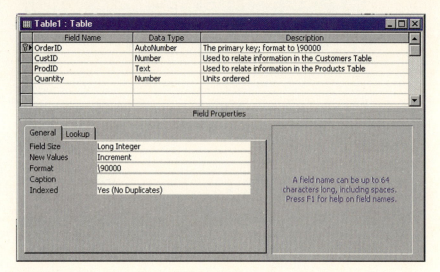

Figure 8.16

6 Close the table design grid. Name the table *Orders*, and select the option to have Access assign a primary key.

Establishing Relationships

Your table structure is almost complete. Microsoft Access utilizes a graphical design window for establishing relationships between tables. Once the tables are added to the workspace, the relationships are created using drag-and-drop techniques.

TASK 4: TO ESTABLISH RELATIONSHIPS:

1 Select Relationships from the Tools menu. The Show Table dialog box should appear.

> **Troubleshooting** If the Show Table dialog box does not appear, select Show Table from the Relationships menu.

2 Select the *Customers* table with the left mouse button, and while holding down the left mouse button, extend the selection to include all tables, as shown in Figure 8.17.

Project 8: Creating Additional Tables and Establishing Relationships ACC-199

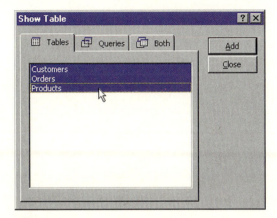

Figure 8.17

3 Click Add, and then click Close to make the Show Table dialog box disappear. The three tables you specified for adding to the database now appear in the Relationships window with their attributes listed. The primary key for each table appears in bold text.

4 Select the CustID field in the *Customers* table. While holding down the left mouse button, drag this field name over the CustID field name in the *Orders* table, as shown in Figure 8.18. Release the mouse button.

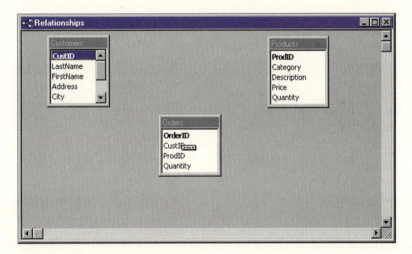

Figure 8.18

5 Notice that a one-to-many relationship is being established. In the Relationships dialog box, check the option to enforce referential integrity, as shown in Figure 8.19. **Referential integrity** is a system of rules that Microsoft Access uses to ensure that relationships between records in related tables are valid, and that you don't accidentally delete or change related data.

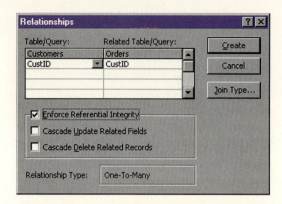

Figure 8.19

> **Tip** For more information on the other two options in the Relationships dialog box (Cascade Update Related Fields and Cascade Delete Related Records), search for "referential integrity" in the Help system.

6 Click the Create button. The relationship shown in Figure 8.20 will appear in the Relationships window. Notice the number 1 and the infinity symbol. In Access, these indicate a one-to-many relationship.

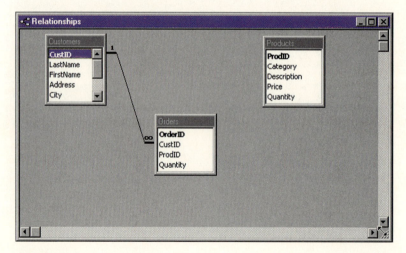

Figure 8.20

7 Using the same procedure, create a one-to-many relationship between the ProdID field in the Products table, and the ProdID field in the Orders table. Make sure you select the option to enforce referential integrity. Click Create.

8 Select Save from the File menu.

9 The relationships, with the *Customers* table resized to display all attributes, should now look like Figure 8.21.

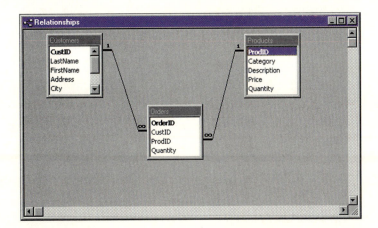

Figure 8.21

10 Close the Relationships dialog box.

> **Tip** You may view or edit the relationships at any time by selecting Relationships from the Tools menu.

The Conclusion

Your database is now ready to store sales transaction data. Although data can be entered into each related table manually, a query object can be used to view and update data in multiple tables simultaneously. In Project 9 you will construct a sophisticated query for adding transaction data to the database.

Summary and Exercises

Summary

- Cardinality determines how many records are related between two tables.
- Cardinalities can be optional or mandatory.
- ✡ one-to-one cardinality relates exactly one record in the child table to each record in the other parent table.
- ✡ one-to-many cardinality relates one or more records in one table to each record in the related table.
- Relationships represented in an E-R diagram must be read in two directions to determine the cardinalities.
- Normalization is the process of simplifying complex data structures.
- Relations normalized to the third normal form are considered efficient.
- Normalization to the third normal form remedies the problem of update anomalies.

Key Terms and Operations

Key Terms
$A \rightarrow B$
Boyce-Codd normal form (BCNF)
cardinality
deletion anomaly
determinant
first normal form (1NF)
functional dependency
insertion anomaly
mandatory cardinality
modification anomaly
multivalued attributes
normal form
normalization
one-to-many relationship
one-to-one relationship
optional cardinality
partial functional dependency
referential integrity
repeating groups
second normal form (2NF)
third normal form (3NF)
transitive dependency

Operations
copy a database file
define cardinality
interpret a high-level E-R diagram
apply the 1NF rules to isolate repeating groups
apply the 2NF rules to eliminate partial functional dependencies
apply the 3NF rules to eliminate transitive dependencies
create a data table by importing ASCII-delimited data
create a data table using the Table Design View grid
create one-to-many relationships between tables that enforce referential integrity

Study Questions

Multiple Choice

1. The process of converting complex data structures to a more simple form is called
   a. cardinality.
   b. referential integrity.
   c. normalization.
   d. functional dependency.
   e. update anomaly.

2. A database in the second normal form has eliminated all
   a. multivalued attributes.
   b. repeating groups.
   c. functional dependencies.
   d. transitive dependencies.
   e. all of the above.

3. A database in the third normal form has eliminated all
   a. multivalued attributes.
   b. repeating groups.
   c. partial functional dependencies.
   d. transitive dependencies.
   e. all of the above.

4. A database in the first normal form has eliminated all
   a. multivalued attributes.
   b. repeating groups.
   c. functional dependencies.
   d. transitive dependencies.
   e. a and b above.

5. A *Customers* table is related to an *Orders* table. The cardinality from the *Customers* table to the *Orders* table is most likely
   a. optional one-to-many.
   b. mandatory one-to-one
   c. optional one-to-one
   d. mandatory one-to-many.
   e. none of the above.

6. A relation without transitive dependencies has been normalized to the
   a. first normal form.
   b. second normal form.
   c. third normal form.
   d. Boyce-Codd normal form.
   e. a and b.

7. A relation without repeating groups has been normalized to the
   a. first normal form.
   b. second normal form.
   c. third normal form.
   d. Boyce-Codd normal form.
   e. b and c.

8. A relation without partial functional dependencies has been normalized to the
   a. first normal form.
   b. second normal form.
   c. third normal form.
   d. Boyce-Codd normal form.
   e. c and d.

9. A high level E-R diagram contains a graphical representation of
   a. entities, attributes, and primary keys.
   b. entities.
   c. entities, attributes, primary keys, and cardinalities.
   d. entities and attributes.

10. In Microsoft Access, the many sides of a one-to-many relationship are represented in the Relationships window by which of the following?
   a. , (comma)
   b. 1
   c. 100
   d. * (the asterisk symbol)
   e. ∞ (the infinity symbol)

Short Answer

1. What is the name for the procedure required to simplify complex data structures?

2. A database is considered efficient when it is normalized to what form?

3. What term is used to describe how records in one table relate to those in another table?

4. A relation in which not all nonkey attributes are dependent on the primary key attribute includes at least one what.

5. What graphically represents entities, attributes, relations, and cardinalities?

6. If a database is not normalized, what can potentially occur?

7. What kind of relationship relates only one record in the parent table to many records in the child table?

8. Normalizing a database to the third normal form eliminates what?

9. A relation will always be in the second normal form if it contains what item based on a single attribute?

10. In a database containing *Customers* and *Orders* relations, what term describes the fact that a customer may never have placed an order?

For Discussion

1. What is database normalization? Why is it important?

2. What is referential integrity?

3. How do the second and third normal forms differ?

4. Describe the difference between mandatory and optional cardinality.

Review Exercises

1. Modifying the Employee Database

The *Employee* database you created in Review Exercise 1 of Project 7 needs an additional table that lists employee time card data. Follow these steps to update the database:

1. Open the *Employees* database (the file *employees.mdb*) on your floppy diskette.

2. In the Database window, click the Tables tab if it is not the active tab.

3. Click New.

4. Create a new table in Design View with the fields listed in Table 8.1.

Table 8.1

Field Name	Data Type	Field Size or Format
EmpID	Text	11
DateStart	Date/Time	Short Date
WeekEnd	Date/Time	Short Date
Hours	Number	Long Integer

5. Select the EmpID field. Type **000\-00\-0000;;_** as an input mask for this field.
6. Close the table design grid. Save the table as *Time Card*.
7. Do not set a primary key.
8. Select Relationships from the Tools menu.
9. Add both tables to the Relationships window.
10. Create a one-to-many relationship between the tables, using the EmpID field.
11. Enforce referential integrity.
12. Close the Relationships window, Save the changes, and close the database.

2. Adding Records to the Employees Time Card Table

The employees *Time Card* table you just created does not have any records. To add records, complete the following steps:

1. Open the *Employees* database file.
2. Open the *Time Card* table in Datasheet View.
3. Add the four records listed in Table 8.2 to the *Time Card* table.

Table 8.2

EmpID	WeekStart	WeekEnd	Hours
123-45-6789	1/5/98	1/11/98	20
322-11-2333	1/5/98	1/11/98	18
123-45-6789	1/12/98	1/18/98	15
322-11-2333	1/12/98	1/18/98	17

When complete, the *Time Card* table should look like the table at the top of the screen in Figure 8.22.

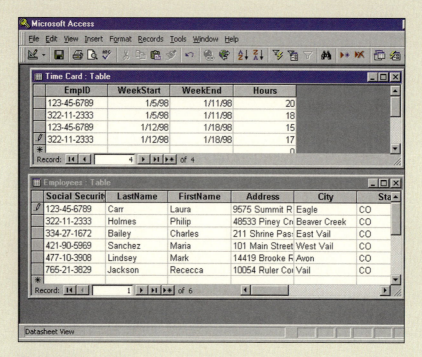

Figure 8.22

4. Close the table, and close the database.

Assignments

1. Updating the Student Database
The student database you created in Assignment 1 of Project 7 needs to be modified so as to contain a table listing course information. This table will consist of four fields: CourseID (the primary key), Course Title, Course Description, and Credit Hours. Determine the appropriate data types. Name the table *Courses*. Create a third table named *Enrollment*. This table will contain the following fields: CourseID, StudentID, Term, and Enrolled. Enrolled will be a yes/no data type. Establish a one-to-many relationship between the *Students* and *Enrollment* tables, and also between the *Courses* and *Enrollment* tables. Save the database.

2. Updating the Vail Eating Establishments Database
Open the Access database about Vail restaurants you created in Assignment 2 of Project 7. Change the structure of the database so that it contains two tables: one listing the restaurants, and another listing categories of cuisine. Create a relationship between the two tables, and modify the table data accordingly. Revisit the Vail Web site to obtain more information if necessary.

PROJECT 9

Creating a Sales Transaction Query and a Customer Form

In Projects 7 and 8 you completed the basic structure of the sales transaction database for Resort Sales Incorporated, including normalizing it. Now you are ready to use this sophisticated tool. You will discover, however, that although data can be related between tables, working with tables in design view or queries in datasheet view is a tedious task. Working with table data is made easier through the use of forms.

Both queries and forms are versatile objects that serve a variety of purposes in a Microsoft Access database. Queries are used to display data from one or more tables. Forms provide a more appealing user interface when working with table or query data. In this project you will broaden your knowledge of queries and forms.

Objectives

After completing this project, you will be able to:

➤ Use the query design grid to construct a query based on three tables
➤ Add AutoLookup fields to a query
➤ Add a calculated field to a query
➤ Create a form based on a table object
➤ Add Visual Basic controls to a Microsoft Access form

The Challenge

In order to use the *Resort Sales* database, you need a method for quickly entering sales transaction data into it. The end users—who may be employees in the order entry department in the company—have requested a simple way for processing sales online that includes a menu system. Your first task as database developer will be to design a screen for entering and verifying sales. This screen needs to behave something like a table but be capable of using the current customer and product data. That screen will be a query, a database object you learned about in Project 4.

The Solution

The key to exploiting the one-to-many relationships you have created in this database is to design a query that searches multiple tables for data. Because you normalized the database to the Boyce-Codd normal form, it is efficient: the product and customer data will rarely need editing, and therefore can be used when adding orders to the database.

Think of a query as having the same capabilities as a table. After you have designed a query that meets your needs, it can also serve as the basis for the screen form the end users have requested. (Actually, the end users will need many such forms to use the database.) One common task for end users will be searching for a specific customer by name, and if the customer record does not exist, adding a new record to the *Customers* table. Figure 9.1 shows a completed *Customers* form allowing users to carry out these tasks.

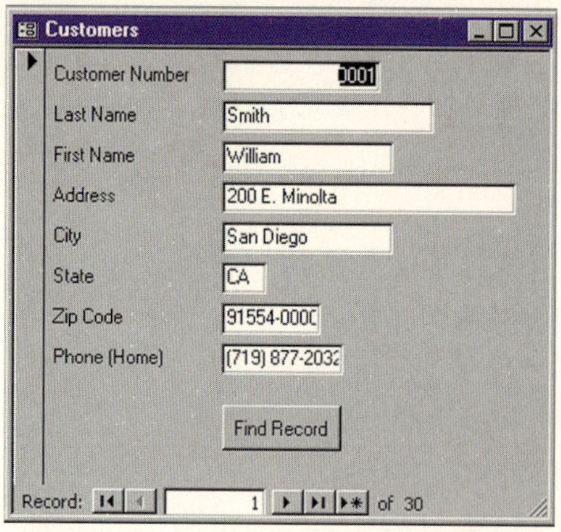

Figure 9.1

The Setup

To complete the steps in this project, you first need to make a copy of the *Resort Sales 2* database.

TASK 1: TO MAKE A COPY OF THE ACCESS DATABASE FILE:

1. Minimize Microsoft Access.
2. Open My Computer on the Desktop.
3. Using the procedures introduced in Task 1 of Project 7, create a copy of the *Resort Sales 2* database (*Resort Sales 2.mdb* file). Rename this copy as *Resort Sales 3*.
4. Restore Access and open the *Resort Sales 3.mdb* database.

> **Troubleshooting** If you are having trouble copying and renaming this file, ask your instructor for assistance.

To complete this project, make sure you do the following in Access:

- If you do not see a toolbar on the screen after launching Access, choose View, Toolbars, and click the Database toolbar option. If additional toolbars are visible, close them.
- Most of the figures in this project will display the Database dialog box and other Access dialog boxes in a restored state. You may resize any dialog boxes by clicking the Restore button in each dialog box.

Close the Microsoft Office Shortcut bar. In this project, you will not need to launch any additional applications.

Working with Queries

Queries are flexible and versatile database objects. In addition to displaying data that meet many criteria, they can display data from many tables simultaneously and update the data in each table underlying the query.

Designing Multitable Queries

The first step in turning your database into an application is to create a multitable query.

TASK 2: TO CREATE A MULTITABLE QUERY:

1. Select the Queries tab in the Database dialog box.
2. Click the New button.

3 Select the Design View option in the New Query dialog box, as shown in Figure 9.2. Then click OK.

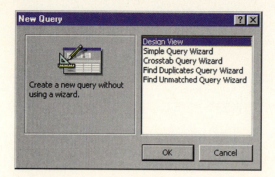

Figure 9.2

4 The Show Table dialog box will appear. Select the *Customers*, *Orders*, and *Products* tables, and click Add, as shown in Figure 9.3. Click Close.

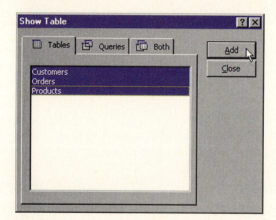

Figure 9.3

5 Maximize the query design grid.

6 Drag the OrderID field from the *Orders* table to the left-most cell of the Field row in the design grid, as shown in Figure 9.4.

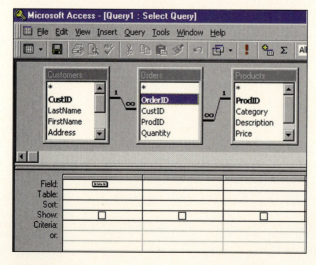

Figure 9.4

Project 9: Creating a Sales Transaction Query and a Customer Form   ACC-211

7 Drag the CustID field from the *Orders* table to the next cell in the Field row.

> **Hint** Make sure you select the CustID field from the *Orders* table, and not from the *Customers* table. This is important, since later in the project AutoLookup fields will be defined, and you must meet specific design conditions when using AutoLookup fields.

8 From the *Customers* table, drag the FirstName, LastName, Address, City, State, ZipCode, and HomePhone fields to the next available cells of the Field row.

9 Drag the ProdID field from the *Orders* table to the next available cell in the Field row. Make sure the ProdID field originates from the *Orders* table.

10 Drag the Description and Price fields from the *Products* table to the next two available cells in the Field row.

11 Drag the Quantity field from the *Orders* table to the next cell.

12 Select Save from the File menu. Type **Customer Orders** as the name of the query, as shown in Figure 9.5. Click OK to save the query.

Figure 9.5

Adding AutoLookup Fields to the Query

When end users enter orders for existing customers, they will be adding very little new data to the database. Information for current customers is already there, as are the product numbers, descriptions, and prices.

Entering orders would be an easy task if you could incorporate the existing customer and product information into the orders query. You can do this by including AutoLookup fields in your query. An **AutoLookup field** is a field in a query that evokes a list of data items when the field is selected for data entry. Before you can create AutoLookup fields, your database must meet certain conditions. First, there must be a one-to-many relationship between the tables that will support the lookup functions. Second, the field that will have its properties set to automatically lookup data from another table must be on the "many" side of the relationship. That is why you added both the CustID and ProdID fields from the *Orders* table to the Query Design grid. Since the tables involved (*Orders* and *Customers*) meet these conditions, you will be able to add AutoLookup fields to the query. You will begin by adding a customer AutoLookup field.

ACC-212

TASK 3: TO ADD A CUSTOMERS AUTOLOOKUP FIELD TO THE QUERY:

1 In the query design grid, use the lower horizontal scroll bar to move the view to the CustID field.

2 Right-click the CustID field column and select Properties from the shortcut menu, as shown in Figure 9.6.

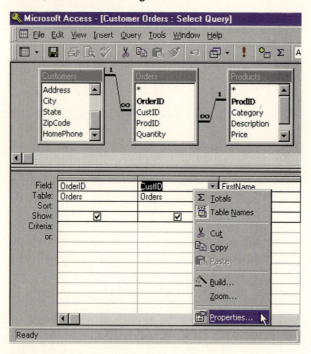

Figure 9.6

3 When the Field Properties dialog box appears, enter **\0000** in the Format text box of the General tab, as shown in Figure 9.7. This will cause the lookup value to be displayed in a four-digit format.

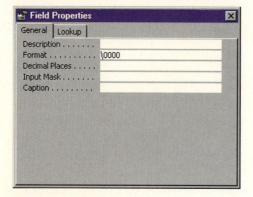

Figure 9.7

4 Click the Lookup tab to make it active.

5 Click the Display Control drop-down arrow, and select List Box, as shown in Figure 9.8. This specifies what kind of control will be added to the field in the query datasheet.

Project 9: Creating a Sales Transaction Query and a Customer Form   ACC-213

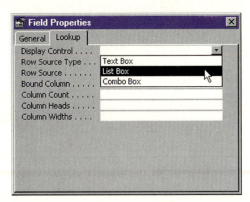

Figure 9.8

6. Click inside the Row Source Type pane, to activate the drop-down list. A button for opening the drop-down list will appear.

7. Select Table/Query, as shown in Figure 9.9. This specifies that the data in the list will originate from a table or query object.

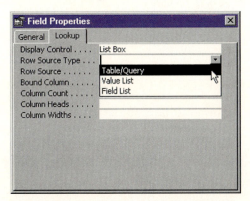

Figure 9.9

8. Select Customers as the Row Source, as shown in Figure 9.10. This specifies the *Customers* table as the data source for the drop-down list.

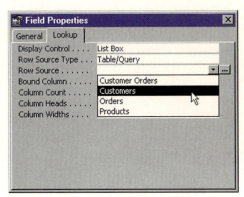

Figure 9.10

9. Select Save from the File menu to update your changes.

TASK 4: TO ADD A PRODUCTS AUTOLOOKUP FIELD TO THE QUERY:

1. Use the horizontal scroll bar in the query design grid to make the ProdID field visible. Right-click anywhere in the ProdID field column. and select Properties from the shortcut menu.

2. Click the Lookup tab to make it active.

3. Select List Box as the Display Control, Table/Query as the Row Source Type, and Products as the Row Source, as shown in Figure 9.11.

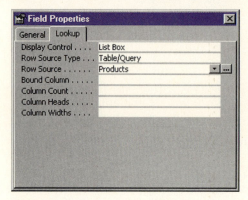

Figure 9.11

4. Close the Properties dialog box.

5. Select Save from the File menu to update the query.

6. Run the query. The results should look like Figure 9.12.

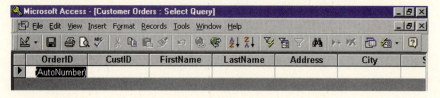

Figure 9.12

You will notice that no data is returned by the query. This is because you did not specify a customer and a product (by customer number and product number). As you will see, you will need to specify three data fields to use the Customer Orders query: customer number, product id number, and order quantity.

Using the Customer Orders Query to Enter Sales Data

One advantage of Microsoft Access query objects is that a user can use a query both to view data from multiple tables and to make changes in the underlying table data. You will now add transaction data to the database.

TASK 5: TO ADD RECORDS TO THE ORDERS TABLE USING THE *CUSTOMER ORDERS* QUERY:

1 In Datasheet View, click inside the CustID cell to activate the drop-down list arrow.

2 Click the arrow button, and select customer 0003 from the list, as shown in Figure 9.13. Once you select a customer number, the name and address information will appear in the query, and the OrderID number will appear as 90001.

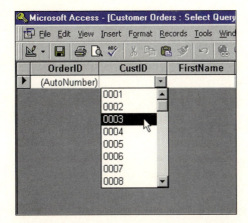

Figure 9.13

3 Click inside the ProdID cell and select product RA100201 from the drop-down list, as shown in Figure 9.14. The description and price data will appear in the datasheet.

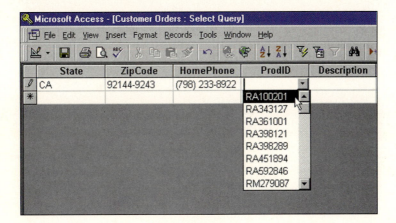

Figure 9.14

4 Double-click inside the Quantity field to select the contents of the cell. Type **1** as the quantity for this order.

5 Press the TAB key twice. The insertion point should once again be in the CustID field, ready to accept data for the second record.

6 Using Table 9.1 as a guide, enter the remaining customer numbers, product numbers, and quantities in the query datasheet.

> **Tip** When entering data in Datasheet view, you can use the TAB key to move between fields.

Table 9.1 Customer Transaction Data

CustID	ProductID	Quantity
0023	RA100201	1
0001	RA361001	2
0025	RA361001	3
0026	RM279087	3
0014	RA451894	1
0027	RA451894	1
0004	RS354671	4
0018	RS354671	1
0015	RM389562	2
0021	RM389562	5
0005	RS652908	2
0017	RA592846	3
0026	RM501835	2
0015	RA398289	5
0002	RM400582	1
0023	RA343127	3
0003	RA398121	2
0015	RS896231	4
0025	RA361001	1

When you are finished entering the transaction data, your query datasheet should look like Figure 9.15.

Project 9: Creating a Sales Transaction Query and a Customer Form   ACC-217

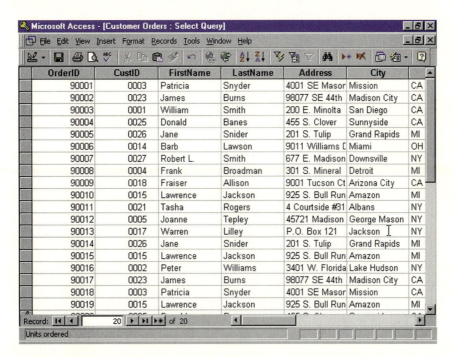

Figure 9.15

7   Close the *Customer Orders* query.

8   Select the Tables tab in the Database dialog box, and double-click the *Orders* table to open it in Datasheet View. Figure 9.16 shows how the table data will appear.

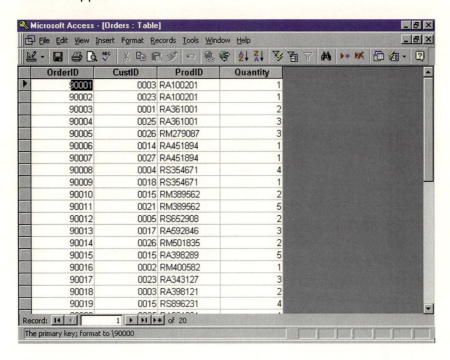

Figure 9.16

The OrderID data is incremented by 1 for each record in the table. The CustID and ProdID data were added to the table automatically using the

AutoLookup field in the *Customer Orders* query. You added the Quantity data to the table from within the query datasheet.

9. Close the *Orders* table.

Calculating the Total Cost for Each Sale

As you entered the sales transaction data, you may have noticed that the total amount of each order is not displayed. One way to enter this data would be to calculate the total and add the value to a numeric field in the *Orders* table. This approach, however, has two problems. First, any time a value is calculated and the result entered manually, there is potential for error. Second, adding data to the database manually when Microsoft Access can calculate and display the figures automatically is inefficient: such data becomes redundant, and the purpose of a relational database is to share data among relations.

To eliminate these two problems, you can add a calculated field to your query. A *calculated field* displays data as if you entered it into a table but the data will appear only when needed for display or printing. How does this work? In general, think of a query as behaving almost like a table. In our example, the *Customer Orders* query displays information from all three tables in the database in a format that simulates a new table. Some RDBMSs refer to this as a **virtual view** or **virtual table**. The totals will appear in the query's Datasheet View as a calculated field.

After creating the calculated expression, you will name the calculated field.

TASK 6: TO CREATE A CALCULATED FIELD:

1. In the Database dialog box, click the Queries tab to make it active. Since there is only one query object in the database, the *Customer Orders* query will be selected by default.

2. Click the Design button to open the Query Design window.

3. Using the bottom horizontal scroll bar, change the view until the first available column becomes visible on the screen. This will be the column to the right of the Quantity field in the grid.

4. Right-click inside the Field cell for this column.

5. Select Build from the shortcut menu, as shown in Figure 9.17.

Project 9: Creating a Sales Transaction Query and a Customer Form ACC-219

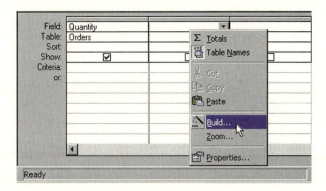

Figure 9.17

The Expression Builder dialog box will appear. This tool will allow you to build an expression that creates the calculated field. Notice that a list of fields comprising the query appears in the lower middle pane of the Expression Builder dialog box.

6 Use the vertical scroll bar to move to the bottom of the list. Double-click Price in the middle pane. This field will appear in the Expression pane at the top of the dialog box, as shown in Figure 9.18.

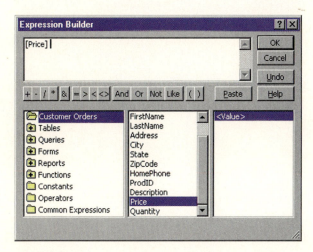

Figure 9.18

7 In the button bar immediately below the Expression pane, click the asterisk symbol (fourth button from the left). This adds an asterisk, which represents multiplication, to your expression.

8 Double-click the Tables folder in the lower left pane of the Expression Builder dialog box. This will display all available tables. Click the *Orders* table. The Expression Builder should now look like Figure 9.19.

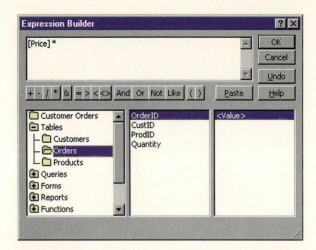

Figure 9.19

9. Double-click the Quantity field name in the lower middle pane of the dialog box. The table name and Quantity attribute will appear in the expression, as shown in Figure 9.20.

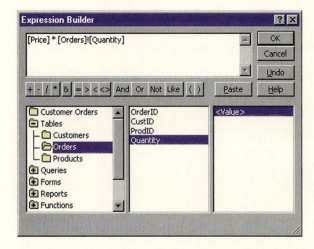

Figure 9.20

10. The expression is now complete. Click OK to enter the expression into the Query Design grid.

11. Save the updated query.

12. Run the query. Using the horizontal scroll bar, scroll to the right of the Query datasheet so that the results of the calculation are visible. The results should appear as shown in Figure 9.21.

Project 9: Creating a Sales Transaction Query and a Customer Form ACC-221

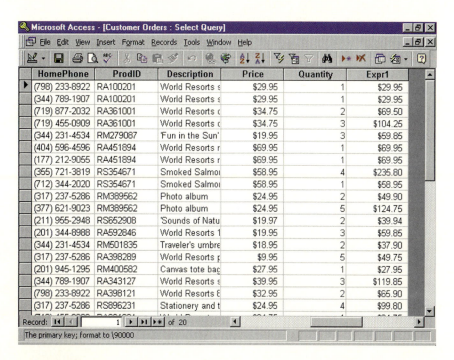

Figure 9.21

Notice that the calculated field has the default name Expr1. You can rename the field using the Query Design grid.

TASK 7: TO RENAME THE CALCULATED FIELD:

1. Switch from Datasheet View to Design View.
2. Highlight Expr1 in the Query Design grid, as shown in Figure 9.22.

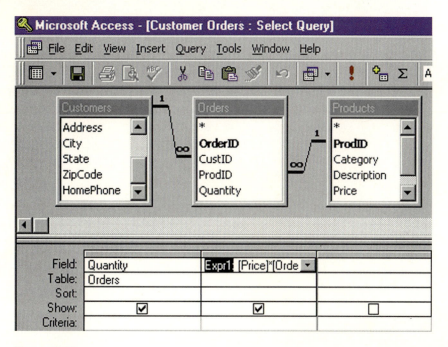

Figure 9.22

> **Caution** Make sure you do not highlight the colon character. This is needed to separate the field name from the field expression.

3 Type **Total Sale**, and press ENTER.

4 Save the query.

5 Run the query. The field name should now appear as shown in Figure 9.23.

Figure 9.23

6 Close the query.

Working with Forms

Creating a Form to Edit the Customers Table

As you entered data into the query in Datasheet View, you probably noticed how cumbersome it is to work in this mode. As you learned in Project 5, forms are used to present database information on the screen in a more aesthetically pleasing format. In addition, forms often display only one record at a time, making the database easier to use.

Think of the kind of tasks the typical database user would encounter. When an order is placed, the first task is to determine whether the customer is already in the database, and if so, whether the information is current. If this is a new customer, the user needs to add a new record to the *Customers* table. Before creating a form based on the *Customers* table, you will add captions to the database structure. A *caption* is a name or title that identifies field data on a form or in a report. If no caption exists, the field name becomes the caption by default. After creating captions, you will create a form using the Form Design View. Then you will modify the form to make it more usable.

TASK 8: TO ADD CAPTIONS TO THE *CUSTOMERS* TABLE:

1 Click the Tables tab in the Database window to make it active.

2 Highlight the *Customers* table, and click the Design button.

3 The caption is a property of each field. Using the data in Table 9.2, add captions for each field in the table. Note that not all fields will require captions.

Project 9: Creating a Sales Transaction Query and a Customer Form   ACC-223

Table 9.2   Captions for Customers Table

Field Name	Caption
CustID	Customer Number
LastName	Last Name
FirstName	First Name
ZipCode	Zip Code
HomePhone	Phone (Home)

4 Save your changes to the table design, and close the table.

You are now ready to create a form. Since the form will include all the fields in the table, you will use the Form Wizard to create the form. The *Form Wizard* is a tool that creates a form based on the specifications that you provide.

TASK 9: TO CREATE A FORM:

1 In the Database dialog box, click the Forms tab to make it active.

2 Click the New button.

3 In the New Form dialog box, select Form Wizard and from the drop-down list, select *Customers* as the table to base the form on, as shown in Figure 9.24. Click OK.

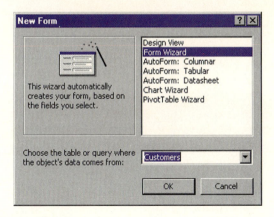

Figure 9.24

4 In the Form Wizard dialog box, click the >> button, as shown in Figure 9.25, to automatically add all fields to the form. When all fields are added, click Next.

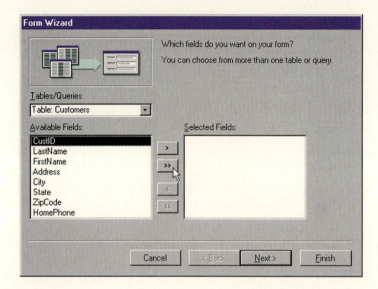

Figure 9.25

5 Select Columnar as the form layout, and click Next.

6 Select Standard as the Form style, and click Next.

7 Select the default name (in this case Customers) for the form. Click Finish. Your form should look like Figure 9.26. Notice how the captions appear on the form.

Figure 9.26

8 Close the form.

Modifying a Form by Adding a Visual Basic Control

Microsoft Access shares many components with Microsoft Visual Basic, a programming environment for creating Windows-based applications. These include **Visual Basic controls,** which are objects programmed to respond to certain events. The form you just created is an object, as are the captions (technically termed *labels*) and the text boxes that display the field data. Visual Basic controls include labels, text boxes, and command buttons. By providing the capability for incorporating Visual Basic controls on forms, Microsoft Access gives you latitude as a database developer to add features to your forms.

Project 9: Creating a Sales Transaction Query and a Customer Form   ACC-225

TASK 10: TO ADD A VISUAL BASIC CONTROL TO THE *CUSTOMERS* FORM:

1 In the Forms window, highlight the *Customers* form, and click the Design button.

2 Maximize the Form Design window.

3 Place the mouse pointer directly over the Form Footer bar, until it appears as a directional arrow, as shown in Figure 9.27.

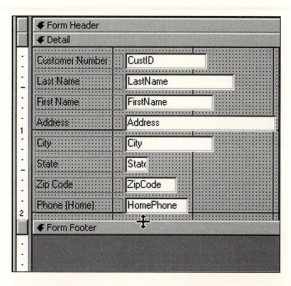

Figure 9.27

4 While holding down the left mouse button, pull down the bottom edge of the form about ½ inch.

5 From the View menu, select Toolbox, as shown in Figure 9.28.

Figure 9.28

6 When the toolbox appears over the Form Design window, select the Command Button tool, as shown in Figure 9.29.

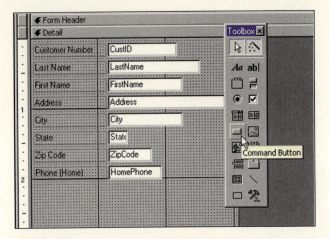

Figure 9.29

7 Drag a command button over the Form Design window just below the HomePhone text box, as shown in Figure 9.30.

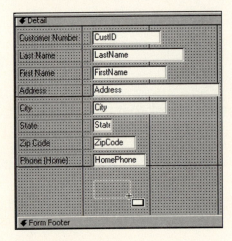

Figure 9.30

8 When you release the mouse button, the Command Button Wizard will appear. In the Categories pane, select Record Navigation and in the Actions pane select Find Record. Click Next, as shown in Figure 9.31.

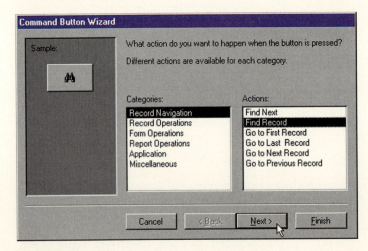

Figure 9.31

9. Select the option to add text to the button, as shown in Figure 9.32. Click Next.

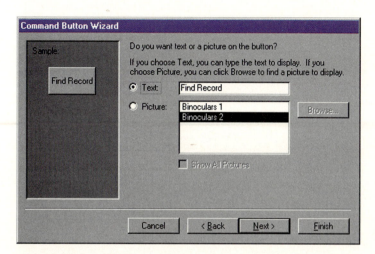

Figure 9.32

10. Type **cmdFindRecord** as the name for the button, as shown in Figure 9.33. Click Finish.

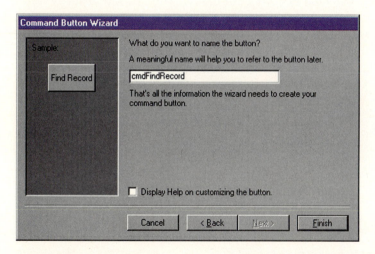

Figure 9.33

11. Select Form View from the View menu.

12. Restore the form. It should appear as shown in Figure 9.34.

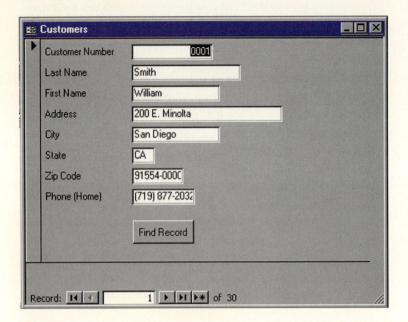

Figure 9.34

13 Click the Find Record button you added to the form. When the Find dialog box appears, type **Smith** as the search string, and uncheck any check boxes. Click Find Next, as shown in Figure 9.35.

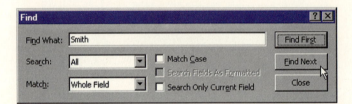

Figure 9.35

The Find dialog box will remain on the screen until you close it. As you continue to click the Find Next button, the record pointer will move through all the records, stopping on each one that contains Smith.

14 Close the Find dialog box.

15 Close the form. When prompted to save changes to the form, update the form.

> **Tip** As you add objects to the database, its size may become quite large. To reduce the size of the database file, select Database Utilities from the Tools menu, and then select the Compact Database option. This will reduce the file size.

The Conclusion

You have greatly improved the usability of the database! In addition to being able to enter and review sales transaction data, the AutoLookup fields in the *Customer Orders* query automatically add the appropriate data to the *Orders* table. The calculated field you created displays the order total. Finally, by using the *Customers* form you created, you can work with records in the *Customers* table more easily than when you tried to work with the table directly.

Summary and Exercises

Summary

- A multitable query will display data from multiple tables simultaneously.
- AutoLookup fields in queries can be used to automatically update table data.
- Data entered in a multitable query will automatically update data in multiple tables.
- A calculated field in a query will display virtual field data.
- The Form Wizard quickly designs a form according to your specifications.
- Visual Basic controls add functionality to forms.

Key Terms and Operations

Key Terms	Operations
AutoLookup field	add AutoLookup fields to a query
calculated field	add a Visual Basic control to a form
caption	add captions to a table design
Form Wizard	create a calculated field
labels	create a form using the Form Wizard
virtual table (virtual view)	create a multitable query
Visual Basic control	update data tables using a query

Study Questions

Multiple Choice

1. Which Microsoft Access object can contain a calculated field?
    a. table
    b. query
    c. form
    d. report

2. Which Microsoft Access object can be used to create a query?
    a. table
    b. query
    c. form
    d. report
    e. a and b above

3. Which Access database object is used to display a single record on the screen?
    a. table
    b. query
    c. form
    d. calculated field
    e. a and b above

4. Which of the following data attributes would be best represented through a calculated field?
    a. employee name
    b. employee address
    c. employee hours worked
    d. employee pay rate
    e. employee gross pay

5. Visual Basic controls are most appropriate for
   a. tables.
   b. forms.
   c. queries.
   d. reports.
   e. none of the above.

6. A database contains two tables, one listing employee data including pay rate, the other listing time card data, such as hours worked. How would you create a calculated query to determine gross pay?
   a. Create a calculated field in the employee data table.
   b. Create a query based on both the employee data and time card tables.
   c. Create a calculated field in the time card table.
   d. Create a screen form and add a calculated field as a Visual Basic control.
   e. Add an AutoLookup field to the time card table.

7. Captions improve the appearance of
   a. tables.
   b. queries.
   c. forms.
   d. reports.
   e. c and d above.

8. The easiest method for creating a calculated field is to use the
   a. Expression Builder dialog box.
   b. Form Wizard.
   c. AutoLookup field.
   d. Query Datasheet View.

9. To modify a form, you must use the
   a. Query Design grid.
   b. Query Datasheet View.
   c. Table Datasheet View.
   d. Form Design View.
   e. Expression Builder dialog box.

10. Which of the following displays one record on the screen in a table format?
    a. Table Datasheet View
    b. Query Datasheet View
    c. Form View
    d. Form Design View
    e. a and b above

Short Answer

1. What Access object is used as the basis of a query?
2. Visual Basic controls are most appropriate for which database object?
3. An AutoLookup field must be based on related data in what kind of relationship?
4. In general, a query behaves like which database object?
5. Captions are used to enhance what objects?
6. Which procedure results in the creation of virtual field data?
7. Which database object can be based on multiple objects?
8. What can be added to a query to add data automatically to tables?

9. Which Microsoft Access object is required before any others can be used?

10. What can be added to a form to increase its usefulness?

For Discussion

1. How do Visual Basic controls add functionality to Access forms?

2. Why are AutoLookup fields useful?

3. What is a virtual table? Why is virtual data desirable?

4. Describe how a multitable query exploits the power of a normalized relational database.

Review Exercises

1. Adding a Query to the Employees Database

Add a query object to the *Employees* database that displays all time cards for each employee. Complete this task as follows:

1. Open the *Employees* database. Click the Queries tab, and click the New button.

2. Add both tables to the Query Design grid. Add the EmpID, LastName, PayRate, WeekStart, WeekEnd, and Hours fields to the query.

3. Run the query.

4. Close the query. Save the query as *Gross Pay*.

2. Creating a Calculated Field in the *Gross Pay* Query

For the *Employees* database you modified in Review Exercise 1 of Project 8, create a calculated field to determine gross pay:

1. Open the *Gross Pay* query in Design View.

2. In the design grid, create a calculated field using the Expression Builder dialog box.

3. Name the Expression field Gross Pay.

4. Run the query to verify that the calculated field is working properly.

5. Update the query, and close the database.

Assignments

1. Updating the Student Database

Open the Student database you modified in Assignment 1 of Project 8. Add two records for each student in the *Courses* table. Then add eight records to the *Enrollment* table, two for each student.

Create a query that displays the courses taken by each student. Save the database.

2. Adding a Query to the Vail Eating Establishments Database

Open the Access database about Vail restaurants you modified in Assignment 2 of Project 8. Add a query to the database that displays the category of cuisine corresponding to each restaurant. Add records for three more establishments. Revisit the Vail Web site to obtain more information if necessary.

PROJECT 10

Creating Forms Based on Multiple Tables

In Project 9 you developed a screen form for allowing the user to interact with the *Customers* table for the Resort Sales Incorporated database. In this project you will further develop the user interface for your application by creating forms based on more than one table, and forms containing subforms. By the end of Project 11, after developing additional forms and reports, you will have created a complete database application.

Objectives

After completing this project, you will be able to:

➤ Modify the *Customers* form
➤ Create a form based on the *Customer Orders* query
➤ Create a main form using Form Design View
➤ Create a subform using Form Design View
➤ Add a subform to a main form

The Challenge

As you learned previously, the purpose of a form is to provide users with the capability of working with a database more efficiently than by using a table or query's datasheet. Think of tables as data repositories, or places for storing data. Think of queries as a way of extracting data meeting various criteria from one or more tables. Users of the database work through a user interface, which consists of the various objects, such as forms and reports, that are presented to the user on the screen in such a way as to make interacting with the data repositories through queries as easy as possible.

The users of your database will need to be able to easily fill new orders and review the data in existing orders. The *Customer Orders* query provides the necessary information from the *Customers* and *Orders* tables, but working with the data returned by a query in Datasheet View would be difficult. So your task is to create two forms to make this easier: one for placing new orders, and one for reviewing a customer's order history. The first form must allow the salespeople to search the database for a specific customer or add a record to the database for new customers. The second form must prevent users from inadvertently changing the order or customer data.

The Solution

In the same way that Microsoft Access allows you to access data from one or more tables in a query, you can create a form that displays data from more than one source. There are two methods for doing this. One method is to create a form based on a query that has multiple tables as its data source. A form based on the *Customer Orders* query (which draws data from two tables) will be sufficient for entering new orders into the database. Figure 10.1 shows the form you will create for entering new orders.

Figure 10.1

The other way to create a form showing data from two or more sources is to create a main form containing a subform. The **main form** is just like any other form, except that it linked to another form, the **subform**, which contains data from a separate table or query and is embedded visually on the main form. The form you will create for displaying a customer's order history should be a form containing a subform. It is shown in Figure 10.2. The Customer Order History data is the subform.

Project 10: Creating Forms Based on Multiple Tables ACC-235

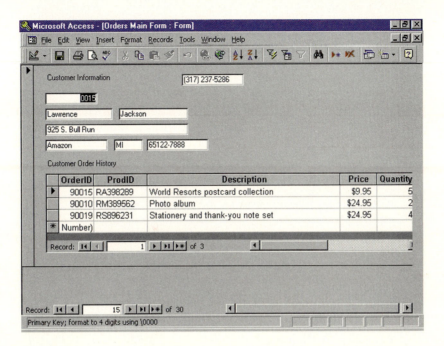

Figure 10.2

The Setup

To complete the steps in this project, you will first need to make a copy of the *Resort Sales 3* database.

TASK 1: TO: MAKE A COPY OF THE ACCESS DATABASE FILE:

1. Minimize Microsoft Access.
2. Click My Computer on the Desktop.
3. Using the procedures introduced in Task 1 of Project 7, create a copy of the *Resort Sales 3* database (*Resort Sales 3.mdb* file). Rename this copy *Resort Sales 4*.
4. Restore Access and open the *Resort Sales 4.mdb* database.

> **Troubleshooting** If you are having trouble copying and renaming this file, ask your instructor for assistance.

To complete this project, make sure you do the following in Access:

- If you do not see a toolbar on the screen after launching Access, choose View, Toolbars, and click the Database toolbar option. If additional toolbars are visible, close them.

- Most of the figures in this project will display the Database dialog box and other Access dialog boxes in a restored state. You may resize any dialog boxes by clicking the Restore button in each dialog box.

Close the Microsoft Office Shortcut bar. In this project, you will not need to launch any additional applications.

Learning More about Controls on Forms

The *Customers* form you created in Project 9 is based on the *Customers* table. In Microsoft Access, forms are always based on a specific data source termed a recordset. A **recordset** represents the records in a base table or the records that result from running a query.

Everything you add to a form or report is a called a **control**. Controls can be categorized according to their function. Text boxes, labels, list boxes, option buttons, command buttons, and lines are examples of specific controls with different functions.

So far you have encountered three of these controls. In Project 5 you worked with text box and label controls, and in Project 9 you added a command button to your *Customers* form. In this project you will continue to work with all three kinds of controls. In addition, you will add data controls to your forms. A **data control** is the set of buttons appearing in a table, query, or form that allow the user to navigate through the recordset or add new records.

Controls can also be classified according to how they are linked to table and query data. Some controls, such as text boxes that display record data, are **bound controls,** which are each tied to a field in an underlying table or query. Other controls, such as lines or descriptive text are **unbound controls**, meaning that they do not have a data source. Another category is **calculated controls,** which uses an expression as its data source. The expression performs one or more calculations using table data.

Recall from Project 9 that the controls use for designing forms are from the Visual Basic programming environment. Microsoft Access uses Visual Basic controls and procedures extensively whenever a Wizard is used to create a form or add capabilities to an object such as a command button.

> **Note** In Project 12 you will learn more about Visual Basic controls and procedures.

Modifying the *Customers* Form

To be really useful, the *Customers* form you created in Project 9 needs modification. Currently it contains a Find Record control button to search for a specific customer. The form should also contain two more buttons: one allowing the user to add a new record if a customer is searched for and not found, and a second to close the form once the user has finished using the customer data.

As with all command buttons, an ***event procedure*** specifies what actions will occur inside the computer when the user clicks the button. Event procedures in Microsoft Access are written in Visual Basic programming code. When you construct command buttons using the Command Button Wizard, Access creates the code for the event procedure automatically.

TASK 2: TO MODIFY THE *CUSTOMERS* FORM:

1. Click the Forms tab. Since only one form object in this database has been created, it is highlighted automatically.

2. Maximize the Form Design window.

3. Click the Design button to open the form in Design View.

4. Select Toolbox from the View menu if the Toolbox is not visible on the screen. This will display the Toolbox.

5. Using the technique you learned in Task 8 of Project 9, create a command button to the left of the Find Record button, as shown in Figure 10.3. The Command Button Wizard will appear.

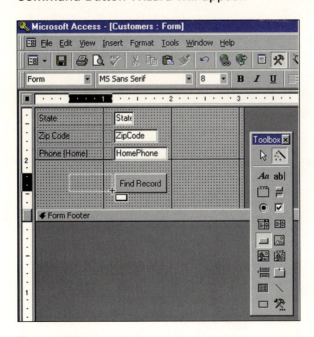

Figure 10.3

6 Select Record Operations from the Categories pane, and Add New Record from the Actions pane, as shown in Figure 10.4. Click Next.

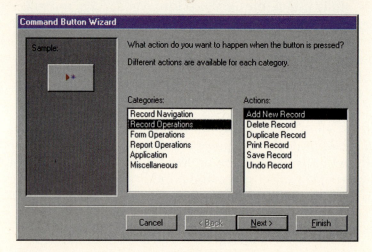

Figure 10.4

7 Select the option to add text to the button, and click Next.

8 Type **cmdNewCustRecord** as the name for the button.

> **Tip** You will learn about the conventions for naming Visual Basic controls in Project 12.

9 Click Finish.

10 Using the techniques you learned in Project 5, resize the button on the form if necessary.

11 Select the Command Button tool from the Toolbox, and create an additional button on the form immediately to the right of the Find Record button.

12 In the Command Button Wizard, select the settings shown in Figure 10.5, and click Next.

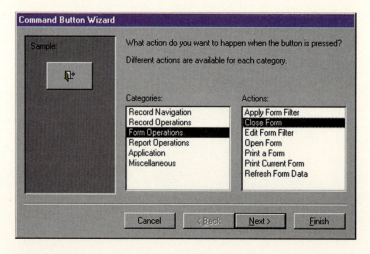

Figure 10.5

Project 10: Creating Forms Based on Multiple Tables ACC-239

13. For a consistent look among buttons, select the option to display text on the button. Click Next.

14. Type **cmdCloseCustForm** as the name for the button. Click Finish.

15. Select Form View from the View menu, and restore the form. The Add Record button will appear on the form as shown in Figure 10.6.

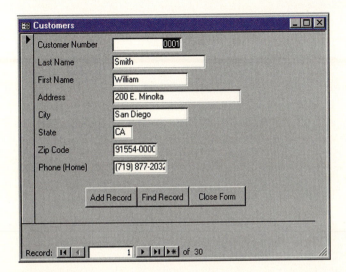

Figure 10.6

16. Close the form. Make sure you save the changes you have made.

Creating a Form Based on a Multitable Query

The query you created in Project 9 provides users with the ability to add sales transaction records to the database with a minimal amount of effort. It is difficult, however, to enter new sales using the query, since users must interact with the query in datasheet view. Providing a form based on the query simplifies data entry, since users can interact with one record at a time, and see all field data on the screen simultaneously.

TASK 2: TO CREATE A FORM BASED ON THE *CUSTOMER ORDERS* QUERY:

1. In the Database Dialog box, click the Forms tab.

2. Click the New button.

3. In the New Form dialog box, select Form Wizard to create a form, and *Customer Orders* as the table or query on which to base the form, as shown in Figure 10.7. Click OK.

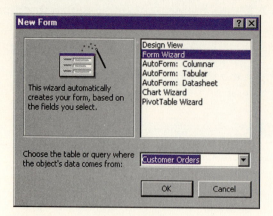

Figure 10.7

4. In the Form Wizard, use the >> button to copy all fields from the Available Fields list in the form. The Available Fields list provides a list of all fields available in the table or query that underlies the form you are creating. The Selected Fields list should now appear as shown in Figure 10.8. Click Next.

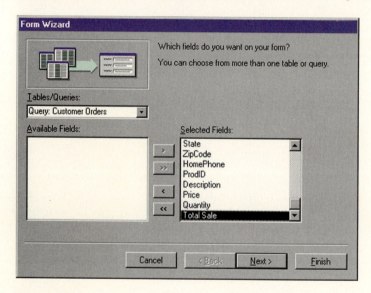

Figure 10.8

5. Select Columnar for the format, and click Next.

6. Select International for the style of form, as shown in Figure 10.9, and click Next button.

Project 10: Creating Forms Based on Multiple Tables   ACC-241

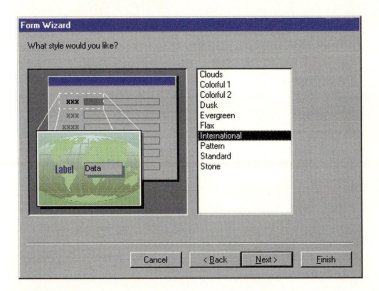

Figure 10.9

7 Type **Add Customer Orders** as the name of the form, and click Finish. The form will appear as shown in Figure 10.10. You will notice that some of the labels and text box controls are truncated. This can be easily corrected in Design View.

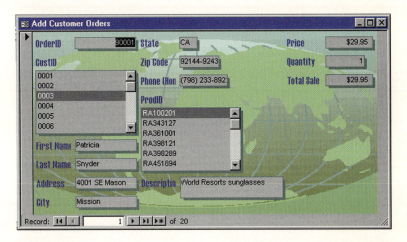

Figure 10.10

8 Make any changes to the form in Design View, save the form, and close the form.

This form has four limitations. First, the form (and its underlying *Orders* table) is set up to accept only one product per order. If an actual company were implementing this database, the users would need to have the capability of recording more than one product on each order. Second, the customer and order data appear scattered throughout the form rather than organized visually into separate areas. You can easily modify the layout of the form by using Design View. Third, although the form can be used to fill orders for existing customers, it does not accommodate new customers. You can overcome this limitation by adding a command button to the form that opens the *Customers* form. This form allows the user to add records to the *Customers* table, where they become available to the *Customer Orders* query. Fourth, and perhaps most serious, is that, although the form is intended only for adding new orders to the database, it also allows users to edit existing orders. This limitation compromises the integrity of the original data. One solution would be to create a new table, named something like *New Orders*. Users would enter and verify new orders into this table, thereby protecting the data in the master *Orders* table. Once the data was verified, each additional record could be appended to the master *Orders* table. Project 11 will present a simpler solution.

Creating a Form That Includes a Subform

There may be times when users of the database need to review a customer's order history, and view simultaneously on the screen all the orders for a given customer. You can accomplish this by creating a main form listing the customer information, and adding to this form a subform containing the order information for that customer.

> **Note** You can only include subforms on a form where a one-to-many relationship exists between the tables included on the form.

You will create the customer form with a subform in three steps. First, you will make a main form and add label controls to it. In general, a **label control** is used to add text that the user will never need to change. Then you will create the subform. And finally, you will add the subform to the main form.

TASK 3: TO CREATE THE MAIN FORM:

1. Click the Forms tab, if it is not active. Click New.
2. Select Design View, and the *Customers* table, as shown in Figure 10.11. Click OK.

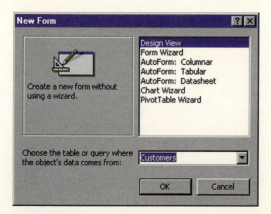

Figure 10.11

Project 10: Creating Forms Based on Multiple Tables ACC-243

3 A blank form will appear in Design View. Maximize the Form window.

4 Select Toolbox from the View menu to display the Toolbox, if it is not visible. Remember that the Toolbox allows you to add controls to the form in Design View.

5 Select the Label control tool, as shown in Figure 10.12.

Figure 10.12

6 Draw a label control in the upper left corner of the form, as shown in Figure 10.13.

Figure 10.13

> **Tip** While you are creating a label control, the insertion point will include a cross and a capital letter, indicating the kind of control being created. This will disappear once you finish creating the control.

7 Type **Customer Information** as the label text.

8 Select Field List from the View menu, to display a list of available fields for the form.

9 Drag the first field in the list (CustID) to the form, as shown in Figure 10.14.

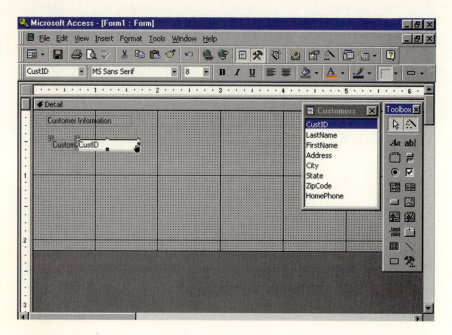

Figure 10.14

10 In similar fashion, drag the remaining fields (LastName, FirstName, Address, City, State, ZipCode, and HomePhone) to the form. Position the controls on the form in approximately the positions of the controls shown in Figure 10.15.

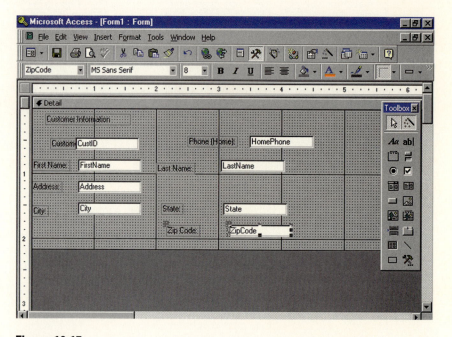

Figure 10.15

11 Place the mouse pointer directly over the label Phone (Home), and select it. Selection handles should appear around the label control, but not around the text box control, as shown in Figure 10.16.

Project 10: Creating Forms Based on Multiple Tables   ACC-245

Figure 10.16

> **Hint** There should be one selection handle in the upper left corner of the text box control. This indicates that the label is bound to the text box.

12 Press the DEL key. The label, but not the text box control, will disappear.

13 While holding down the SHIFT key, select all the remaining labels visible on the screen except for Customer Information.

14 Press DEL to remove these controls.

15 Using the techniques learned in Project 5, resize and reposition the text box controls on the form so that they appear as shown in Figure 10.17.

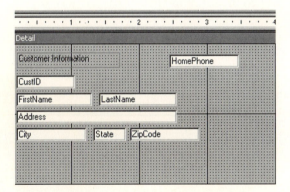

Figure 10.17

16 Select Save from the File menu. Name the form **Orders Main Form**.

17 Close the form.

Now that you have created the main form, you are ready to create the subform.

TASK 4: TO CREATE THE SUBFORM:

1 Click New in the Forms window of the Database dialog box.

2 In the New Form dialog box, select Form Wizard for the *Customer Orders* query. Click OK.

3 In the Form Wizard dialog box, add the fields OrderID, ProdID, Description, Price, Quantity, and Total Sale from the Available Fields list to the Selected

Fields list, using the > button. Your screen should then look like Figure 10.18. Click Next.

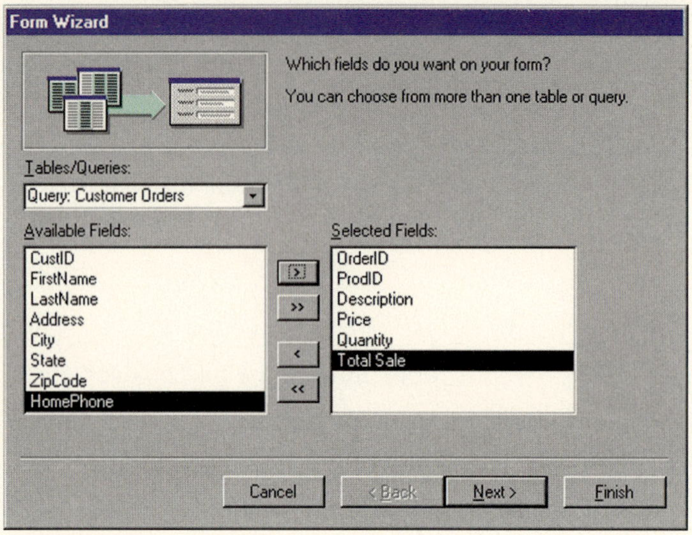

Figure 10.18

4 Select Datasheet as the layout, and click Next.

5 Select Standard as the form style, and click Next.

6 Type **Orders Subform** as the name of the form, and click Finish.

7 Switch to Datasheet view and resize the width of each column in the form to an appropriate width. Your *Orders* subform should look similar to Figure 10.19.

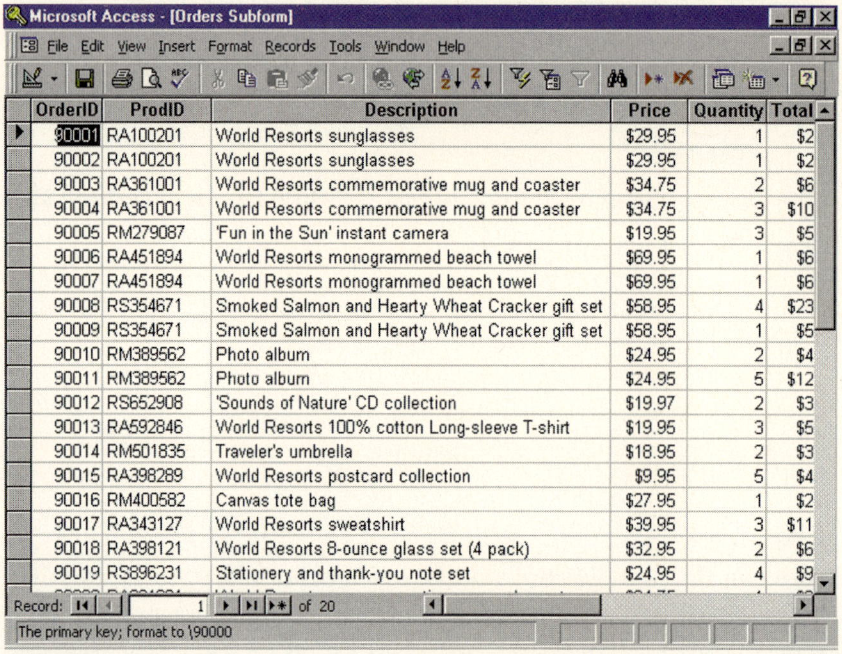

OrderID	ProdID	Description	Price	Quantity	Total
90001	RA100201	World Resorts sunglasses	$29.95	1	$2
90002	RA100201	World Resorts sunglasses	$29.95	1	$2
90003	RA361001	World Resorts commemorative mug and coaster	$34.75	2	$6
90004	RA361001	World Resorts commemorative mug and coaster	$34.75	3	$10
90005	RM279087	'Fun in the Sun' instant camera	$19.95	3	$5
90006	RA451894	World Resorts monogrammed beach towel	$69.95	1	$6
90007	RA451894	World Resorts monogrammed beach towel	$69.95	1	$6
90008	RS354671	Smoked Salmon and Hearty Wheat Cracker gift set	$58.95	4	$23
90009	RS354671	Smoked Salmon and Hearty Wheat Cracker gift set	$58.95	1	$5
90010	RM389562	Photo album	$24.95	2	$4
90011	RM389562	Photo album	$24.95	5	$12
90012	RS652908	'Sounds of Nature' CD collection	$19.97	2	$3
90013	RA592846	World Resorts 100% cotton Long-sleeve T-shirt	$19.95	3	$5
90014	RM501835	Traveler's umbrella	$18.95	2	$3
90015	RA398289	World Resorts postcard collection	$9.95	5	$4
90016	RM400582	Canvas tote bag	$27.95	1	$2
90017	RA343127	World Resorts sweatshirt	$39.95	3	$11
90018	RA398121	World Resorts 8-ounce glass set (4 pack)	$32.95	2	$6
90019	RS896231	Stationery and thank-you note set	$24.95	4	$9

Figure 10.19

Project 10: Creating Forms Based on Multiple Tables   ACC-247

8 Save your changes and close the form.

Now you have created both the main form and the subform, you can combine the two. To do this requires adding a *subform/subreport control,* which links data from another table or query to the existing report or form.

TASK 5: TO ADD THE *ORDERS* SUBFORM TO THE *ORDERS* MAIN FORM:

1 In Design View, open the *Orders* main form.

2 In the Toolbox, select the Subform/Subreport tool shown in Figure 10.20.

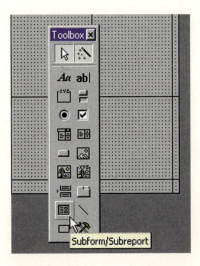

Figure 10.20

3 Draw a Subform/Subreport control on the main form approximately in the position shown in Figure 10.21.

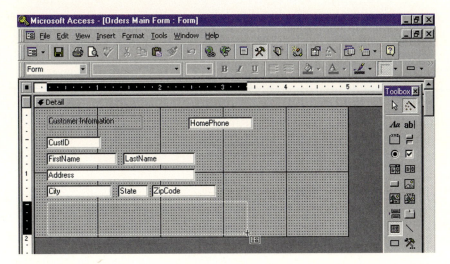

Figure 10.21

4 The Subform/Subreport Wizard will appear. Select the Forms option, and in the drop-down list, select the *Orders* subform, as shown in Figure 10.22. Click Next.

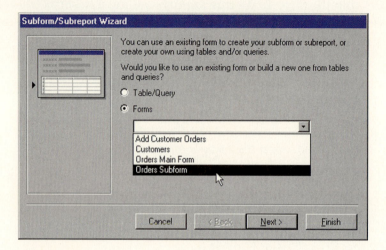

Figure 10.22

5 Select the option for linking the subform to the main form by choosing the first option from the list, as shown in Figure 10.23. Click Next.

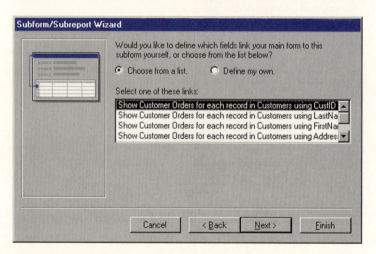

Figure 10.23

6 Type **Customer Order History** as the name of the subform, and click Finish.

7 Resize and move the label control and Subform control as necessary. Save the form.

8 Select Form View from the View menu. Your form/subform should look similar to Figure 10.24.

Project 10: Creating Forms Based on Multiple Tables   ACC-249

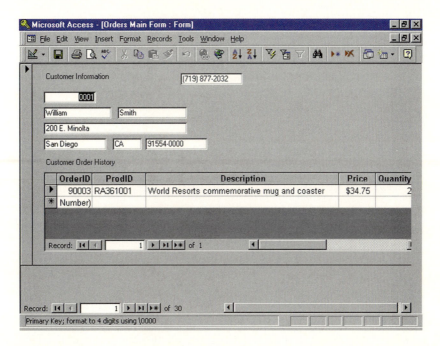

Figure 10.24

9   Notice that there are two data controls (sets of navigation buttons) on the form. A data control is a set of buttons and a record counter appearing in a table, query, or form that is used to move through the recordset or add new records. The upper data control is bound to the subform. Since not all of the columns in the subform are visible at the same time, you can use the horizontal scroll bar to move the view on the subform to the right. The lower data control is bound to the *Orders* main form. Using the lower data control, change the view to customer record 15, as shown in Figure 10.25. Notice that both the Customer Information and Customer Order History have changed.

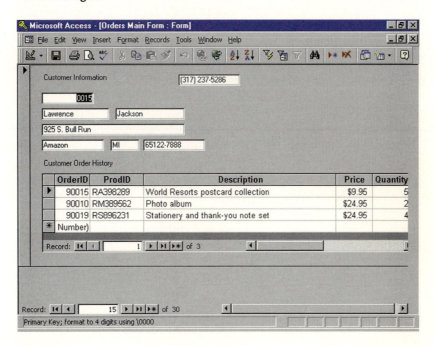

Figure 10.25

10 Close the form. Make sure you save the changes you have made to the form design.

The Conclusion

Forms are an integral part of a database, since they provide the user interface for working with the underlying data. As you have learned in this project, Microsoft Access includes many options for creating forms based on one or more tables or queries.

There are many other ways to customize forms. Although fully customizing the forms you have created in this project is beyond the scope of this book, you will make some modifications to the forms in Project 11.

Summary and Exercises

Summary

- Forms are bound to a table or query, which are based upon an underlying recordset.
- A form based on a multitable query can be constructed using the Form Wizard.
- A form consisting of a main form with a subform can be used to display record information from multiple tables or queries simultaneously.
- All objects added to forms are called controls.
- There are three kinds of controls: bound, unbound, and calculated.
- A command button is an example of an unbound control.
- Text boxes displaying field data are examples of bound controls.

Key Terms and Operations

Key Terms
bound control
calculated control
control
data control
event procedure
label control
main form
recordset
subform
Subform/Subreport control
unbound control

Operations
add command button controls to an existing form
create a form based on a multitable query
create a main form
create a subform
add a subform to a main form

Study Questions

Multiple Choice

1. A text box is what kind of control?
   a. bound
   b. unbound
   c. calculated
   d. Subform/Subreport control
   e. command button control

2. The data source underlying a table or query is called a(n)
   a. unbound control.
   b. data control.
   c. subform.
   d. recordset.
   e. bound control.

3. The forms that users interact with when using a database are part of the
   a.   data control.
   b.   user interface.
   c.   recordset.
   d.   subform.
   e.   main form.

4. A form in an Access database contains record information from two database tables. The lower portion of the form displays multiple records. The data here is displayed using a(n)
   a.   text box control.
   b.   command button control.
   c.   label control.
   d.   unbound control.
   e.   Subform/Subreport control.

5. A label is what kind of control?
   a.   bound
   b.   unbound
   c.   calculated
   d.   Subform/Subreport control
   e.   command button control

6. What kind of control is most appropriate for actions such as closing a form?
   a.   bound
   b.   unbound
   c.   calculated
   d.   Subform/Subreport
   e.   command button

7. What kind of relationship is required for adding a subform to a form?
   a.   one-to-one
   b.   one-to-many
   c.   many-to-many
   d.   No relationship is required.

8. Which kind of control normally has an event procedure attached to it?
   a.   text box
   b.   label
   c.   command button
   d.   bound
   e.   Subform/Subreport

9. Which of the following objects normally contains a subform?
   a.   text box
   b.   label
   c.   command button
   d.   bound control
   e.   main form

10. A data control is used to
    a.   navigate within a recordset.
    b.   display field data in a text box.
    c.   add records to a recordset.
    d.   display data in a label control.
    e.   a and c above.

Short Answer
1. What word applies to every object added to a form?
2. A text box is what kind of control?
3. What term describes specific source on which a table or query is based?
4. A label is what kind of control?
5. A subform can be added to a form only if what condition is true?
6. Is a subform used to display a single record or multiple records?
7. When a subform is added to a form, how many data controls will appear on the form?
8. Which kind of control is used to display text that the user will never edit?
9. Controls are added to forms using which view?
10. Field data from multiple tables can be added to one form when the data source is what object?

For Discussion
1. What is the difference between a main form and a subform?
2. How does a bound control differ from an unbound control?
3. What is the Subform/Subreport tool? When would you use it?
4. When would you use a subform?

Review Exercises

1. Creating an Employees Main Form and Subform
The *Employees* database you have been working on in Review Exercise 1 of previous projects needs to be modified to display all time cards for each employee. A form containing a subform will be the best method for accomplishing this. Follow these instructions to create a main form that will contain a subform:

1. Open the *Employees* database you modified in Project 9.
2. Click the Forms tab.
3. Click New.
4. Create a form that is based on the *Employees* table and that contains the following fields: EmpID, LastName, FirstName, and PayRate.
5. Select Columnar format, and whatever style you desire.
6. Save the form as *Employees,* and close the form.
7. Create an additional form based on the *Gross Pay* query.
8. Add the WeekStart, WeekEnd, Hours, and GrossPay fields to the form.
9. Select Datasheet as the format, and Standard as the style.
10. Save the form as *Time Cards,* and close the form.

2. Adding the *Employees* Subform to the Main Form

To display the time card data from each employee on a single form, the subform containing the time card data needs to be added to the form listing each employee. To accomplish this task, complete the following steps:

1. Open the *Employees* form in Design View.

2. Using the subform/subreport tool, add a subform/subreport control near the bottom of the *Employees* form.

3. Select the Forms option, and in the drop-down list, select the *Time Cards* subform. Click Next.

4. In the Subform/Subreport Wizard, select the first option in the drop-down list for linking the subform to the main form. Click Next.

5. Type **Employee Time Cards** as the name of the form, and click Finish.

6. Select Design View from the View menu to review the form.

7. Close the form. Make sure you save the changes you have made to the form design.

Assignments

1. Creating a Form Displaying Student Course Data

Open the Student database you modified in Assignment 1 of Project 9. Using the Form Wizard, create a form based on the query displaying student courses. Review the form in Form View, and make any necessary changes in Design View before saving the form.

2. Creating a Form Displaying Restaurant Information

Open the Access database about Vail restaurants. Using the query you created in Exercise 2 of Project 9, create a form displaying the restaurant and cuisine information. Decide whether a single form will accomplish this task, or a main form containing a subform will best display the data. Save any changes you make to the database.

PROJECT 11

Creating a Database Application

After you become familiar with Microsoft Access and know how to create tables, queries, forms, and reports, you can add macros and Visual Basic for Applications code to tie these objects together as a database application. In this project you will construct a database application using Microsoft Access.

Objectives

After completing this project, you will be able to:

➤ **Create a report based on a query**
➤ **Customize a form by altering the properties of the form's controls**
➤ **Add a macro to a form specifying the form's behavior**
➤ **Specify a validation rule for field data**
➤ **Create a startup form containing command buttons**
➤ **Add an image control to the startup form to enhance its appearance**

The Challenge

An *application* organizes related tasks so that the user can focus on the task at hand, not on how the application works or on how a specific program is used to develop the application. By now the future users of this database you have been developing for Resort Sales, Incorporated have seen the forms you created for the database. They have provided additional recommendations for developing it into an application. First, they think the database should include the capability of printing an invoice for each customer order. Second, the users want a screen for entering orders that automatically displays a blank record. Third, they want you to develop some sort of menu system for accessing the various database components. And finally, they want to see the company's logo integrated into the database.

The Solution

You will be able to develop a solution for each recommendation for improving the database. First you will create a *report* object based on the *Customer Orders* query that will print an invoice for each customer. Recall from Project 6 that a *report* summarizes data from database tables and normally gets printed on paper, whereas forms remain on-screen. Then you will remove the navigation controls from the Add Customers form and create a *macro* that automatically adds a new record to the query recordset when the form opens, so new customers can easily be added to the database. Third, you will create a *startup form*, the form that first appears on the screen when the user opens the database application. Since the startup form will contain command buttons for opening various database objects, it will serve as a menu system. And fourth, you will add an *image control* to display a graphic image of the company logo on the form. When the database opens, the startup form will look like Figure 11.1.

Figure 11.1

The Setup

To complete the steps in this project, you will first need to make a copy of the *Resort Sales 4* database.

TASK 1: TO MAKE A COPY OF THE ACCESS DATABASE FILE:

1. Minimize Microsoft Access.
2. Open My Computer on the Desktop.

Project 11: Creating a Database Application   ACC-257

3 Using the procedures introduced in Task 1 of Project 7, create a copy of the *Resort Sales 4* database (*Resort Sales 4.mdb* file). Rename this copy as **Resort Sales 5**.

4 Copy the file *Logo.bmp* from your campus network to the root directory of your data diskette.

> **Tip** If you do not have access to this file, it is also available from the Addison-Wesley Web site, http://www.awl.com.he/is/.

5 Restore Access and open the *Resort Sales 5.mdb* database.

> **Troubleshooting** If you are having trouble copying and renaming this file, ask your instructor for assistance.

To complete this project, make sure you do the following in Access:

- If you do not see a toolbar on the screen after launching Access, choose View, Toolbars, and click the Database toolbar option. If additional toolbars are visible, close them.
- Most of the figures in this project will display the Database dialog box and other Access dialog boxes in a restored state. You may resize any dialog boxes by clicking the Restore button in each dialog box.

Close the Microsoft Office Shortcut bar. In this project, you will not need to launch any additional applications.

Creating a Report Based on a Query

In order to print a copy of a customer invoice, you must first create a report object. As you will recall from Project 6, you can create report objects using the Report Design window. This window contains three main design areas: the Page Header section, the Detail section, and the Page Footer section. To create a report you add controls to each of these sections of the Report Design window.

In Project 6 you created an AutoReport, whereby Access placed each object onto the Report Design window. In this project you will add controls to the report directly using the Toolbox. You will create the report in three tasks, one for each section of the Report Design window.

TASK 2: TO CREATE A REPORT AND ADD CONTROLS TO THE PAGE HEADER SECTION:

1 Select the Reports tab in the Access Database dialog box, and click the New button.

2 Select Design View, and base the report on the *Customer Orders* query, as shown in Figure 11.2. Click OK.

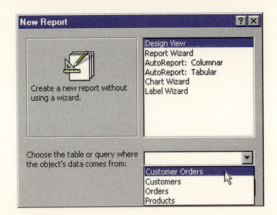

Figure 11.2

3 Maximize the Report Design window. Use the View menu to display the Toolbox and Field List, if they are not currently visible.

4 Select the Label control tool, as shown in Figure 11.3.

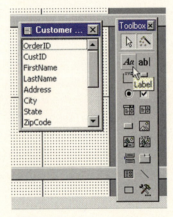

Figure 11.3

5 Draw a label control in the Page Header section approximately in the position shown in Figure 11.4.

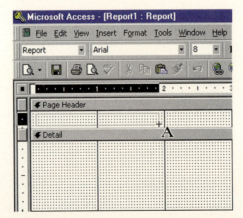

Figure 11.4

Project 11: Creating a Database Application ACC-259

6 Type **Resort Sales Incorporated** as the text for the label. With the insertion point immediately after the text, hold down the (CTRL) key and press (ENTER). The insertion point will now appear at the beginning of the next line in the label control. Type **Customer Invoice**, and press (ENTER) to accept the text.

7 Right-click the label control, and the shortcut menu shown in Figure 11.5 will appear. This menu sets the properties for the selected control.

Figure 11.5

8 Select Properties from the menu. The dialog box for the selected control will appear, as shown in Figure 11.6.

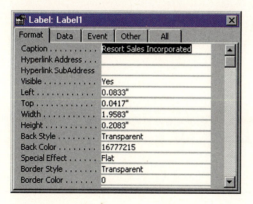

Figure 11.6

> **Tip** The properties for each kind of control will differ.

9 With the Format tab active, scroll down the list of available options, and change the Font Name property to Arial, the Font Size to 12, and the Font Weight to Bold, as shown in Figure 11.7.

ACC-260

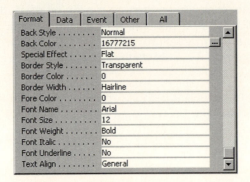

Figure 11.7

10 Click the mouse inside the Back Color field. Click the small button with the ellipsis when it appears. Change the color to gray, as shown in Figure 11.8. Click OK.

Figure 11.8

11 Resize the label control as necessary, so the entire caption is displayed.

12 Select Layout Preview from the View menu. The label in the Page Header of the invoice should now look similar to Figure 11.9.

Project 11: Creating a Database Application   ACC-261

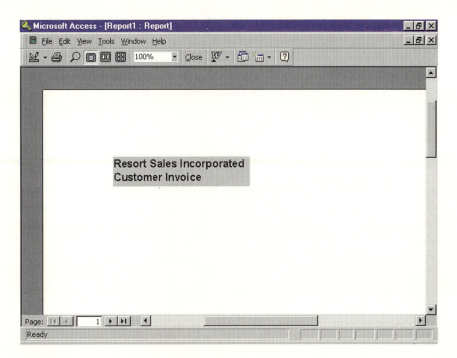

Figure 11.9

> **Tip** Click the Zoom icon if necessary.

13. Switch to Design View.

Now that you have defined the Page Header section, you are ready to add controls to the Detail section. The controls appearing here will display data from the query's recordset.

TASK 3: TO ADD CONTROLS TO THE REPORT'S DETAIL SECTION:

1. Add a text box control to the upper left corner of the report's Detail section of the Report Design window, as shown in Figure 11.10. The control consists of two components: a label (with the default name Text1), and a text box (identified as Unbound).

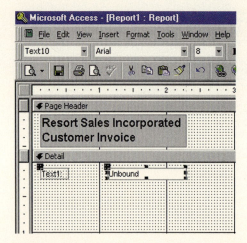

Figure 11.10

2 Using the left mouse button, double-click inside the label control to edit the label text. Replace Text1 with **Customer Number**, and click outside the label to accept the new text.

3 Right-click the text box. Select Properties from the right-click menu.

4 With the All tab active, click inside the Control Source field. Select CustID from the drop-down list, as shown in Figure 11.11.

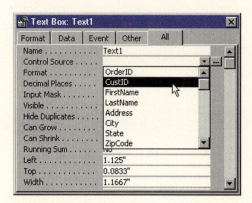

Figure 11.11

5 Select the Format property of the text box control, type **\1000** as the format.

6 Select the Text Align property for both the text box and the label control, and change the alignment to Right.

7 Select the OrderID field in the field list, and drag a copy of the field control to the Detail section, immediately below the Customer Number control.

8 Change the Align property of the OrderID label and text box to Right, and move the label closer to the OrderID text box.

9 Drag the FirstName, LastName, Address, City, State, ZipCode, and HomePhone controls from the Field List to the Detail section.

10 Highlight the label for each control you added in the previous step and press (DELETE).

Project 11: Creating a Database Application   ACC-263

> **Tip** You are deleting these labels because the field contents do not need a label for clarification. You may select multiple labels for deletion by holding down the SHIFT key while selecting each label.

11 After deleting all these labels, arrange the field data on the screen to approximate the layout shown in Figure 11.12.

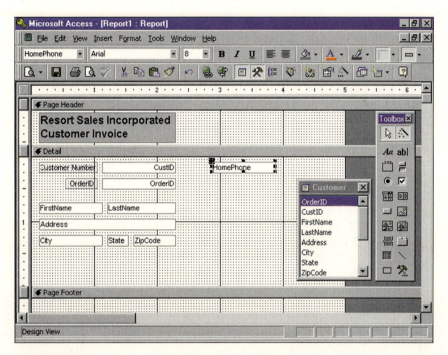

Figure 11.12

12 Using the same procedures listed in Steps 1 to 4 above, add a text box control below the address information. Make the text of the label **Product Number**, and set Font Weight to Bold.

13 Set the Control Source of the text box for this field to ProdID. Position the text box control below the label control, as shown in Figure 11.13. Increase the size of the Detail area of the Report Design window if necessary.

ACC-264

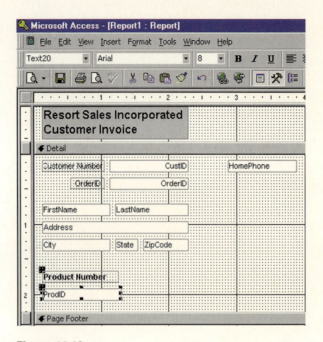

Figure 11.13

14 Using the Field List, add the Description, Price, Quantity, and Total Sale fields to the Detail section of the Report Design window to the right of the Product Description text box and label.

15 Change the font weight of the labels accompanying these fields to Bold, and remove any colon characters following the descriptive label.

16 Change the Text Align property of the Price, Quantity and Total Sale text box and label controls to Right. Resize the Detail section if necessary. Your screen should now look like Figure 11.14.

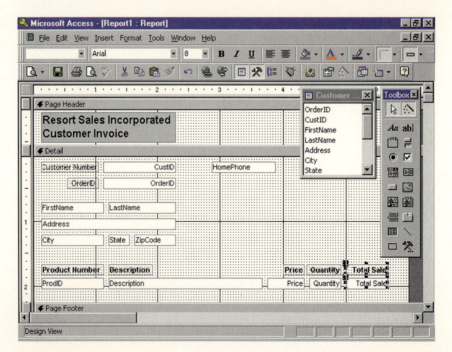

Figure 11.14

Project 11: Creating a Database Application ACC-265

You are now ready to add information to the Page Footer area of the Report Design window. You will first add a page break control in the Detail section.

TASK 4: TO ADD CONTROLS TO THE PAGE FOOTER SECTION:

1 Select the Page Break Tool, as shown in Figure 11.15.

Figure 11.15

2 Drag the Page Break control tool to just below the ProductID text box. This will instruct Access to print only one customer invoice per page.

3 From the Insert menu, select Insert Date and Time. The Date and Time dialog box will appear.

4 Change the settings to match Figure 11.16, and click OK.

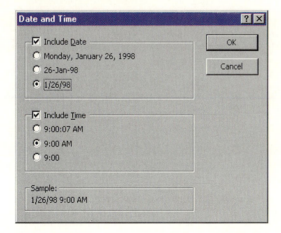

Figure 11.16

5 By default, the date and time controls are added to the top of the Detail section. Move the Date and Time field to the left side of the Page Footer section, as shown in Figure 11.17.

Figure 11.17

6 Change the view using the horizontal scroll bar, until the rest of the Detail section is visible. Select the Line control tool from the Toolbox, as shown in Figure 11.18.

Figure 11.18

7 Draw a horizontal line in the Detail section immediately above the product heading information. The line should extend across the entire Detail section.

8 Using Copy and Paste, copy the line and paste the copy in the Detail section. Move the second line to a position immediately below the product heading information.

9 Select Print Preview from the File menu, and set Zoom control to 100%. Your report should look similar to Figure 11.19.

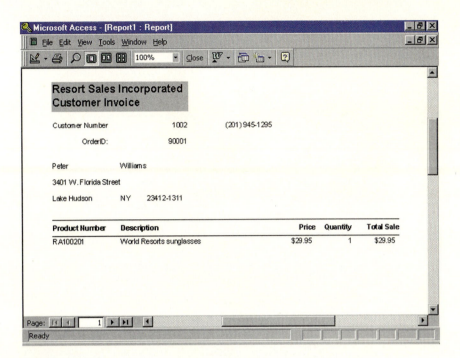

Figure 11.19

10 Select Save from the File menu.

11 Type **Customer Invoice** as the name of the report.

12 Close the report.

Customizing the *Add Customer Orders* Form by Altering Its Properties

You will need to customize the form you created in Project 10 for adding new customer orders. You will now modify the form as follows. First, you should remove the field controls containing redundant information from the form. Second, the fields represented on the form are based on both the *Customers* and the *Orders* tables, and the form currently allows users to edit the data in those tables. You will change the properties of these controls to protect data entry personnel from inadvertently altering the form. Third, the form should only allow users to add new orders to the database, and not navigate between records. Removing the data control from the form and adding a command button to close the form will prevent users from navigating to other records in the recordset. You will then write a macro that creates a new record whenever the form opens. Next you will add an additional command button to the form that will bring the *Customers* form onto the screen whenever the person placing the order is a new customer (that is, one for whom no record currently exists). Finally, you will add a validation rule to the Quantity field so that a value greater than zero must be entered when an order is placed.

TASK 5: TO DELETE AND REPOSITION FIELD CONTROLS ON THE *ADD CUSTOMER ORDERS* FORM:

1. Open the *Add Customer Orders* form in Design View.
2. Maximize the Form Design window.
3. Using the SHIFT key, select each label control associated with a name, address, or phone number field.
4. Press DELETE to delete the selected label controls.
5. Change the text of the OrderID label to **Order Number**, the ProdID label to **Product Number**, and the CustID label to **Customer Number**.
6. Change the location of all controls so your form looks similar to Figure 11.20.

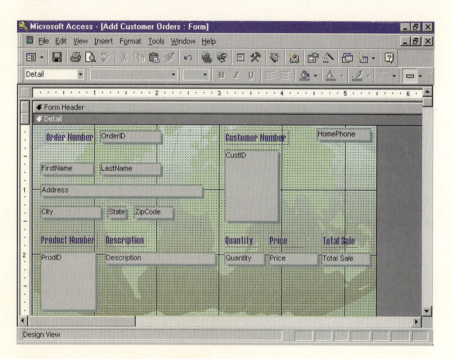

Figure 11.20

You are now ready to change the properties of the field controls to make portions of the *Add Customer Orders* form **read-only**. This will prevent users from changing this data in the *Customers* and *Orders* tables when using the form. To make the field contents of the form read-only, you will alter the value of two properties. First you will change the **Locked property** from No to Yes. By itself this change will make the field contents of the control read-only, but it will also make them appear dimmed. A **dimmed control** appears light gray, indicating that the field is unavailable for selecting or changing. Another way of saying this is that the field cannot **receive the focus.** However, you want the user to be able to read easily all the information in all the fields on the form, including those that cannot receive the focus. To make this possible, you will change value of the Enabled property to No. With both of these settings, the text in each field will appear normal (undimmed), even though the field cannot receive the focus.

Project 11: Creating a Database Application   ACC-269

TASK 6: TO MAKE FIELD DATA IN THE FORM READ-ONLY:

1. Using the SHIFT key, select all text box controls except CustID, ProdID, and Quantity. (Data entry personnel will need to be able to change the Customer Number, Product Number, and Quantity field data.)

2. Right-click one control in the selection to evoke the Properties dialog box. Notice that the title bar of the dialog box specifies that the properties will apply to a multiple selection.

3. Click the All tab in the Multiple selection dialog box to display the Locked property.

4. Change the value of the Locked property from No to Yes, as shown in Figure 11.21.

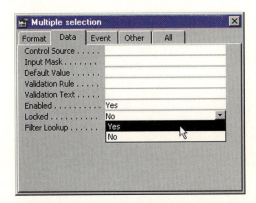

Figure 11.21

5. Using the same procedure, change the value of the Enabled property to No.

6. Save the form.

Although you modified the form so certain fields cannot be changed, users will still have access to three of the fields. To prevent them from modifying any records in the existing recordset on which these fields are based, you will next remove the data control (navigation buttons) from the form. Then you will add a command button that allows users to close the form after entering new orders, thus returning program control to the *Add Customer Orders* form.

TASK 7: TO REMOVE THE DATA CONTROL FROM THE FORM AND ADD A COMMAND BUTTON FOR CLOSING THE FORM:

1. Make sure you are in Design view and the Properties dialog box is visible. Choose Select Form from the Edit menu.

2. In the Form properties dialog box, click the Format tab.

3. Change the setting of the Navigation Buttons property to No. This will remove the data control from the form.

4. Set the Scroll Bars property to Neither. This will remove the scroll bars from the form.

5	Select the Command Button tool from the Toolbox, and add a command button to the lower right corner of the form.
6	In the Command Button Wizard, select Form Operations and Close Form in the first dialog box. Click Next.
7	In the next dialog box, select the option to display text on the button. Click Next.
8	Type **cmdCloseAddOrdersForm** as the name of the command button. Click Finish.
9	Reposition the button if necessary.
10	Switch to Form View. Your form should now resemble Figure 11.22.

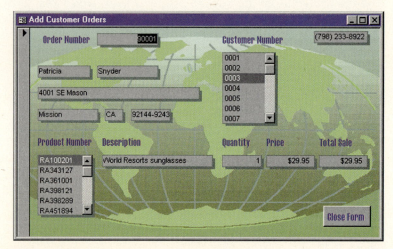

Figure 11.22

Now you will modify the form so that every time a user opens the form, the database creates a new record.

TASK 8: TO CREATE A MACRO THAT AUTOMATICALLY OPENS A NEW RECORD:

1	With your *Add Customer Orders* form in Design View, choose Select Form from the Edit menu.
2	In the Properties dialog box for the form, click the Event tab.
3	Scroll to the On Open property, and place the insertion point inside the field for this property.
4	Click the small button with the ellipsis to the right of the On Click property line.
5	Select Macro Builder from the Choose Builder dialog box, as shown in Figure 11.23, and click OK.

Project 11: Creating a Database Application ACC-271

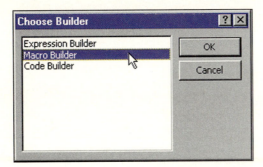

Figure 11.23

6 Type **NewRecord** as the name for the macro. Click OK.

7 The Macro Design window that appears resembles the Table Design grid. You will use this window to specify one or more macro actions and to enter comments explaining what action each step of the macro performs.

8 In the Action drop-down list for the first row in the grid, select GoToRecord.

9 In the Comments cell, type **Create a new record**.

10 In the Record drop-down list in the Action Arguments pane, select New. The Macro Design grid should now look like Figure 11.24.

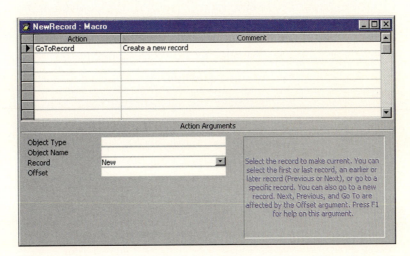

Figure 11.24

11 Select Save from the File menu to save the macro.

12 Close the NewRecord:Macro dialog box.

Since the only data entry required to place an order is a Customer number, product number, and order quantity, you need to make two final changes to the form. The form needs a button so the user can add new records to the *Customers* table. Also, the Quantity field needs a **validation rule** specifying what kind of data the user can enter into the field. Accompanying the validation rule is **validation text,** the message displayed on the screen when the user violates the validation rule. Usually the validation text also states how to correct the entry.

ACC-272

TASK 9: TO ADD A COMMAND BUTTON TO THE FORM AND SET A VALIDATION RULE:

1. Make sure the *Add Customer Orders* form is in Design View.

2. Using the Command Button tool, create a command button to the left of the Close Form button.

3. Select Form Operations and Open Form in the first dialog box of the Command Button Wizard. Click Next.

4. Select the *Customers* form as the form to open when the button is selected. Click Next.

5. Select the option to open the form and display all records, and Click Next.

> **Tip** Remember that the *Customers* form contains a Search button to search for a specific customer.

6. Select the option to display text on the button and type **Add a Customer** as the caption for the button. Click Next.

7. Type **cmdOpenCustForm** as the name for the control, and click Finish.

8. Resize and reposition the control as necessary.

9. Select the properties for the Quantity field and click the All tab.

10. Type **>0** in the Validation Rule property.

11. Type **The quantity ordered must be greater than zero** as the validation text.

12. Switch to Form View. The form should now look like Figure 11.25. Notice that only the field data boxes for Order Number, Customer Number, and Production Number have any data in them. Compare with Figure 11.22. Save and close the form.

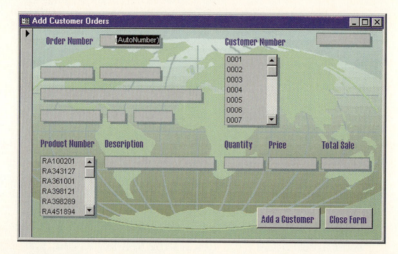

Figure 11.25

Project 11: Creating a Database Application   ACC-273

Creating a Startup Form

Your database is almost complete! However, it still lacks a menu system for accessing the necessary forms and reports for adding orders, checking the status of existing orders, adding new customer records, and printing a customer invoice.

Microsoft Access allows you to create a form that will act as a menu for the database. This form is not bound to a particular table or query object, and since it is usually the first database object to display when the database opens, it is called the startup form. In this section you will create the startup form, which will contain four command buttons. To enhance its appearance, in the following section you will add the company logo and a copyright notice.

TASK 10: TO CREATE A STARTUP FORM:

1. Select New from the Forms window in the Database dialog box.
2. Without specifying a table or query, select Design View in the New Form dialog box. Click OK.
3. Maximize the Form Design window.
4. Choose Select Form from the Edit menu.
5. Set the properties listed in Table 11.1 for the form.

Table 11.1

Property	Value
Caption	Resort Sales Incorporated
Scroll Bars	Neither
Record Selectors	No
Navigation Buttons	No
Dividing Lines	No
Border Style	Dialog
Min Max Buttons	None

6. Add a command button near the upper right of the form. Design the button to open the *Add Customer Orders* form. Type **Add Order** as the caption for the button, and give the button an appropriate name.

7. Add three additional command buttons below the one you just created: Print *Customer Invoice* to print the customer invoice report, View Order History to open the *Orders Main Form* form, and Quit to close the database application.

ACC-274

> **Tip** For the Quit button, select Application as the Action Category.

8 Save the form as **Resort Sales Startup**.

9 Switch to Form View. The form should look similar to Figure 11.26.

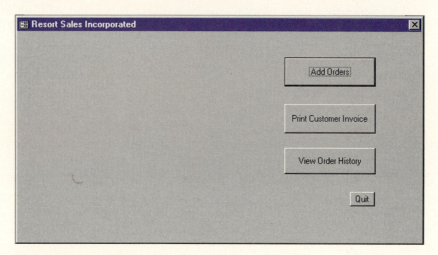

Figure 11.26

10 Select Startup from the Tools menu.

11 Type **Resort Sales Incorporated** as the application title.

12 Select *Resort Sales Startup* in the Display Form drop-down list. When your settings match those shown in Figure 11.27, click OK. Save the changes to your database.

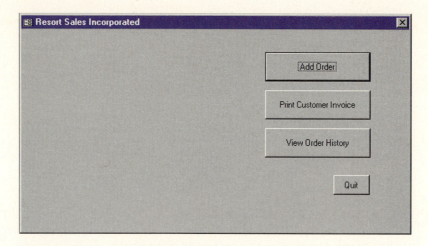

Figure 11.27

Adding an Image Control to the Startup Form

Adding the company logo to the form will enhance its appearance. Microsoft Access supports the Visual Basic *image control,* which is used to display a bitmap image or clip art file on a form.

Project 11: Creating a Database Application ACC-275

In this section you will also add a label control for the copyright statement.

TASK 11: TO ADD ADDITIONAL CONTROLS TO THE STARTUP FORM:

1. Switch to Design View for the *Resort Sales Startup* form.
2. Select the Image control tool from the Toolbox, as shown in Figure 11.28.

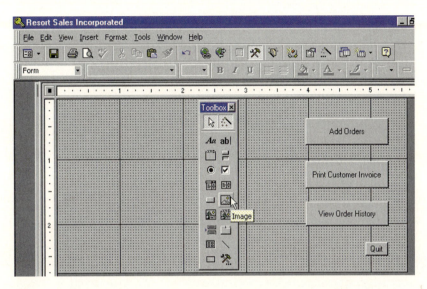

Figure 11.28

3. Place an image control to the left of the command buttons.
4. When the Insert Picture dialog box appears, select the *Logo.bmp* file from your student data diskette. Access then inserts the logo in the image control, as shown in Figure 11.29.

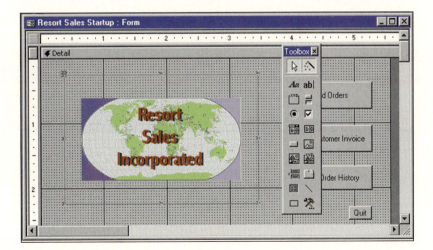

Figure 11.29

5. Set the Special Effect property of the image control to Sunken. Resize the control down to the size of the image.
6. Add a label control below the image control.
7. Type **Copyright 1998** as the first line of the label.

8. Hold down the (CONTROL) key and press (ENTER). **Type Resort Sales Incorporated** as the second line of the label.
9. Save your changes to the form.
10. Switch to Form View. Your form should look similar to Figure 11.30.

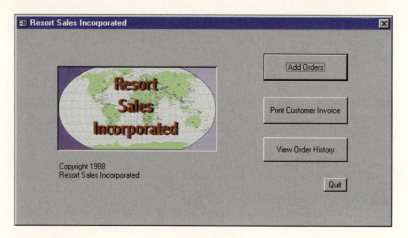

Figure 11.30

Each command button is a **tab stop,** meaning that as you press the (TAB) key the next button on the form will receive the focus.

11. Press the (TAB) key a few times to see how each button receives the focus.
12. Close the form.

The Conclusion

Your database application is now fully functional. There are additional enhancements you could make, such as customizing the *Customer Invoice* report to print specific customer invoices, or refining the *Orders Sub Form* to improve the display of order information Detail section.

You have gained some understanding of the power of controls for adding functionality to an application. In Project 12 you will learn how to create a Visual Basic application that serves as an interface to Microsoft Access database objects.

Summary and Exercises

Summary

- You can use the Report Design window to create a report based on a query object.
- You create a report using the Report Design window by adding controls to the Page Header, Detail, and Page Footer sections of the window.
- Each control that you add to a form or a report has specific properties, which you can change.
- You can make the data in some or all of the fields read-only by changing the Lock and Enabled properties of their field controls.
- You specify validation rules for forms by changing the format properties of specific controls.
- A startup form often serves as a database menu.
- An image control can display a bitmap image on a form.

Key Terms and Operations

Key Terms
application
dimmed control
image control
locked property
macro
read-only
receive the focus
report
startup form
tab stop
validation rule
validation text

Operations
create a report using Design View
reposition field controls appearing on a form
remove the data control from a form
delete field controls appearing on a form
add controls to the Page Header, Detail, and Page Footer sections of the Report Design window
make a form's data read-only
set a validation rule for a form's field control
create a startup form
add controls to a startup form

Study Questions

Multiple Choice

1. Which section of the Report Design window do you put information that will appear in a report for all records in the recordset on which the report is based?
   a. Page Header
   b. Page Footer
   c. Detail
   d. a and b above
   e. none of the above

2. Which of the following controls allow you to add text such as copyright information to a form?
   a. label
   b. text box
   c. command button
   d. image
   e. page break

3. What property of a text box control prevents the field information from being changed?
   a. Text align
   b. Enabled
   c. Back Color
   d. Locked
   e. b and d above

4. How would you describe an object that is currently not available or cannot be selected?
   a. locked
   b. enabled
   c. visible
   d. dimmed
   e. a control

5. Which of the following properties specifies the kind of data entered into a field control?
   a. Enabled
   b. Validation Rule
   c. Locked
   d. Validation Text
   e. Tab Stop

6. Which of the following properties specifies the message that Access will display when a user enters invalid data into a field control on a form?
   a. Enabled
   b. Validation Rule
   c. Locked
   d. Validation Text
   e. Tab Stop

7. When a user can enter data into a control on a form, the control is said to have or be which of the following?
   a. a validation rule
   b. the focus
   c. enabled
   d. locked
   e. a tab stop

8. What kind of control displays a bitmap file on a form?
   a. text box
   b. label
   c. page break
   d. command button
   e. image

9. To add an object to a database that will be the first object displayed when the user opens the database, and that is not bound to a recordset, you will create what kind of object?
   a. main form
   b. subreport
   c. subform
   d. startup form
   e. query

10. Which database object contains statements that can be executed by evoking the object?
    a. table
    b. query
    c. form
    d. report
    e. macro

Short Answer

1. What kind of control do you use to display a bitmap file on a form?
2. You add controls to the Detail section of a report when using which method of creating a report?
3. Which control adds a page break to a report?
4. What kind of form is often used to create a menu for a database application?
5. To display the data and time at the top of every page in a report, you add the appropriate control to which section of the report using Design View?
6. What kind of control is added to a Startup form to open other form objects in the database?
7. What kind of control gives descriptive information such as a copyright statement on a form?
8. The data displayed in a text box of a form is set to read-only by changing which properties of the control?
9. What control do you use to display data from a subform in a report?
10. Which Access menu do you use to specify that a form is to be used as a startup form?

For Discussion

1. What is a startup form? Why is it a useful addition to a database?
2. How does a validation rule differ from an input mask?
3. What additional validation rules could you specify for the *Add Customer Orders* form?
4. Should you design a report using the AutoReport Wizard, the Report Wizard, or Design View? Explain the benefits of each.

Review Exercises

1. Adding a Time Card Report to the *Employees* Database

The *Employees* database presently includes a main form/subform that displays time card data from each employee. Create a report object in Design View that prints the time card data from each employee. To complete this task, do the following:

1. Open the *Employees* database.
2. Select New from the Reports tab.
3. Select Design View, and base the report on the *Employees* table.
4. Add a label control to the report's Page Header.
5. Type **Employee Time Cards** as the text for the label.
6. Add the EmpID, LastName, FirstName, and PayRate fields to the report's Detail section.
7. Using the Subform/Subreport tool, add a subreport control to the report's Detail section, below the name information.
8. Specify the *Time Cards Sub Form* as the object on which to base the subreport.
9. Add a page break control immediately following the subreport control.
10. Save the report as *Employee Time Cards*.

2. Adding a Startup Form to the *Employees* Database

The *Employees* database will be easier to use if it contains a startup form. Create a menu for the database by completing the following tasks:

1. Open the *Employees* database, if it is not currently open.
2. Select New from the Forms tab to create a new form.
3. Select Design View for the form. Do not base the form on an existing table or query object.
4. Add a label control to the form. Type **Employee Database Application** as the text for the label.
5. Add a command button to the upper right portion of the form. Use the Command Button Wizard to specify a form operation that opens the *Employees* table.
6. Create an additional command button below the one you just created. Using the Command Button Wizard, specify a form operation that opens the *Employee Time Cards* form.
7. Add a command button to the form that closes the database.
8. Save the form as **Employee Startup**.
9. Select Startup from the Tools menu. Change the settings in the Startup dialog box so that the form you just created loads whenever a user opens the database.
10. Update the database.

Assignments

1. Creating a Grade Report for the Student Database

Open the student database file you last modified in Assignment 1 of Project 10. Create a report object in Design View that lists each student's first and last name, social security number, course name, course number, and course grade. View the report in Layout View, and make any necessary changes to the report before saving it.

2. Adding a Startup Form Displaying Restaurants in Vail, Colorado

You can greatly enhance the appearance of the database about restaurants in Vail by adding a startup form to the database. Search the Web for an appropriate image file to include on the form. Create three buttons: one that displays restaurant information, one that displays the main form/subform data, and one that closes the database.

PROJECT 12

Using Microsoft Access Data in Other Applications

The database application you have created in Projects 7 through 11 is now fully functional within Microsoft Access. But how will you share the database with users who do not have Access installed on their computers? There are a variety of methods for sharing data from a Microsoft Access database with other applications. In this project you will learn about two of them. One method is to publish any or all of the information from the database on the World Wide Web or on a corporate Intranet. The other is to use a programming environment such as Visual Basic to create a stand-alone application, called a front end, which allows the user to interact with the database more easily.

Objectives

After completing this project, you will be able to:

- ➤ **Create a query object to publish as an HTML document**
- ➤ **Publish a Microsoft Access table on the World Wide Web or on a corporate intranet as an HTML document**
- ➤ **Modify the HTML document**
- ➤ **Create a Visual Basic application as a front-end application to the Access database**
- ➤ **Add functionality to the Visual Basic application using the data control**
- ➤ **Add controls to a Visual Basic form**
- ➤ **Create a Visual Basic form load event**
- ➤ **Save your application as an executable file and create an installable distribution set**

The Challenge

Upper management is so impressed with the database you have created that they want to make it available in two ways. First, they want you to figure out a way to post the *Products* table on the Internet so customers can receive product data at their convenience. Second, they want others in the corporation to be able to use your database. Since not all employees have Microsoft Access installed on their computers, management has asked you to find a way to make the data available through another application.

The Solution

Publishing information from the *Products* table to the Internet is a simple task. With Access 97 you can easily create a document written in HTML from any Access database object. **HTML**, or *HyperText Markup Language*, is a format used for text documents that specifies how the information will be displayed on the World Wide Web using a Web browser such as Microsoft Internet Explorer. After creating the document, you can modify it using a text editor. The finished HTML document you will create is shown in Figure 12.1.

Figure 12.1

The second requirement presents more of a challenge. Since Microsoft Access and Visual Basic share many of the same database components, you can write an application in Visual Basic that will act as a front end to the Access database. A database *front end* is an application containing a user interface and methods for interacting with data stored in a table structure. Once you have created the application, you can use the Visual Basic Setup Wizard to create a distribution set for it. This is the set of floppy diskettes that the Information Systems department can use to install the application on computers throughout the enterprise.

The Setup

To complete this project in its entirety, you need to have Microsoft Visual Basic version 5 installed on your computer. If it has not been, ask your instructor where the installation files are for the Visual Basic application like the one created here. You may install the application and see how it uses data from the *Customers* table.

To complete the steps in this project, you will first need to make a copy of the *Resort Sales 5* database file:

TASK 1: TO PREPARE YOUR DISKETTE TO COMPLETE THIS PROJECT:

1. Minimize Microsoft Access.
2. Open My Computer on the Desktop.
3. Place your data diskette in the computer's floppy disk drive.
4. Click the icon for the floppy diskette drive.
5. Create two folders on your floppy diskette: one named HTML, and one named VB5.
6. Copy the file *Logo.gif* from the root directory of your diskette into the HTML folder.
7. Copy the file *Border.gif* from the root directory into the HTML folder.
8. Move the file *Logo.bmp* from the root directory to the VB5 directory of your floppy diskette.
9. Using the procedures you learned in previous projects, copy the Resort Sales 5 database (Resort Sales 5.mdb file), and rename the copy **Resort Sales 6.**
10. Restore Access and open the *Resort Sales 6.mdb* database.

> **Troubleshooting** If you are having trouble copying and renaming this file, ask your instructor for assistance.

To complete this project, make sure you do the following in Access:
- If you do not see a toolbar on the screen after launching Access, choose View, Toolbars, and click the Database toolbar option. If additional toolbars are visible, close them.

Project 12: Using Microsoft Access Data in Other Applications   ACC-285

- Most of the figures in this project will display the Database dialog box and other Access dialog boxes in a restored state. You may resize any dialog boxes by clicking the Restore button in each dialog box.

Close the Microsoft Office Shortcut bar. In this project, you will not need to launch any additional applications.

Publishing Access Data on the World Wide Web or a Corporate Intranet

Each application in the Microsoft 97 Office suite includes the capability for saving data in the HTML format. This feature is becoming more important as corporations increasingly use Intranets for publishing information electronically. An *Intranet* is a private network using Web technology to publish information in HTML. You can read about publishing Microsoft Access in HTML on their Web site at http://www.microsoft.com/Access/Internet/WebWiz/.

The first step in publishing on the Web or on an Intranet is to create a query object for the specific data you want to publish.

TASK 2: TO CREATE A QUERY CONTAINING INFORMATION TO PUBLISH ON THE WEB:

1 In Microsoft Access, select Unhide from the Windows menu.

2 The Unhide Window dialog box lists Resort Sales 6: Database as the only hidden object, as shown in Figure 12.2.

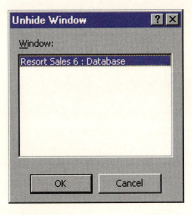

Figure 12.2

3 Click OK. The Database dialog box will appear.

4 Click the Queries tab to make it the active window. Click New.

5 In the New Query dialog box, select Design View. Create a query based on the *Products* table. Include the field data shown in Figure 12.3.

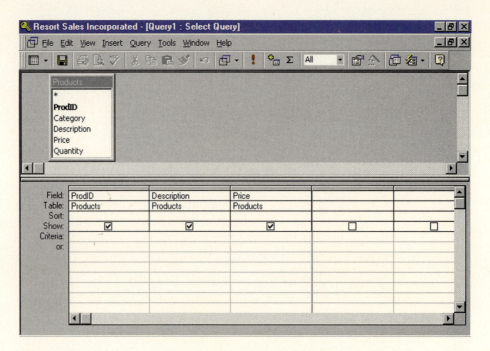

Figure 12.3

6 Set the caption property of the ProdID field to Product Number.

7 Save the query as *Product List*.

You are now ready to publish the query as an HTML document. You will use a Microsoft Access Wizard to complete this task.

TASK 3: TO CREATE AN HTML DOCUMENT FROM THE *PRODUCT LIST* QUERY:

1 Select Save As HTML from the File menu.

2 The Publish to the Web Wizard will appear, as shown in Figure 12.4. Click Next.

Project 12: Using Microsoft Access Data in Other Applications   ACC-287

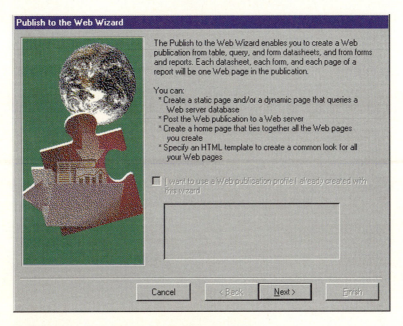

Figure 12.4

3   Click the Queries tab, and highlight *Product List*. Click the check box before the Product List entry. A check mark will appear in front of the *Product List* name, as shown in Figure 12.5. Click Next.

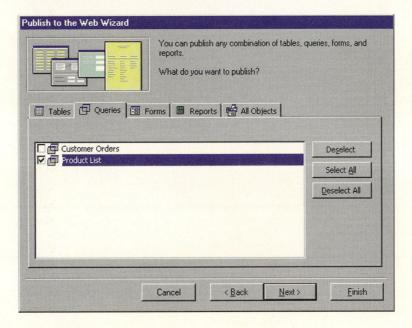

Figure 12.5

4   The Publish to the Web Wizard now prompts you to specify an HTML template, as shown in Figure 12.6. Since you do not have a template, click Next.

ACC-288

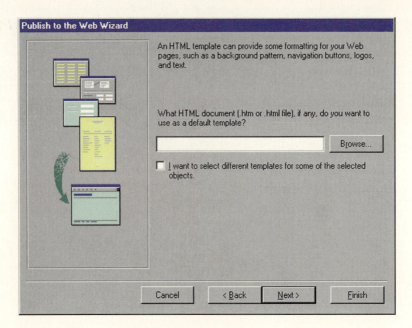

Figure 12.6

5 The wizard next asks you to specify whether you want the page to be static or dynamic. Select Static HTML as shown in Figure 12.7, and click Next.

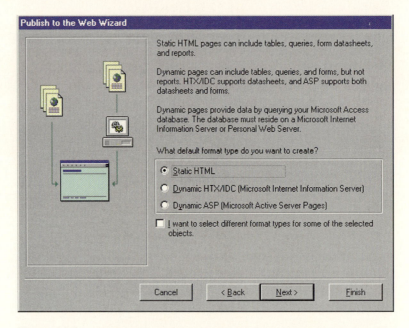

Figure 12.7

6 You will now specify a location (drive and folder) for your Web publication and how widely you want to publish. Select A:\HTML and the option to publish locally, as shown in Figure 12.8. Click Next.

Project 12: Using Microsoft Access Data in Other Applications   ACC-289

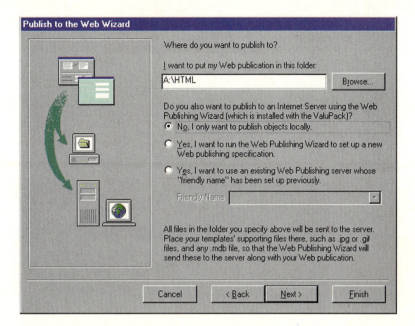

Figure 12.8

7   The wizard now asks whether you want a home page. Leave the home page check box unchecked, as shown in Figure 12.9. Click Next.

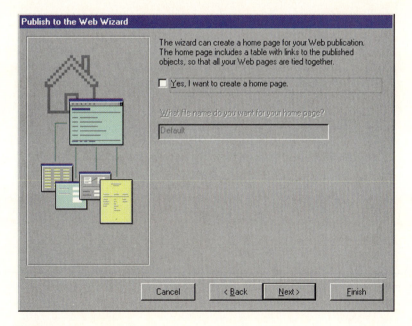

Figure 12.9

8   The last step of the Wizard is shown in Figure 12.10. Since you do not need a Web publication profile, leave the box unchecked and click Finish.

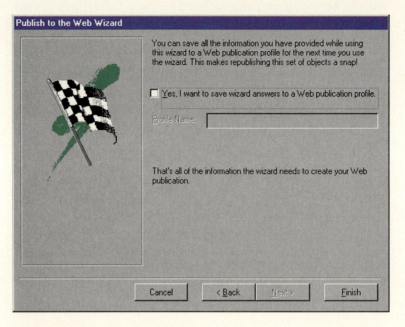

Figure 12.10

9 Close the database. You do not need to save the database file because you did not make any changes to it.

10 Exit Microsoft Access.

Your Web page has been created with the filename *Product List_1.html*. You may view your page using the Web browsers Microsoft Internet Explorer or Netscape Navigator. Figure 12.11 displays the HTML page you just created.

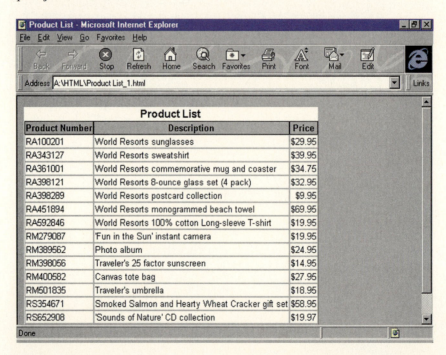

Figure 12.11

Project 12: Using Microsoft Access Data in Other Applications   ACC-291

> **Troubleshooting** If you are having problems using the Publish to the Web Wizard, highlight the *Product List* query in the Database dialog box, and select Save As/Export from the File menu. Select the HTML file format when you save your file.

Modifying HTML Documents

HTML documents are simple ASCII text files that include text and HTML codes specifying how the Web will format text and display media objects on the page. These codes, also called *tags*, are usually enclosed between the < and > characters. Figure 12.12 displays some of the HTML tags for the document you just created.

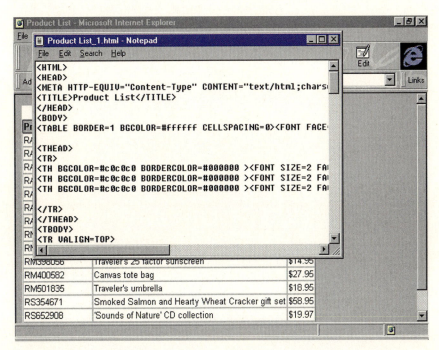

Figure 12.12

When you saved the *Product List* query you saved as an HTML document, Access converted it into a ***static HTML page***, meaning that the page represents the information in the database at a specific point in time. If a dynamic link existed between the Web page and the database file, the Web page would reflect any modifications made to the database over the course of time, and it would be a ***dynamic HTML page***.

When Access creates a static HTML page, it formats the recordset for the database object you specified as an HTML table. An ***HTML table*** represents text information in a specific row-and-column format, in which the HTML tags indicate exactly how the table will appear when viewed with a Web browser. Access generates the HTML table tags and adds these to the database field and record text.

The Web page should also include information identifying the company. Next, using Internet Explorer to open the HTML file, you will modify the HTML document by adding the company logo and text about the company.

TASK 4: TO MODIFY THE HTML DOCUMENT:

1 Launch Microsoft Internet Explorer.

> **Troubleshooting** If you are running this Web browser without accessing the World Wide Web, you may receive an error message, depending upon how your computer or network is configured. You will still be able to open your HTML document without accessing the Web by clicking OK.

2 Select Open from the File menu. The Open dialog box shown in Figure 12.13 will appear.

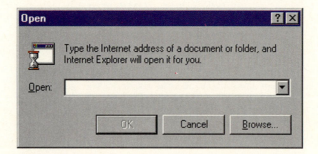

Figure 12.13

3 Click the Browse button, and select the Html folder from your floppy diskette, as shown in Figure 12.14. Open the Html folder.

Figure 12.14

4 Select the *Product List_1.html* file, and click Open. When the path and filename appear in the Open dialog box, click OK to open the document. Explorer will now display the HTML document.

Project 12: Using Microsoft Access Data in Other Applications ACC-293

> **Tip** You can also accomplish Steps 3 and 4 by entering the path and file name directly in the Address text box in the Open dialog box shown in Figure 12.13.

5 Select Source from the View menu. Explorer will open your HTML file using the Notepad text editor.

> **Caution** Notice that the task bar includes two buttons: one for the *Product List* HTML document in Internet Explorer, and a second for the same HTML document in Notepad. If you continue to select Source from the View menu, you will be launching multiple instances of Notepad.

6 Place the insertion point at the end of line 6 of the document, immediately after <Body>.

7 Press ENTER twice to add two blank lines to your document. Any blank lines you add in HTML will not appear on the Web page.

8 Type **<P Align= "Center"> <Img Src = "Logo.gif">** , and press ENTER. This tag specifies that the graphic file *Logo.gif* will appear centered on the page.

> **Tip** When entering HTML tags, spaces are inconsequential, unless the spaces occur between quotes, such as in a filename.

9 Type **<P><P>** , and press ENTER. This will display two paragraph returns on your page.

10 Type **<HR>**, and press ENTER twice. This tag will add to your document a **horizontal rule,** a shadowed line extending horizontally across the page.

11 Select Save from the File menu. Your HTML document should now look like Figure 12.15.

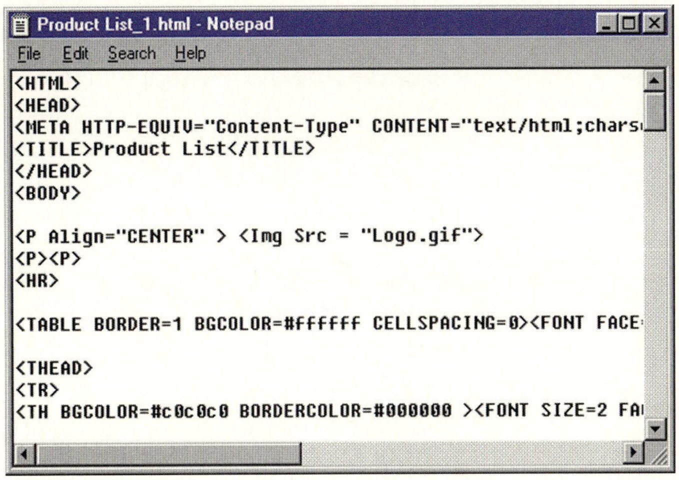

```
Product List_1.html - Notepad
File  Edit  Search  Help
<HTML>
<HEAD>
<META HTTP-EQUIV="Content-Type" CONTENT="text/html;chars
<TITLE>Product List</TITLE>
</HEAD>
<BODY>

<P Align="CENTER" > <Img Src = "Logo.gif">
<P><P>
<HR>

<TABLE BORDER=1 BGCOLOR=#ffffff CELLSPACING=0><FONT FACE

<THEAD>
<TR>
<TH BGCOLOR=#c0c0c0 BORDERCOLOR=#000000 ><FONT SIZE=2 FA
```

Figure 12.15

12 Using the Windows 95 task bar, switch to Explorer.

13 Press the Refresh button, or if the toolbar is not currently visible, select Refresh from the View menu. Your document should look like Figure 12.16. Notice the added company logo.

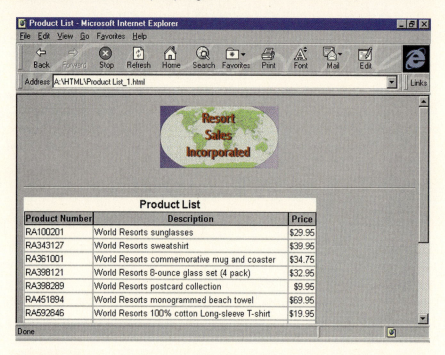

Figure 12.16

14 Switch to Windows Notepad, and place the insertion point in the line following the <HR> tag.

15 Type **<H1> <P Align ="Center"> Resort Sales Incorporated </H1>**, and press ENTER. This will enter a centered title formatted as a Level 2 heading.

16 Type **<HR></HR>**, and press ENTER.

17 Type **<H3> <P Align = "Left"> Welcome to the Resort Sales Incorporated Home Page! Below you will find a listing of our products. To place an order, please contact our Sales Department.</H3>**, and press ENTER. This will add a descriptive paragraph as a Level 3 heading.

18 Place the insertion point immediately after the word "BODY" in the sixth line of the text document. Make sure the insertion point is between the letter Y and the > character.

19 Press the spacebar once, and type **leftmargin = 80 Background = Border.gif**. This will add an additional graphic to the background.

20 Select Save from the File menu, and close Notepad.

21 Switch to Microsoft Internet Explorer, and refresh the screen. Your document will look like Figure 12.17. When you are finished viewing your document, close Explorer.

Project 12: Using Microsoft Access Data in Other Applications   ACC-295

Figure 12.17

Creating a Database Front-End Application with Microsoft Visual Basic

As you learned in Project 10, Microsoft Access and Visual Basic share many of the same components for developing information solutions. Microsoft Access uses Visual Basic controls for developing forms, reports, and applications. Visual Basic is a programming environment for developing computer applications for the Microsoft Windows operating system. Visual Basic also supports connectivity between applications and Microsoft Access database objects. Both Visual Basic and Microsoft use the *Jet database engine*, the DBMS that retrieves data from and stores data in user and system databases.

You can use Visual Basic to create a front-end or stand-alone application to an Access database. Forms created in Microsoft Access are similar to front-end applications, in that they provide an interface that shields users from working directly with database tables and query recordsets. Why is a separate front end needed, then? Access forms are a part of the Access application, while a front end written in Visual Basic will allow your database to be used on computers that have Windows installed but not Access. Moreover, since Visual Basic is a full-featured programming environment, you can build more flexibility into your database application by using it than you could if you created your database using Access alone.

In Visual Basic there are two modes of operation. **Design time** refers to the work environment used to create the application. You create forms, add controls to forms, and write code in design time. **Run time** refers to the application as it is being executed. In the Visual Basic environment, you can view your application in run time from within design time.

The remaining tasks in this project are devoted to building a *stand-alone application,* one that can be run independent of Microsoft Access. You will build an application that connects to the *Customers* data table in the Resort Sales 6 database. Although a working knowledge of Visual Basic version 5 is helpful, even without that, many of the concepts and procedures introduced here will be familiar to you. The application you will create appears as shown in Figure 12.18.

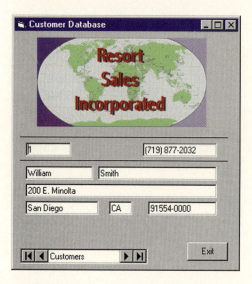

Figure 12.18

The procedures for building this application are similar to working with forms and reports in Microsoft Access. You will construct a *Visual Basic project* that consists of at least one form. The form will contain various controls, some containing Visual Basic code. You will save the form and project as files for later use by the Setup Wizard in creating a set of diskettes for installing the application.

You will complete five tasks to create your database application. First, you will create the new Visual Basic project. Second, you will add a data control to your application's form. Third, you will add text box, label, and command button controls to the form. Fourth, you will write a *form load event,* which specifies what occurs when the application is run. Finally, you will create a set of installation diskettes for installing your application.

TASK 5: TO CREATE A NEW VISUAL BASIC PROJECT:

1. Launch Visual Basic version 5.

   Troubleshooting If you do not know how to launch Visual Basic, ask your instructor for assistance.

2. In the New Project dialog box, select Standard EXE, as shown in Figure 12.19.

Project 12: Using Microsoft Access Data in Other Applications   ACC-297

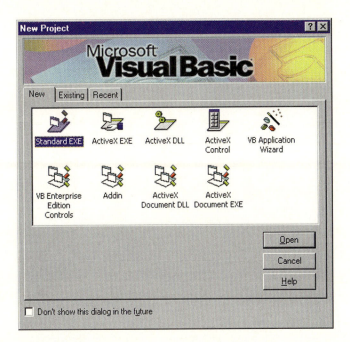

Figure 12.19

3 Select Form 1 from the drop-down list at the top of the Properties window, and resize it to about the same size as the form shown in Figure 12.20.

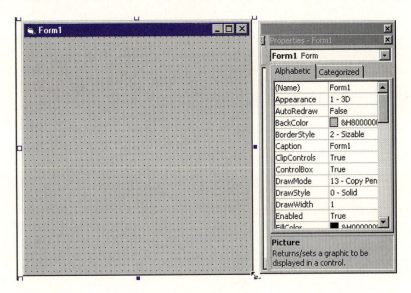

Figure 12.20

4 Using the Toolbox, create an image control in the upper center portion of Form 1.

5 In the Properties window, select the Picture property for the control you just created, and click the small button with the ellipsis (three dots), as shown in Figure 12.21.

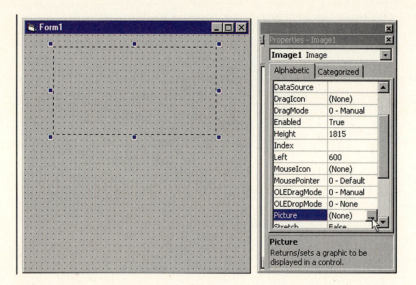

Figure 12.21

6. Select the *Logo.bmp* file, which is in the VB5 folder on your floppy diskette, and click Open. The image will appear in the image control.

7. Right-click the gray portion of the form. The title bar of the Properties window will change to Form 1. Type **Customer Database** as the caption property in the Properties window for the form. Select Save Project from the File menu. The Save File As dialog box will appear.

8. Type **frmCustomers.frm** as the name of the form, and select Vb5 as the folder on your floppy diskette to save the form in, as shown in Figure 12.22. Click Save to save the form.

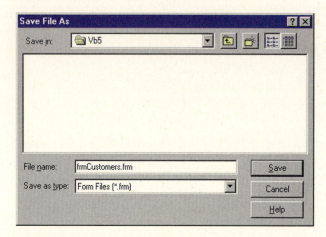

Figure 12.22

9. Since this is a new project, you will need to save the project file as well. Type **Customers.vbp** as the name of the project, as shown in Figure 12.23. Click Save to save the project.

Project 12: Using Microsoft Access Data in Other Applications   ACC-299

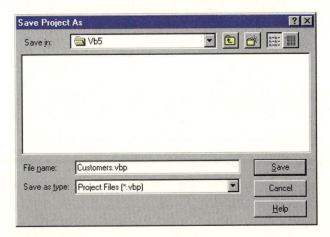

Figure 12.23

Visual Basic Naming Conventions

Visual Basic programmers usually name Visual Basic objects in a consistent manner. Each control has a three-character identifier that specifies the control type. Table 12.1 lists the three-character identifier for certain objects. After the identifier comes the descriptive name, explaining what the control does. The descriptive name usually begins with a cap letter, consists of one or more words, and avoids spaces and special characters.

Table 12.1 Visual Basic Naming Conventions

Object	Three-Character Identifier
Form	Frm
Text box	Txt
Label	Lbl
Command button	Cmd
Data control	Dat

Using the Visual Basic Data Control

To display Microsoft Access data in a Visual Basic application, you must first establish a connection between the data source (the Access recordset) and the application. You can easily do this by adding a data control to your Visual Basic form. Recall from Project 10 that the data control enables you to move from record to record and to display and manipulate data from the records in bound controls. After adding a data control to the form, you can then bind controls to the data control.

ACC-300

TASK 6: TO ADD A DATA CONTROL TO YOUR APPLICATION:

1. Select the Data Control tool from the Toolbox, as shown in Figure 12.24.

Figure 12.24

2. Draw a data control near the lower left of the form.

3. Right-click over the data control to display its default properties in the Properties window.

4. Type **datCustomers** as the Name property, and **Customers** as the Caption property.

5. Click inside the DatabaseName field, and select the ellipsis button. Select *Resort Sales 6.mdb* from your floppy diskette as the file name for the database, and click Open, as shown in Figure 12.25.

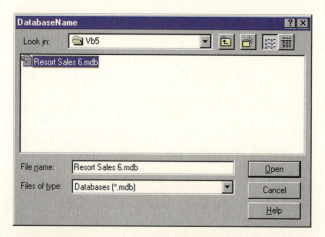

Figure 12.25

Project 12: Using Microsoft Access Data in Other Applications   ACC-301

6 Scroll down the Properties window until RecordSource is visible. You will use this property to specify a database object to bind the database to.

7 Click inside the RecordSource field, and click the drop-down list arrow. Select Customers in the list, as shown in Figure 12.26.

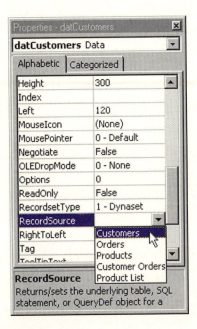

Figure 12.26

8 Select Save from the File menu to save your project.

9 Select Start from the Run menu, as shown in Figure 12.27. This will allow you to view your application in run time.

Figure 12.27

10 The form will display in run time, as shown in Figure 12.28. Notice that the caption for the form appears in the data control, and that the image is displayed on the form.

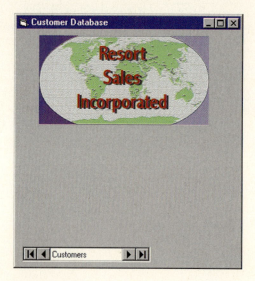

Figure 12.28

11 Select End from the Run menu to return to design time.

Adding Controls to a Visual Basic Form

Now that you have established a connection between the Access database object and your *Customers* form (the Visual Basic front-end application), you may add controls to the form. In Project 10 you learned the difference between bound and unbound controls. In this section you will bind text box controls to the data control, and add unbound line and command button controls to the form to enhance its appearance and functionality.

TASK 7: TO ADD CONTROLS TO THE VISUAL BASIC FORM:

1 Select the Line Control tool from the Toolbox, and add a line control immediately below the image control. Extend the control across the entire form, leaving only a small margin on the left and right edges of the form.

2 With the line still selected, select Copy and then Paste from the Edit menu, to make a copy of the control.

3 The dialog box shown in Figure 12.29 will display. You do not want to create a control array, so click No.

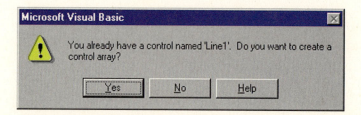

Figure 12.29

4 Notice that Visual Basic has added a new line control at the very top of the form. Its selection handles should be visible. Move the control below the other line control you created.

5 Select the Text Box tool from the Toolbox, and draw a text box control between the two lines, near the left side of the form.

6 Notice that the properties for the control appear in the Properties window. Enter **txtCustID** as the Name property, select datCustomers from the drop-down list as the DataSource, enter **CustID** as the DataField, and **Customer Number** as the Text.

7 Select Start from the Run menu. In run time, the form should look like Figure 12.30.

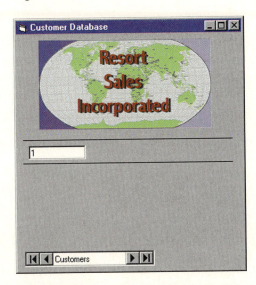

Figure 12.30

8 Select End from the Run menu to return to design time.

9 Highlight the text box control on the form, and select Copy from the Edit menu.

10 Paste seven additional text box controls to the form, each time indicating that you do not wish to create a control array.

11 Position and size the controls on the form as shown in Figure 12.31.

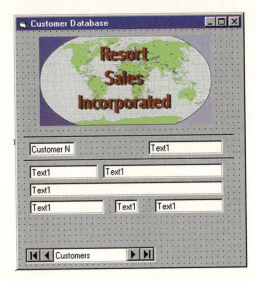

Figure 12.31

12 Using the values displayed in Table 12.2, change the Name, DataField, and Text properties of each control. Refer to Figure 12.32 if necessary.

Table 12.2 Employee Identification Data

Control Name	Control DataField	Control Text
TxtPhone	HomePhone	Phone
TxtFirstName	FirstName	First
TxtLastName	LastName	Last
TxtAddress	Address	Address
TxtCity	City	City
TxtState	State	State
TxtZipcode	ZipCode	ZipCode

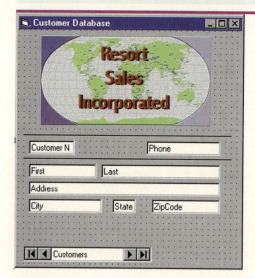

Figure 12.32

13 Using the Command Button control tool, create a command button on the lower right side of the form.

14 Set the Name property to cmdExit and the Caption property to Exit.

15 Right-click the command button, and select View Code from the shortcut menu, as shown in Figure 12.33.

Project 12: Using Microsoft Access Data in Other Applications   ACC-305

Figure 12.33

16 The code window will open. Select cmdExit as the control in the left drop-down list, as shown in Figure 12.34. This control will contain code to exit the application when the user clicks this button.

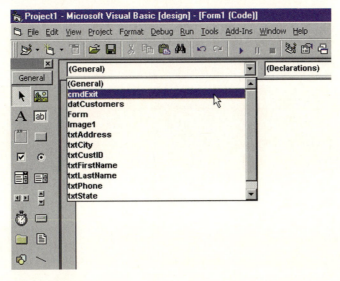

Figure 12.34

17 Type **End** between the Private Sub and End Sub statements, as shown in Figure 12.35. This code specifies that in response to a button click event, the command button control will close the application.

Figure 12.35

18 Save your project.

19 Run your project. The application should look similar to Figure 12.36. Notice that the bound controls display data from a single record shown in the data control.

Figure 12.36

20 Click the Exit button. The application will close and Visual Basic will return to design time.

Creating a Form Load Event

Your Visual Basic application for accessing the *Customers* database table is almost complete. Before compiling it into an executable file and creating a set of installation diskettes, however, you need to make one last change.

When you set the properties for the data control, you specified that it should look for the *Resort Sales 6.mdb* database in the VB5 directory on your floppy diskette. Since the DatabaseName property of the data control contains the names of both the database file and the path, the application will always look for the database file in the VB5 directory on a floppy diskette. This will cause a run time error if the application is installed to and running from a hard disk.

Visual Basic will allow you to set the path of your Access database file in the directory where the executable file (the front-end application) resides. As long as both files are located in the same directory, an error will not occur. You can write code to set the path of the database file to the same path as the application to the event of the form being loaded into memory when users run the front-end application. In this way, the application is *path-independent,* meaning that the front-end's data control will look for the database in the same path as the front end itself, regardless of where it is physically located. The Visual Basic App object has a Path property specifying the application path at runtime. Therefore, adding the ***App.Path statement*** to the form load event will set the path for both the Access database file and the Visual Basic executable file.

TASK 8: TO ADD CODE FOR THE FORM LOAD EVENT:

1. Select the datCustomer data control, and delete the value of the DatabaseName property. When deleted, the cell should be blank.

2. Right-click somewhere over Form 1, but not on a specific control. Select View Code from the shortcut menu.

3. Select Form from the drop-down list located in the left side of the code window.

4. The code should look like Figure 12.37, with the insertion point should be between the Private Sub Form_Load() and End Sub statements.

Figure 12.37

5 Type **datCustomers.DatabaseName = App.Path & "\Resort Sales 6.mdb"**, and press ENTER.

6 Type **datCustomers.Refresh**, and press ENTER. The code window should now look like Figure 12.38.

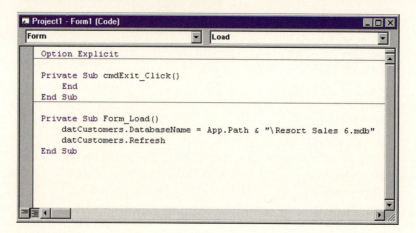

Figure 12.38

7 Save the project.

8 Run the project. It should run without errors.

9 Return to design time.

10 Select Make Customers.exe from the File menu, as shown in Figure 12.39.

Figure 12.39

11 Select the default file name *Customers.exe*, and specify that the executable file should be stored in the Vb5 directory on your floppy diskette, as shown in Figure 12.40. Click OK.

Project 12: Using Microsoft Access Data in Other Applications   ACC-309

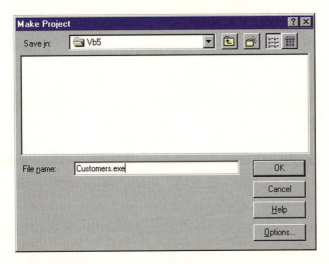

Figure 12.40

12 Exit Visual Basic. Save any changes you have made to your project.

Using the Visual Basic Setup Wizard to Make Your Application Installable

With the help of the Visual Basic Application Setup Wizard, you will now create a distribution set of diskettes for installing your application. You will need three blank 1.44-megabyte floppy diskettes for this task.

TASK 9: TO CREATE AN INSTALLATION SET USING THE SETUP WIZARD:

1 Create a temporary folder VbSetup on the C drive.

> **Tip** You are creating this folder because you will need to use the floppy diskette drive to create the distribution diskettes.

2 Copy all the files in the Vb5 folder on your floppy diskette to VbSetup. When all the files are copied, remove your data diskette from the drive.

3 Launch Visual Basic's Application Setup Wizard, as shown in Figure 12.41.

ACC-310

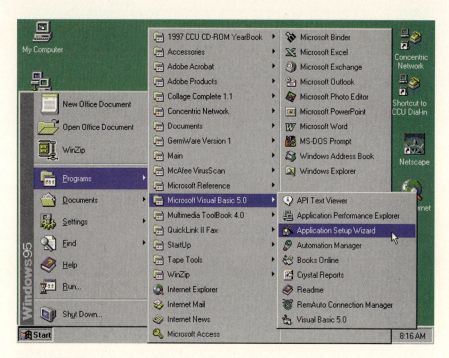

Figure 12.41

4 If the Introduction screen shown in Figure 12.42 appears, click Next.

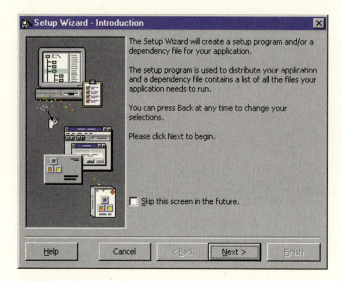

Figure 12.42

5 The Setup Wizard should find your project on the C drive in the VbSetup folder. When the path and filename for your project file match Figure 12.43, click Next.

Project 12: Using Microsoft Access Data in Other Applications   ACC-311

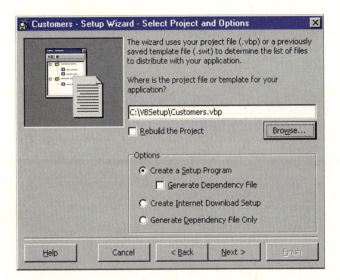

Figure 12.43

Troubleshooting If you created the VBSetup folder on a drive other than C, make sure the appropriate drive letter appears in the path.

6. Select the option to distribute your application on floppy disk, as shown in Figure 12.44. Click Next.

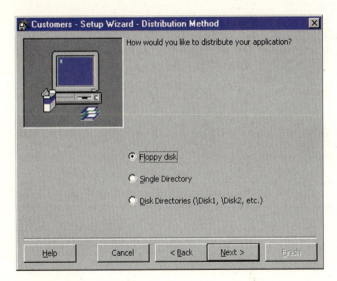

Figure 12.44

7. In the Floppy Disk dialog box shown in Figure 12.45, select the appropriate drive letter and disk size, and click Next.

ACC-312

Figure 12.45

8. In the Data Access dialog box, make sure the check box for dbUseJet is selected (since your application uses a Microsoft Access database), as shown in Figure 12.46. Leave all the check boxes for installable ISAMs unchecked, and click Next.

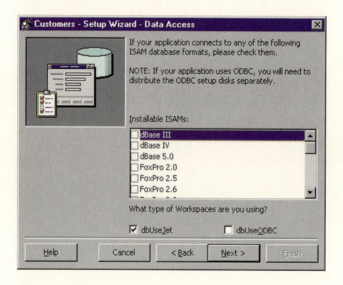

Figure 12.46

9. When the ActiveX Server Components dialog box shown in Figure 12.47 appears, click Next since your application does not use any of these components.

Project 12: Using Microsoft Access Data in Other Applications ACC-313

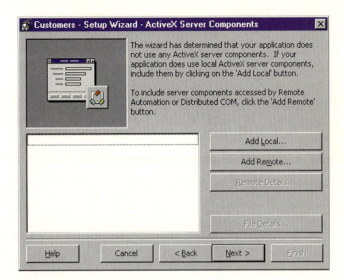

Figure 12.47

10 In the Confirm Dependencies dialog box, assume that the dependencies listed in Figure 12.48 are correct, and click Next.

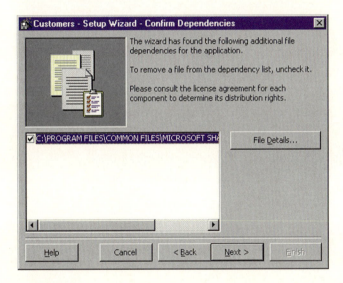

Figure 12.48

11 When the File Summary dialog box appears, click the Add button, as shown in Figure 12.49. You will need to specify the location of your Resort Sales 6.mdb database file so it can be added to the file list.

ACC-314

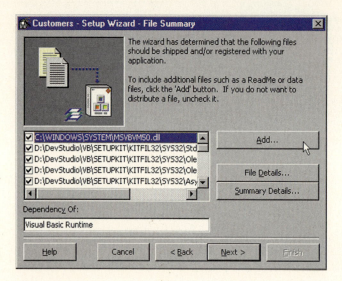

Figure 12.49

12 In the Add Files dialog box shown in Figure 12.50, select the *Resort Sales 6.mdb* file in the VbSetup folder on the C drive. Click Open.

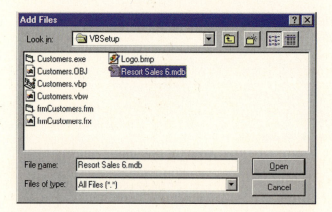

Figure 12.50

13 Notice that the Setup Wizard has added the database file to the list of files to be included in the distribution set, as shown in Figure 12.51. Click Next.

Project 12: Using Microsoft Access Data in Other Applications   ACC-315

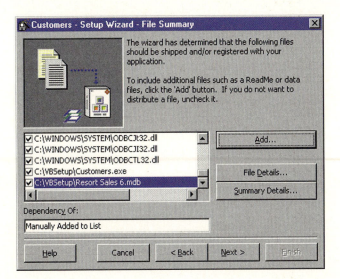

Figure 12.51

14 The Setup Wizard now has all the information it needs to create your diskettes. You do not need to create a template, so click Finish in the dialog box shown in Figure 12.52.

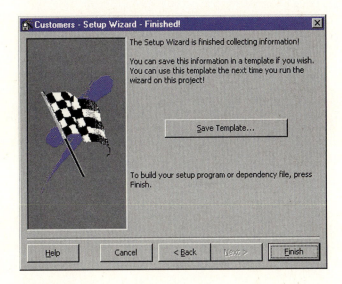

Figure 12.52

15 The wizard will begin compressing the files in the list. When this task is finished, the dialog box shown in Figure 12.53 appears. Place a diskette in the A drive, and press OK.

Figure 12.53

16 Follow the instructions that appear on the screen, inserting a new disk when prompted.

> **Tip** Make sure you label your diskettes as they are created!

17 The dialog box shown in Figure 12.54 appears when your diskettes have been created successfully. Click OK.

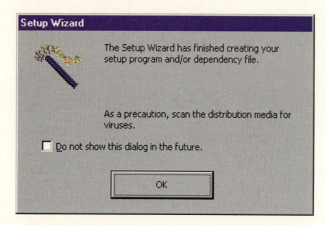

Figure 12.54

18 Delete the VbSetup folder from the C drive.

> **Troubleshooting** On some computer systems you will not see the dialog box shown in Figure 12.54 because it has been disabled.

To install your application on another computer, place the first diskette of the set in the floppy disk drive, and select Run from the Start menu on the Windows Taskbar. Run the Setup.exe program from the floppy diskette and follow the directions on the screen.

The Conclusion

In this project you have learned two methods for using Microsoft Access data in other applications. Publishing Access data as HTML documents makes information available on the World Wide Web or on a corporate intranet. You can also use Visual Basic to write a database front-end application, so that users without Microsoft Access installed on their computers can still work with the database.

Summary and Exercises

Summary

- By using the Save to HTML feature in Microsoft Access, database objects can be converted to static and dynamic HTML documents.
- Once an HTML document has been created, it can be modified using a text editor such as the Windows Notepad.
- Visual Basic and Microsoft Access share the same Jet database engine.
- A data control establishes a connection between a Visual Basic application and a Microsoft Access database.
- You can make a Visual Basic application connected to an Access database path-independent by adding an App.Path statement to the form load event.
- Once a Visual Basic project is complete, you use the Application Setup Wizard to create a distribution set.

Key Terms and Operations

Key Terms
app.path statement
design time
dynamic HTML page
form load event
front-end application
horizontal rule
HTML (HyperText Markup Language)
HTML table
Intranet
Jet database engine
path-independent
run time
stand-alone application
static HTML page
tags
Visual Basic project

Operations
add bound and unbound controls to a Visual Basic form
create a distribution set
create a Microsoft Access query object
create a Visual Basic application as a database front end
establish a connection between a Visual Basic application and a Microsoft Access database using a data control
export query data to an HTML document
modify an HTML document to display additional text and images

Study Questions

Multiple Choice

1. Which of the following do you use to create a set of diskettes for installing a Visual Basic application?
   a. the Jet database engine
   b. Visual Basic
   c. the Visual Basic Setup Wizard
   d. Microsoft Access
   e. Microsoft Internet Explorer

2. Which tag is used to display a line across an HTML page?
   a. <H1>
   b. <P>
   c. <Align = "Center">
   d. <Body>
   e. <HR>

3. The HyperText Markup Language is used to
   a. add event procedures to a Visual Basic form.
   b. specify which fields to include in a query.
   c. add functionality to a Microsoft Access form.
   d. add tags to a Web page document.
   e. link one table to another.

4. Which of the following is a bound control?
   a. command button control
   b. image control
   c. line control
   d. label control
   e. data control

5. The App.Path statement is used to
   a. avoid path dependence.
   b. set the path for opening an HTML document.
   c. Specify the first form displayed in a Visual Basic application.
   d. bind the data control to a text box control.
   e. display images on a Web page.

6. Visual basic supports how many modes (also called time)?
   a. none
   b. one
   c. two
   d. three
   e. four

7. Which control displays a bitmap on a Visual Basic form?
   a. text box
   b. data control
   c. line control
   d. image control
   e. form control

8. A front-end application usually provides an interface to what?
   a. a web browser
   b. an HTML document
   c. a Visual Basic application
   d. a text editor
   e. a database

9. What do HTML documents primarily consist of?
   a. ASCII text
   b. programming code and event procedures
   c. images
   d. data from an Access table
   e. tags

10. Visual Basic is which category of software?
    a. a Web browser
    b. a database file
    c. a programming environment
    d. a text editor
    e. a database management system

Short Answer

1. Database field information is displayed in a Visual Basic application using what kind of control?

2. What items in HTML documents indicate how a Web browser will display data?

3. What is the term for a series of diskettes used to install software applications?

4. A static HTML page created from an Access report represents what?

5. What does HTML stand for?

6. An HTML document consists of what kind of data?

7. What item establishes a connection between a Visual Basic application and a Microsoft Access database object?

8. You add controls to a Visual Basic application in what mode?

9. What tag do you use to add a line appearing in an HTML document?

10. Microsoft Access and Visual Basic both use what engine to work with database information?

For Discussion

1. What is an HTML document? What does it contain?

2. How does an HTML document display images?

3. What is a database front end?

4. Why is the App.Path statement useful when a Visual Basic application is connected to a Microsoft Access database?

Review Exercises

1. Creating a Visual Basic Front-End Application for the *Employees* Database

Some of the data entry personnel in your company do not have Microsoft Access installed on their computers, but they need to be able to use the *Employees* database you created and modified in previous projects. To create a Visual Basic front end for the database, complete the following:

1. Launch Visual Basic.

2. Create a Standard.exe project.

3. Set the caption property of the default form to frmGrossPay.

4. Add a data control to the form and name it **datGrossPay**.

5. Set the DatabaseName property of the control to the *Employees.mdb* database.

6. Set the RecordSource property of the data control to the *GrossPay* query.

7. Create a text box control for each field data element. Give each text box control an appropriate name, and set the DataSource and Field properties for each.

8. Remove the value from the DatabaseName property from the data control.

9. Add a form load event procedure with an App.Path statement linking the data control to the Access database file.

10. Save the form as *frmGrossPay.frm* and the Visual Basic project as *Gross Pay.vbp*.

2. Creating a Distribution Set to Install the *Gross Pay* Database Front-End Application

To install the database front end you just created, you will need to create a distribution set:

1. Create a temporary folder on the hard drive of your computer.
2. Copy the appropriate files into this folder.
3. Launch the Visual Basic Application Setup Wizard.
4. Complete the steps required for creating a distribution set. Make sure you include the database file.
5. When finished, delete the temporary folder you created.
6. Test your installation.

Assignments

1. Creating a Visual Basic Front-End Application for the Student Database

Open the student database you have worked with in previous projects. Design a Visual Basic application with one form that returns data from the query listing courses taken by each student. Save the form and project files.

2. Create an HTML Page of Restaurants

Open the Vail eating establishments database you have been working with in Assignment 2 of previous projects. Create an HTML document from the query displaying cuisine categories according to restaurant. Add additional text as necessary.

Operations Reference

Function	Mouse Action or Button	Menu	Keyboard Shortcut
Database, close	Click ✕	Choose File, Close	
Database, create new		Choose File, New Database	Press CTRL+N
Display page of Database window	Click page tab	Choose View, Database Objects, *Object*	Press CTRL+TAB until the database window page appears
Database, open existing	Click 📂	Choose File, Open	Press CTRL+O
Datasheet View, Query	Click	Select Datasheet View from the View menu	
Datasheet View, Table	Click	Select Datasheet View from the View menu	
Design View, Form	Click	Select Design View from the View menu	
Design View, Query	Click	Select Design View from the View menu	
Design View, Table	Click	Select Design View from the View menu	
Exit	Click ✕	Choose File, Exit	
Field, delete	Display table in Design view, click field row, and click	Display table in Design view, click field row, and choose Edit, Delete Rows	
Field, sort	Activate field and click A↓ or Z↓	Activate field and choose Records, Sort, Sort order	Display table in Design view, click field row, and press DELETE
Field List, Display	Click	Select Field List from the View menu	
Form, create new	Display table or query and click	Select table or query name in database window and choose Insert, Form	
Form, design	Select form name in database window and click Design button OR Open form and click	Open form and choose View, Design View	
Form, open	Select form name in database window and click Open button		Select form name in Forms page of database window and press ENTER
Form View Form	Click	Select Form View from the View menu	
HTML, creating from a database		Select Save As HTML from the File menu	
Key Field, assign		Display table in Design view, click field, and choose Edit, Primary Key	
Object, create new	Click New button on object page of database window		Press ALT+N on object page of database window

EM-1

Function	Mouse Action or Button	Menu	Keyboard Shortcut
Preview	Click	Choose File, Print Preview	
Print	Click	Choose File, Print	Press CTRL+**P**
Properties, Display	Click	Select Properties from the View menu	
Query, add fields	Double-click field name		
Query, add table	Click	Choose Query, Show Table	
Query, design	Select query name in database window and click Design button OR Open query and click	Open query and choose View, Design View	
Query, open	Select query name in database window and click Open button		Select query name in Forms page of database window and press ENTER
Query, run	Click	Choose Query, Run	
Query, save	Click	Choose File, Save	Press CTRL+**S**
Query, delete		Select the record and choose Edit, Delete Record	Select record and press DEL
Record, insert	Display table to contain record and click	Open table to contain record and choose Insert, New Record	
Relationships, creating		Select Relationships from the Tools menu	
Report, create	Display table or query and select AutoReport from drop-down list arrow	Select table or query name in database window and choose Insert, Report	
Report, design	Select report name in database window and click Design button OR Open report and click	Open report and choose View, Design View	
Report, Design View	Click	Select Design View from the View menu	
Report, open	Select report name in database window and click Open button		Select report name in Forms page of database window and press ENTER
Report, Print Preview	Click	Select Design View from the View menu	
Save	Click	Choose File, Save	Press CTRL+S
Send		Choose File, Send	Press ALT+**F**, **E**
Spelling check	Click	Choose Tools, Spelling and Grammar	Press F7
Table align		Click in the table and choose Table, Cell Height and Width	

EM-2

Function	Mouse Action or Button	Menu	Keyboard Shortcut
Table, copy structure	Click table name in database window, click 📋, click 📋 and type new table name	Click table name in database window, choose Edit, Paste and type new table name	Click table name in database window, press CTRL+**C**, press CTRL+**V** and type new table name
Table, create		Choose Table, Insert Table	
Table, design	Select table name in database window and click Design button OR Open table and click 🔲	Open table and choose View, Design View	
Table, open	Select table name in database window and click Open button		Select table name in Forms page of database window and press ENTER
Text, copy	Select the text and click 📋	Select the text and choose Edit, Copy	Press CTRL+**C**
Text, cut	Select the text and click ✂	Choose Edit, Cut	Press CTRL+**X**
Text, find	Click 🔍	Choose Edit, Find	Press CTRL+**F**
Text, Import		Select Get External Data and Import from the File menu	
Text, paste	Select the text and click 📋	Choose Edit, Paste	Press CTRL+**V**
Text, replace		Choose Edit, Replace	Press CTRL+**H**
Text, select	Drag through text		Press SHIFT+any cursor movement key, such as → or END
Toolbox, displaying	Click 🧰	Select Toolbox from the View menu	
Undo	Click ↶	Choose Edit, Undo	Press CTRL+**Z**
View, change	Click 📝 or 🔲	Choose View, Type View	
Web	Click 🌐	Choose Help, Microsoft on the Web	

EM-3

Glossary

A → B Symbolic notation representing a functional dependency.

App.path statement A Visual Basic property that specifies the application path at runtime for a given object such as a database file.

Application An application organizes related tasks so that the user can focus on the task at hand, not on how the application works or on how a specific program is used to develop the application.

Ascending order A sort order in which you arrange records alphabetically from A to Z or numerically from smallest to largest.

ASCII text A format for storing computer data, consisting of the letters a through z, the digits 0 through 9, and special characters. ASCII data can be shared among microcomputers using different operating systems.

Attribute One or more characteristics of an entity that distinguish it from other entity instances. In an address database, last name is an example of an entity.

AutoForm A feature that you use to create forms using the fields and information stored as part of the table or query.

AutoLookup field A field in a query that evokes a list of data items when the field is selected for data entry.

AutoReport A feature you use to create simple report formats using the fields contained in a table or query.

Bound control A control that accesses data from a field in an underlying table or query.

Boyce-Codd normal form (BCNF) A stage of database normalization where every determinant in a relation is a candidate key.

Calculated control A control that uses an expression as its data source.

Calculated field A field in a query that contains an expression for performing a calculation using the underlying table data.

Candidate key One or more fields in a database that uniquely identify each record.

Caption A name or title that identifies field data on a form or report.

Cardinality The number of instances of one entity that can or must be associated with instances of a second entity.

Compound key A candidate key consisting of more than one attribute.

Conceptual data model A conceptual model that displays the overall structure of an organization's data flow, and the specific data requirements. The conceptual data model is developed independent of any specific RDBMS.

Control A Visual Basic object that is added to a form or a report. Controls include labels, text boxes, and buttons, to name a few.

Controls Field labels and field data boxes that appear in the Detail section of a form or report in Design view.

Criteria Conditions you set in a grid to limit the information displayed in the datasheet.

Data Raw, unevaluated facts and figures that have not been interpreted in any way.

Data control A control which is bound to a Microsoft Access recordset.

Database design process A systematic approach to designing a database system that includes planning, analysis, design, and implementation phases.

Database management system (DBMS) A computer application used to create and maintain computer databases.

Data dictionary A paper document that lists all the database entities and their attributes that are used to design the structure of a database.

Datasheet view The view in which you can see multiple records on-screen at the same time; this view makes data entry more efficient.

Deletion anomaly Data errors that occur in a database when records are deleted from one, but not all related tables.

Delimited text ASCII text listing database fields where each field is bound by one or more characters so as to differentiate it.

Delimiting character (delimiter) The specific character is a delimited file that differentiates field data.

Descending order A sort order in which you arrange records alphabetically from Z to A or numerically from largest to smallest.

Design time The Visual Basic work environment used to create an application.

Detail section The part of a form or report that holds the field data controls and pulls information from database tables.

Determinant The attribute in a functional dependency that uniquely identifies a second attribute.

Dimmed control   A control that is currently unavailable. Dimmed controls appear in gray.

Dynamic HTML page   A Web page linked to a database that reflects any modifications made to the database over the course of time.

Enterprise data model   A high-level conceptual model listing an organization's entities, and the relationships that exist between them.

Entity   A person, place, thing, or event about which an organization keeps data.

Entity-relationship (E-R) diagram   A diagram displaying entities, attributes, and relationships. E-R diagrams usually include notation for indicating the cardinality of relationships.

Event procedure   A Visual Basic programming statement indicating what actions will occur in response to a user, system, or error event.

Field   The common term for an attribute in a relational database.

Field data box   The part of the field control that connects data from a table to a form or report.

Field label   The part of the field control that identifies data in a form or report.

File processing systems   Manual systems used to manage data. File processing systems are usually characterized by inefficiency and data redundancy.

Filter   To select only those records in a table that contain the specified value in the selected field.

First normal form (1NF)   A stage of normalization in which all multi-valued attributes or repeating groups have been eliminated from a table.

Form   An aesthetically pleasing layout of table data designed to display one record on-screen at a time.

Form Header/Footer   The area of a form in which you supply information such as the form title that you want to display on each screen or printed page.

Form load event   An event specifying what occurs first when a Visual Basic application is run.

Form view   The view which displays records on-screen one at a time in an aesthetically pleasing format.

Form Wizard   A Microsoft Wizard available in Access to assist with designing forms.

Front-end application   An application containing a user interface and methods for interacting with data stored in a database table.

Functional dependency   Attribute B is functionally dependent upon attribute A if the value of A uniquely determines each valid instance of attribute B.

Gridlines   Cell borders in Datasheet view used to separate fields of data and records. Also, lines displayed in Form Design View and Report Design View to mark sections of the form or report to help align fields.

Grid points   Dots displayed on-screen in Form Design or Report Design view that help you align field controls.

Horizontal rule   An HTML tag that places a horizontal line across the page when it is displayed using a graphical browser.

HTML (HyperText Markup Language)   HTML codes specifying how the Web will format text and display media objects on the page.

HTML table   Text information displayed in a row-and-column format, in which the HTML tags indicate exactly how the table will appear with a Web browser.

Image control   A Visual Basic control used to display image files in a form.

Information   Data that has been evaluated, interpreted, or otherwise determined to be of value.

Input mask   A table design specification consisting of a series of characters that control how data is entered in a field.

Insertion anomaly   Errors that occur in a database when new records are added to the database.

Instance   A unique database record for a given entity.

Intranet   A private network using Web technology to publish information in HTML.

Jet database engine   The underlying database system that is used by both Microsoft Access and Visual Basic.

Key field   A field that contains different (unique) data for each record and that you can use to organize records. You can assign only one key field to each table.

Label control   A Visual Basic control that is used to add descriptive text to a form or report.

Labels   A control appearing on a form or report that contains descriptive text that is never changed.

Layout Preview   The view in which Access displays a report using only a few records so that you can check the layout and then make adjustments before printing.

Locked property   A property of certain controls specifying whether they can be selected and changed.

Macro   A mini program that stores a set of instructions designed to perform a particular task.

Main form A Microsoft Access form that will contain a subform.

Mandatory cardinality A circumstance in which a record that exists in one table must also exist in a related table. For example, in a sales database, orders must be placed by a customer.

Menu bar The bar at the top of the window that provides access to commands used to perform tasks. The menu bar changes, depending on the task you're performing.

Migrate data The process of converting existing data for use in a newly designed RDBMS.

Modification anomaly Errors that occur in a database when one or more of the records are changed.

Module A collection of Visual Basic programming procedures stored together to customize the Access environment.

Multivalued attributes Attributes that can have more than one value for each record.

Normal form The stages in Codd's database normalization process.

Normalization The process of applying the normal forms to a database design to improve efficiency, reduce data redundancy, and minimize anomalies.

Object A table, query, form, report, macro, or module in a database.

Office Assistant The new on-the-spot Help feature that pops up frequently to offer help on the task you're performing. Office Assistant enables you to ask questions about the task you want to perform.

One-to-many relationship A cardinality where a record in one table is related to a one or more records in another table.

One-to-one relationship A cardinality where a record in one table is related to a single record in another table.

Online help The help provided by the software and accessible from the computer.

Optional cardinality A cardinality where a record is not required in both tables when the two tables are related.

Page Header/Footer The part of a page displayed in Report Design view in which you place information you want to appear on each printed report page.

Partial functional dependency A partial dependency occurs when one or more nonkey attributes are not fully functionally dependent on the entire primary key.

Path-independent Path independence means that a database front-end application's data control will look for the database file in the same path as the front end itself, regardless of where it is physically located.

Primary key The candidate key that the database designer selects to be the unique identifier for an entity.

Query A structured guideline used to search database tables and retrieve records that meet specific conditions.

Query grid The lower pane of the Query window where you tell Access which fields you want to use or display in a query.

Read-only A property of certain bound controls that prevents users from changing the underlying data.

Receive the focus A property of certain controls meaning that they can be selected. A dimmed control cannot receive the focus.

Record A database record is comprised of the field data (attributes) representing one instance of an entity. An example is all the data for a customer in a customer database.

Recordset The records in a table or query that are displayed when running a query.

Referential integrity Rules applied to relationships ensuring that relationships between records in related tables are valid, and that you don't accidentally delete or change related data.

Relation A database table that has been normalized to Codd's First Normal Form (1NF).

Relational database A database, based on the relational model invented in 1969, that enables you to store data using a variety of different objects and manipulate data using relational operations.

Relational database management system (RDBMS) A database management system designed to utilize Codd's relational model. An RDBMS supports establishing relationships among data tables.

Relational model A database model that differs from both the network and the hierarchical models. Developed by E. F. Codd, the relational model is the model upon which the most powerful microcomputer database management systems are based.

Relationships Connections between fields of tables contained in a database to identify common field data.

Repeating groups Two attributes in one relation that are related to a single attribute in another relation.

Report An organized format for summarizing and grouping database data to provide meaningful information. Also an Access object used to format database information for printing.

Run time The Visual Basic environment used to run an application.

ScreenTips Short explanations that pop up when you point to any toolbar button, identifying the tasks the buttons perform.

Second normal form (2NF) A relation that is in the first normal form and, in addition, contains no partial dependencies.

Select query The most common type of query; it can be used to display selected fields of data in Datasheet view to make it easier to update.

Simple key A candidate or primary key based upon one attribute.

Sort To arrange records in either Datasheet view or Form view in Ascending or Descending order.

Stand-alone application In this context, a stand-alone application is a database front-end application and its underlying database file that can be run independent of Microsoft Access.

Startup form An Access form that can be used as a menu to select additional database forms.

Static HTML page A Web page that represents information from a database at a specific point in time.

Status bar The bar at the bottom of the program window that displays information about the program, instructions for performing selected tasks, active key information, and trouble messages.

Subform A form added to a main form using a mainform/subform control.

Subform/Subreport control A Visual Basic control that links data from another table or query to the existing report or form.

Table The primary object of a database that stores field names, field descriptions, and field data. Tables display multiple records in a row/column format similar to a spreadsheet layout.

Tab stop A property of certain controls specifying whether or not the user can use the tab key to select the control.

Tags See HTML tags.

Third normal form (3NF) A relation that is in both the first and the second normal form, and in addition, contains no transitive dependencies.

Title bar The bar at the top of the program window document or object window that identifies the application name and contains the application icon, Maximize/Restore, Minimize, and Close buttons.

Toolbar A palette of buttons that serve as shortcuts for performing the most common tasks.

Transitive dependency A functional dependency existing between two or more nonkey attributes.

Unbound control A Visual Basic control that does not have a data source.

Update To change the field data contained in a record.

Validation rule Rules governing data input into Access tables. These rules restrict the data can be entered.

Validation text Text that is displayed in a dialog box when a validation rule is violated.

Virtual table (virtual view) The recordset resulting when a query is run.

Visual Basic control A set of objects from the Visual Basic programming environment that add functionality to Access forms and reports.

Visual Basic project The forms, modules, and controls that comprise a Visual Basic application at design time. A project consists of at least one form.

Index

Numerals with "WIN" refer to Windows section. All other numerals refer to Access section.

Access. *See* Microsoft Access
Adding
　AutoLookup fields to queries, 211–215
　captions, 222–223
　controls to page header section, 257–261
　fields to query grids, 96–97
　records to database tables, 34–36
　titles to forms, 125–128
　Visual Basic control, 224–228
Addison-Wesley web site, 257
Aligning
　field controls on reports, 144
　fields on forms, 122–123
Altering table design, 74–91
Application
　explanation of, WIN-1, 255
　starting, WIN-4–WIN-5
App.Path statement, 307
ASCII text
　creating table from, 172–175
　explanation of, 170
　imported into Microsoft Access table, 176
Attributes
　in E-R diagram, 168
　explanation of, 166
　multivalued, 193
AutoForm, 37–38
AutoLookup fields
　added to queries, 211–214
　explanation of, 211
AutoReport
　creating, 83–84, 134–155, 257
　saving, 83–84

Bound control, 236
Boyce-Codd normal form (BCNF), 195
Building databases, 25–49

Calculated control, 236
Calculated fields
　creating, 218–221
　explanation of, 218
　renaming, 221–222
Candidate key
　Boyce-Codd normal form and, 195
　explanation of, 166–167
Captions, 222–223
Cardinalities
　explanation of, 189
　represented in E-R diagrams, 190–191
Check box, 63
Check mark, 63
Chen, Peter P., 166
Clicking
　check box, 63
　explanation of, WIN-3
Closing
　database tables, 32–33
　databases, 20
　Office Assistant, 15–16
　queries, 98–99
　Toolbox, 121
　windows, WIN-5

Codd, E. F., 164
Command Button Wizard, 237, 238, 270, 272
Comparison operators, 100
Compound key, 166, 167
Conceptual data model, 165
Context sensitive Help, WIN-14
Controls
　added to page footer section, 265–267
　added to page header section, 257–261
　added to startup form, 274–276
　added to Visual Basic form, 302–307
　aligning field, 144
　deleting and repositioning field, 268
　to report detail section, 261–265
　types of form, 236
Copying table structures, 84–85
Correcting mistakes, 35
Creating
　AutoForm, 37–38
　AutoReport, 83–84, 134–155
　database tables, 28–33
　databases, 8–10, 169–170
　form based on multitable queries, 239–242
　forms, 37–38, 115–133, 223–224, 242–245
　key fields, 82–83
　multitable queries, 209–211
　new forms, 117–118
　new queries, 94–96
　queries, 92–114
　queries based on fields, 95
　startup form, 273–274
　subforms, 242–247
Criteria
　defined, 96
　setting, 100–103

Data
　creating table object by importing, 170–175
　hidden, 58
　previewing, 40–42
　printing, 40–42
　relationship between information and, 163
　replacing, 57–59
　saving, 36
　searching for, 103
Data control. *See also* Controls
　explanation of, 236
　removing, 269–270
　with Visual Basic, 299–307
Data dictionaries
　design of, 168–169
　explanation of, 165
　updating, 192
Data repositories, 233
Database design phases, 164–165
Database management system (DBMS). *See also* Relational database management system (RDBMS)
　explanation of, 164
　jet database engine as, 295
Database tables. *See also* Tables
　adding records to, 34–36
　checking spelling in, 36–37

closing, 32–33
creating, 28–33
opening, 33–34
saving, 32–33
Databases
　building, 25–49
　closing, 20
　coping, 187–188, 235–236, 256–257
　creating, 8–10, 169–170
　designing, 6–7, 195–201
　maintaining, 50–73
　opening, 27
　programs, 4
　reducing size of, 228
　saving, 8–10
　terminology defined, 2–6
Datasheets
　navigating, 38–40
　views, 37, 39
Deleting
　field controls on forms, 268
　fields, 120, 139
　records, 59–60
　table fields, 81–82
Deletion anomaly, 193
Delimited text, 170, 171
Delimiting character (delimiter), 170
Dependencies
　functional, 192
　partial, 193
　transitive, 194, 195
Design time, Visual Basic, 295
Determinants, 192
Dialog boxes
　Access, 9
　displaying, 13–14
　Find, 53
　Replace, 58
　resizing, 285
　using, WIN-8–WIN-9
　working with, 12–14
Dimmed control, 268
Displaying
　dialog boxes, 13–14
　Form Design view, 117–118
　header sections of forms, 125
　menus, 13–14
　Office Assistant, 15–16
Distribution set, 284
Double-clicking, WIN-3
Dynamic HTML page, 288, 291

Editing queries, 104–107
Enterprise data model, 165
Entities, 166, 188
Entity-relationship (E-R) diagrams
　cardinalities represented in, 190–191
　entities and their relationships represented in, 188, 189
　explanation of, 165, 167–168
Entity-relationship model, 166–167
E-R diagrams. *See* Entity-relationship (E-R) diagrams
Event procedure, 237
Exiting
　Access, 20
　Windows, WIN-16
　Windows programs, WIN-6

EM-8

Features, looking up new, 17–18
Field controls, 144, 268
Field list, 240
Field selection
    clicking check box during, 63
    from forms, 119–120
    from reports, 137–139
Fields
    adding to query grids, 96–97
    adjusting length of, 124–125
    aligning, 122–123
    changing data, 53–55
    creating key, 82–83
    creating queries based on, 95
    deleting, 120, 139
    deleting table, 81–82
    dropping in wrong locations, 79
    explanation of, 3, 170
    filtering different, 65
    labels, 123–124
    moving, 35, 122
    not spell checking, 37
    rearranging, 78–81
    rearranging on forms, 120–122
    removing from forms, 119–120
    searching for data contained in, 103
    of tables, 106
File processing system, 163
Files, WIN-6
Filtering records
    by Form, 63–66
    by Selection, 62–63
Find dialog box, 53
First normal form (1NF), 193, 194
Form Design view
    displaying, 117–118
    identifying features of, 118–119
Form load event
    adding code for, 307–309
    creating, 306–307
    explanation of, 296
Form view, 39
Form Wizard
    explanation of, 223
    using, 236, 240
Forms. *See also* Subforms
    adding image control to, 274–276
    adding titles to, 125–128
    adjusting field lengths on, 124–125
    aligning fields on, 122–123
    altering properties to customize, 267–272
    changing field labels on, 123–124
    controls on, 236
    creating, 37–38, 115–133, 223–224, 242–245
    creating startup, 273–374
    displaying header sections of, 125
    explanation of, 5
    filtering records by, 63–66
    modifying, 115–133, 224, 237–239
    navigating, 38–40
    rearranging fields on, 120–122
    removing fields from, 119–120
    saving, 37–38, 122
    viewing complete, 53
    working with, 222
Front-end application
    explanation of, 283–284
    function of, 282
    using Visual Basic to create database, 295–299

Functional dependency, 192

Getting Help, 14–20
Graphical User Interface, WIN-1
Grid settings, query, 103
GUI, WIN-1

Header sections, 125
Help
    features available for, 14
    from Microsoft Web site, 19–20
    using Help Index for, 18–19
    using Office Assistant for, 15–18
Hidden data, 58
Home page, 289
HTML documents
    created from queries, 286–291
    modifying, 291–294
HTML (Hypertext Markup Language), 183, 285
HTML table, 291

Identifying
    Form Design view features, 118–119
    menu features, 11–12
    Report Design screen features, 135–137
    screen elements, 10–11
Image control
    added to startup form, 274–276
    explanation of, 256
Import Text Wizard, 172–175
Index, Help, 14, 18–19
Information, 163
Input mask, 176, 178
Insertion anomaly, 193
Instance, 166
Internet, 282, 285–296. *See also* World Wide Web (WWW)
Intranet
    explanation of, 285
    publishing Access data on, 282, 285–296

Jet database engine, 295

Key fields, 3, 82–83
Keys, 166–167

Label control
    explanation of, 242, 243
    using, 262
Labels
    changing form field, 123–124
    deleting, 263
Locked property, 268
Looking up new features, 17–18

Macros
    creating, 256, 267, 270–271
    explanation of, 5
Main form, 234
Maintaining databases, 50–73
Mandatory cardinality, 189
Maximize button, WIN-5
Menu bar, WIN-7, 11–12
Menus
    displaying, 13–14
    identifying features in, 11–12
    overview, WIN-7
    using, WIN-7
    working with, 11–12
Microsoft Access
    dialog box, 9
    exiting, 20
    launching, 7–8
    learning about, 9
    looking up features of, 17–18
    object-oriented relational database program, 4
    shared components of Visual Basic and, 283, 295
    sharing data from, 282
    starting, 7–8
Microsoft Internet Explorer
    launching, 292
    using, 283, 290, 293, 294
Microsoft Web site
    Access publishing information on, 285
    gettzing Help from, 19–20
Microsoft Windows
    exiting, WIN-16
    overview, WIN-1
    starting, WIN-2
Migrate data, 162
Minimize button, WIN-5
Mistakes, correcting, 35
Modification
    of forms, 115–133
    of report designs, 140–147
Modification anomaly, 193
Modules, 5
More Files, 27
Mouse, WIN-3–WIN-4
Multitable queries
    creating, 209–211
    creating form based on, 239–242
Multivalued attributes, 193
My Computer, WIN-2

Names, query, 99
Netscape Navigator, 290
Normal forms
    Boyce-Codd, 195
    explanation of, 192–193
    first, 193
    second, 193–194
    third, 194–195
Normalization
    explanation of, 186
    stages of, 192–195
Notepad, 293, 294

Object page tabs, 11
Objects, 3, 20
Office Assistant
    closing, 15–16
    displaying, 15–16
    during first launch of Access, 8
    using, 14–16, 18
One-to-many relationships, 189, 211
One-to-one relationships, 189
Opening
    database tables, 33–34
    databases, 27
    queries, 99–100
    reports, 135–137
Operating systems, WIN-1
Operators, comparison, 100
Optional cardinality, 189
Page footer section
    adding controls to, 265–267
    viewing, 137

Page header section
    adding controls to, 257–261
    moving field labels to, 140

Partial dependency, 193
Path-independent, 307
Previewing database data, 40–42
Primary key, 167
Printing
    database data, 40–42
    Help info, WIN-15
    reports, 148–149
Programs, starting, WIN-4–WIN-5
Publish to the Web Wizard
    problems using, 291
    using, 286–290

Queries
    adding AutoLookup fields to, 211–215
    adding records to orders table using, 215–218
    based on fields, 95
    closing, 98–99
    containing information to publish on Web, 285–286
    creating, 92–114
    creating form based on multitable, 239–242
    creating multitable, 209–211
    creating report based on, 257
    editing, 104–107
    explanation of, 5
    function of, 208
    opening, 99–100
    printing reports based on, 148
    published as HTML documents, 286–292
    running, 97–100
    saving, 98–99
    selecting, 94
    setting sort order for, 100–103
    windows, 106
    working with, 209
Query grids
    adding fields to, 96–97
    settings, 103

RDBM. *See* Relational database management system (RDBM)
Read-only, 268, 269
Rearranging fields
    on forms, 120–122
    in tables, 78–81
Receive the focus, 268
Records
    arrangements of, 53
    creating macros that open new, 270–271
    deleting, 59–60
    explanation of, 3, 170
    filtering, 62–66
    finding, 52–53
    inserting, 55–57
    navigating, 38–40
    order of, 58
    sorting, 60–62, 78
    updating, 53–55
Recordset, 236
Recycle Bin, WIN-2
Referential integrity, 199
Relational database design
    creating data dictionary for, 168–169
    creating Microsoft Access database for, 169–170
    creating table object by importing data for, 170–179
    phases of, 164–165
    process of, 162, 164
    setup for, 162–163
    using database approach for, 163–164
    using entry-relationship model in, 166–168
    using file processing system for, 163
Relational database management system (RDBMS)
    characteristics of, 162
    explanation of, 2, 161, 164
    function of, 188
Relational model, 164, 192, 193
Relations
    explanation of, 166
    in first normal form, 194
    in second normal form, 193, 195
    as tables, 166
    in third normal form, 194
Relationships
    establishing, 198–201
    explanation of, 3
    represented in E-R diagrams, 188, 189
    searching for topics about, 18–19
Repeating groups, 193
Replace dialog box, 58
Replace feature, 57–59
Replacing data, 57–59
Report Design
    identifying screen features of, 135–137
    using, 257, 258, 261
Reports
    aligning field controls on, 144
    based on queries, 257–267
    explanation of, 5, 256
    modifying design of, 140–147
    opening, 135–137
    printing, 148–149
    removing fields from, 137–139
    saving, 139–140
    viewing, 139–140
Restore button, WIN-5
Run time, Visual Basic, 295
Running queries, 97–100

Saving
    AutoForm, 37–38
    AutoReport, 83–84
    changes to objects, 20
    data, 36
    database tables, 32–33
    databases, 8–10
    forms, 37–38, 122
    queries, 98–99
    reports, 139–140
Screen
    accessing area of, 121
    identifying elements on, 10–11
ScreenTip, 12
Scrolling, WIN-5
Second normal form (2NF), 193–194
Select query, 94
Simple key, 166
Sizing, windows, WIN-5–WIN-6
Sort order, query, 100–103
Sorting records, 60–62, 78
Spelling checker, 36–37
Stand-alone application, Visual Basic to create, 295, 296
Starting
    Access, 7–8
    programs via Start Menu, WIN-4–WIN-5
    Windows, WIN-2
Startup forms, 256, 273–274
Static HTML page, 288, 291
Status bar, WIN-5, 11
Subforms. *See also* Forms
    added to main form, 247–250
    creating, 242–247
    explanation of, 234
Subform/Subreport control, 247–248

Tab stop, 276
Table fields
    added to query window, 106
    defining, 29–32
    deleting, 81–82
    inserting, 76–78
Tables. *See also* Database tables
    altering design of, 74–91
    copying structures of, 84–85
    creating orders, 197–198
    creating products, 195–197
    explanation of, 5, 176–179
    rearranging fields in, 78–81
    as relations, 166
    relationships between, 198–201
The Willows, 25–26
Tags, 291
Taskbar, WIN-2
Third normal form (3NF), 194–195
Title bars, WIN-5, 11–12
Titles to forms, 125–128
Toolbars
    explanation of, 11
    overview, WIN-5
    using 13, WIN-7–WIN-8, 14
    working with, 12
Toolbox
    closing, 121
    displaying a, 147
    palette, 127
ToolTips, WIN-7
Transitive dependency, 194, 195

Unbound control, 236
Undo feature, 59, 120, 139
Updating records, 53–55
User interface, 233

Validation rule, 267, 271
Validation text, 271
Viewing
    forms, 53
    reports, 139–140
Views
    datasheet, 37, 39
    displaying Form Design, 117–118
    Form, 39
    list of available, 76
Virtual tables, 218
Visual Basic
    adding controls to, 302–307
    constructing project in, 296–299
    creating front end using, 282–284, 295–296
    explanation of, 295
    launching, 296
    modes of operation of, 295
    naming conventions for, 299
    shared components of Microsoft Access and, 283, 295
    version 5, 284
Visual Basic control
    explanation of, 224

Visual Basic Control (Continued)
   modifying forms by adding, 224–228
   using, 236, 274
Visual Basic Setup Wizard
   creating distribution set using, 284
   creating installation set using, 309–316

Web. *See* World Wide Web (WWW)
What's This? feature, WIN-14, 16
The Willows table, 25–26
Windows
   manipulating, WIN-5–WIN-6
   query, 106
Windows Explorer, WIN-5

World Wide Web (WWW). *See also* Internet
   Addison-Wesley site on, 257
   creating query containing information to publish on, 285–286
   Microsoft site on, 19–20